THE STOIC IN LOVE

*Selected essays on literature
and ideas*

THE STOIC IN LOVE

*Selected essays on literature
and ideas*

A. D. NUTTALL

Fellow of New College, Oxford

BARNES & NOBLE BOOKS
SAVAGE, MARYLAND

First Published in the United States of America 1990 by
BARNES & NOBLE BOOKS
8705 Bollman Place, Savage, Maryland

ISBN 0–389–20887–6

Library of Congress Cataloging in Publication Data
are available from the publisher.

Printed in Great Britain

CONTENTS

PREFACE

Not very long ago, when I was visiting Yale University, the most elegant of
the Deconstructionists said to me, with the air of one successfully exposing a
fatal flaw, 'You always prefer philosophy to Theory.' I cannot be sure that
those were the exact words (though I am fairly sure that I 'heard' the capital
'T' of 'Theory'), but that was the substance. Looking through the essays
printed in this volume, I see that he was right, although I still do not
understand (presumably because of my benighted state) why I should feel
damaged by the charge. The accredited areas of negotiation between
disciplines – aesthetics, say, or sociology or literary theory – have always
seemed less exciting to me than the business of discovering unlooked-for
connections between fundamentally autonomous modes of discourse. I
would rather link Sterne with Hume than Macherey with Miller.

The University of Sussex, where I taught for many years, was famous in
the 1960s for interdisciplinary studies. There it gradually became clear that
the word 'interdisciplinary' could mean either 'linking two disciplines' or
'operating in a field intermediate between two disciplines'. I always preferred
the first, perhaps because, years before, I had read Classical Moderations at
Oxford. The convulsive innovations of the 1960s, forcing English Literature
into contact with History and Philosophy, were to a surprising degree the
reconstitution of something which, in another field, was harmoniously
familiar. Classicists had for years addressed an entire civilisation, simultaneously investigating poetry and the most technical philosophy, sewage
systems, oracles, potsherds, syllogisms. The curious system of invisible
shutters which in traditional English departments fall heavily into place
whenever there is thought to be some danger of straying 'outside the subject'
was virtually unknown to the older generation of classicists. If one could not
solve one's problem without doing some philosophy, one did some
philosophy. Thus Oxford Classics was utterly unlike Oxford English, but
much more like a Sussex School of Studies.

When I was a graduate student I became interested in a certain structural

similarity: an apparently trivial technical problem arises in allegorical poetry
when Mercy (say) is made to triumph over Cruelty in the Battle of the Mind;
how is Mercy to win the fight if she is continually merciful, that is,
continually giving way? Meanwhile in Plato's *Parmenides* a philosophical
problem arises from what is called the 'self-predication of the Forms':
Beauty, say, is conceived as itself supremely beautiful ('beautiful-and-
nothing-else'); but, if Beauty is beautiful, what are we to say of that beauty in
respect of which both Beauty and all the beautiful things are beautiful? Is it,
too, beautiful? And so on. I sensed a kinship here. I began to *hunt*, following
the fiery track of a certain idea; that, before the eighteenth century, what we
call 'abstractions' were imaginatively warmer, having some of the characteristics of super-sensible individuals, so that a Leavisian insistence on
particularity as the sole province of poetic vitality was mistaken – but at this
point I found myself faced with one of the aforementioned shutters: allegory
was literature and therefore available for study, but Plato was philosophy,
and therefore forbidden ground. Of course I broke through in the end (and
wrote a book called *Two Concepts of Allegory*), but I was shocked by what
seemed to me an artificial constraint on intellectual enquiry (though, in due
course, delighted by the sudden freedom of Sussex).

The essays in this book are, apart from a few corrections, as they were first
written. There would be something disingenuous in the application of a
1980s gloss (in both senses of that word) to obstinately unregenerate
materials. One essay in particular, 'Did Meursault mean to kill the Arab?', is
very much of its time. Gilbert Ryle's sustained effort in *The Concept of Mind* to
eliminate interior mental life had an immense effect in the late 1950s and
1960s. Behaviourism, the 'Problem of Other Minds', the necessary publicity
of language – these were, so to speak, unavoidable challenges. I was never
fully persuaded by Ryle, but the essay marks how far I was nevertheless
willing to go. I accepted the suggestion that our notions of purpose and
surprise depended far less crucially on previous interior states (realised or
disconfirmed) than had previously been assumed; that in practice we
confidently describe an action as intentional even when we have no access to
the mind of the agent; that it is conceivable that one might describe one of
one's own actions as intentional, even when there had been no clearly relevant
preceding mental project. Thus, I might answer the door intentionally – not
inadvertently or automatically – without saying to myself, 'Now I will
answer the door.' But if intention is to a considerable extent a matter of
publicly available sequence, might not this dissolve the notorious Intentional
Fallacy of the New Critics? The 'intention' of *Paradise Lost* might then be, not
some irrecoverable moment in Milton's stream of consciousness, but rather
something to be read off from the public sequence of utterance. This essay
may have played a small part in the dissolution of the authorial ego which
has followed, but I am sure that I would, even then, have resisted the full
metaphysical version of the doctrine (as I do now).

'Causal *Dum*' illustrates, as sharply as I know how, the conceptual latitude I ascribe to classical studies. It is a kind of act of homage to E. R. Dodds who in his lectures could draw from some minute point of linguistic analysis a wealth of immense implication. If the essay works, it shows how the tantalising presence of an indicative where a subjunctive might have been expected betrays a radical displacement (in the direction of poetic fiction) of Virgil's conception of an after-life. I do not imagine, of course, that I have matched or even come near what Dodds used to do; *sequiturque patrem non passibus aequis.*

Other essays exhibit other hops or leaps (more or less ungainly) of the mind. That on *Hamlet* follows at first the original transgression of Gilbert Murray, who proposed an intricate analogy between Shakespeare and certain Greeks whose works Shakespeare never read; thereafter the essay transgresses on its own account, taking one further seven-league stride from Empsonian 'mystery' to Wittgensteinian notions of death and negation. 'Fishes in the trees', 'Gulliver among the horses' and 'Moving cities' deal instead with the more or less authorised connection of the eighteenth century with Augustan antiquity but seek to substitute a dynamic, fluid relation for a static one. '*Measure for Measure*: The bed-trick' steps dangerously from legal niceties which were always obscure to that unique combination of emotional alienation with social 'belonging' which marks Shakespearian comedy. 'Adam's dream and Madeline's' returns, after a long interval, to the ontological obsession of *Two Concepts of Allegory*. Here I become absorbed, perhaps in direct reaction to the competitive scepticism of the 1980s, in what might be called, 'Keatsian counter-scepticism': that is, the discovery of substance and palpable reality in a field normally conceded to unreality, in poetry and the fictive imagination. The essay terminates, however, in a kind of blasphemy, for I found, half against my will, that Keats's poetry is not more but less starry-eyed than his letters.

The 'odd man out' is the essay on C. S. Lewis, 'The giant-killer'. Lewis's *Abolition of Man* had an enormous effect on me when I was an undergraduate. I was then an obscurely distressed Blakean subjectivist. Not so many years before I had experienced the painful loss of a quasi-Wordsworthian intuition of glory in the world. The effect of this was to turn the notion of reality, for me, into something inherently imperilled, not to be trusted. My immediate reaction was one of strenuous concession: of course the 'glory' had never been real; a wise man and a fool see not the same tree; aesthetic experience, like poetry, is an exciting flux which means only itself and can never be in any further sense veridical. *The Abolition of Man* amazed me by suggesting that one could without intellectual discredit follow another path. 'Consider', said Lewis (in effect), 'a strange tribe where the people think it possible to draw a distinction between cases in which value is justly ascribed and cases in which it is unjustly ascribed.' First of all it was clear that *we* were that tribe, still: that in off-guard moments, outside lectures and tutorials, most of us operate in this way. Secondly, it was clear that the simplified, subjectivist account, meanwhile, had not been reached by a rigorous refutation of objectivism. In short, I was shaken. The essay 'The giant-killer' is a conscientious attempt to break the thing I had come to respect, an attempt to drag out all the weaknesses, the illicit transitions, the confusions. The outcome is that my essay inflicts some damage on Lewis's superstructure, but (to my great content) he remains sound below the water-line. I still do not know whether aesthetic judgements and value judgements are or are not species of fictions. But I can never recover the automatic contempt with which, in my late teens, I regarded those who viewed them as objective. Epistemological objectivity, on the other hand, now seems to me a profound operational necessity and quite inescapable.

Looking back at what I have so far written in this preface, I find that I may not have been quite honest. I have paraded an austere disregard for the confused, political, intermediate area of theory and a correspondingly intense concentration on particular problematic moments or intersections. But in fact I was always conscious of leaning against the wind. I was never able to join, to step aboard. I never believed in the crassly moralised criticism of F. R. Leavis, in the harmonious 'world-we-have-lost' of Tillyard (or Lewis), in the New Critical Tabus. The current growth of a lavish scepticism also, in its turn, seems to me profoundly implausible. I do not believe, cannot join, still.

But, like Apemantus, I am a very sociable solitary. All these essays grew out of conversations and a *full* list of acknowledgements (which I cannot now put together from memory) would be very long indeed.

A. D. Nuttall
New College
Oxford

ACKNOWLEDGEMENTS

Grateful acknowledgement is made to the following for permission to reprint material in copyright:

Hodder & Stoughton for 'Two unassimilable men', which first appeared in *Shakespearian Comedy*, Stratford-upon-Avon Studies, 14, eds. Malcolm Bradbury and David Palmer, 1972.

Cambridge University Press for 'Moving cities: Pope as translator and transposer', which first appeared in *The Enduring Legacy: Alexander Pope tercentenary essays*, eds. G. S. Rousseau and Pat Rogers, 1988, and for '*Measure for Measure*: The bed-trick', which first appeared in *Shakespeare Survey*, 28, 1975.

The Editor of *Essays in Criticism* for 'Fishes in the trees', first published in *Essays in Criticism*, 24, 1974.

Edinburgh University Press for 'Adam's dream and Madeline's', which first appeared in *The Religious Imagination*, ed. James P. Mackey, 1986.

Basil Blackwell for 'Personality and poetry', which first appeared in *Persons and Personality*, eds. A. Peacocke and Grant Gillett, 1987.

The Higher Education Foundation for 'Is there a legitimate reductionism?', which first appeared in *Reductionism in Academic Disciplines*, ed. A. Peacocke, 1985.

The British Academy for permission to include '*Hamlet*: Conversations with the dead', which was first given as a lecture at the British Academy, 1988.

'Gulliver among the horses' is reprinted from *The Yearbook of English Studies*, 1988 by permission of the Editor and of the Modern Humanities Research Association for this purpose only.

'Jack the giant-killer' is reprinted from *Seven*, 5, 1984 with permission.

'Ovid immoralised: The method of wit in Marvell's "The Garden"' first appeared in *Essays in Honour of Kristian Smidt,* eds. Peter Bilton *et al.*, University Oslo Institute of English Studies, 1986.

'Did Meursault mean to kill the Arab? – The intentional fallacy fallacy' first appeared in *Critical Quarterly*, 10, 1968.

The following essays are published here for the first time:

The Stoic in Love
Shallow's Orchard, Adam's Garden
Causal *Dum*
Hamlet: Conversations with the dead.

TWO UNASSIMILABLE MEN

I

We do not naturally associate Jaques with Caliban; yet a form of association exists, and is demonstrable. Edward A. Armstrong expounded it in his book, *Shakespeare's Imagination* (1946): the same distinctive 'cluster' of images is used for both Jaques and Caliban. For both of them we have a reference to an infected body (*As You Like It*, II. vii. 60; *The Tempest*, I. ii. 370),[1] to food (*AYLI*, II. vii. 14; *Tempest*, I. ii. 330), to music (*AYLI*, II. vii. 5; *Tempest*, III. ii. 130–5, 146). Moreover, there are what may be called coincidences of thought: Duke Senior says of Jaques,

> I think he be transform'd into a beast;
> For I can nowhere find him like a man.
> *(AYLI*, II. vii. 1–2)

And Prospero calls Caliban,

> A freckl'd whelp, hag-born – not honour'd with
> A human shape.
> *(Tempest*, I. ii. 283–4)

Duke Senior calls Jaques,

> a libertine
> As sensual as the brutish sting itself.
> *(AYLI*, II. vii. 65–6)

And Prospero (or, more probably, Miranda) calls Caliban,

> A thing most brutish.
> *(Tempest*, I. ii. 357)

There is nothing about a sting in the quotation from *The Tempest*, nor does the word appear elsewhere in the play; but hedgehogs mount their pricks at Caliban's footfall (II. ii. 11–12) and he is constantly threatened with or fearful of pinches (I. ii. 329, II. ii. 4, IV. i, 232, V. i. 276).

Our first inference from all this is psychological. Shakespeare wrote the parts of Jaques and Caliban from the same quarter of his mind, so to speak. Some will say that no further inference is possible; that the coincidence of imagery is a freak of the poet's psychology which is proved already to be critically irrelevant by our very surprise at the association. That surprise, after all, arises from our sense of each character in his proper setting: from our knowledge that Caliban is uncivilised, natural and earthy while Jaques is cultured, neurotic and austere. This is what the plays teach us, as long as they are read or watched as plays, and such teaching is in a manner invulnerable. For criticism must always concern itself with the work as apprehended, rather than with the material conditions of that apprehension. Statistical analysis may one day show us that Gray is more alliterative than Collins, but if we cannot hear the difference between the two poets we have, as critics, learned nothing; if, on the other hand, we can hear the difference, two things follow: first that the difference is relevant to criticism, and, second, that we had no need of the statistical analyst to tell us what our ears had already picked up. The 'scientific' investigator of poetry is therefore unhappily placed; he is either irrelevant or superfluous.

But this dismissal is much too slick. There are sounds we might never have heard, if we had never been invited to listen for them. And indeed if it were otherwise, it is criticism which would find itself superfluous. Good literature is usually indefinitely rich; we never know what more is to be found in it. The claim that criticism must concern itself with the work as apprehended is correct, but apprehension itself is commonly not instantaneous but progressive. Certainly if we cannot hear the stronger alliteration of Gray the analytic information is critically useless, but we must listen *after* we have read the analysis. Only if it obstinately remains inaudible should we (now of course it becomes an obligation) reject the statistical findings. Thus 'scientific' analysis of literature provides us with no critical imperatives; but we must not conclude too briskly that it therefore offers us nothing. In fact it issues invitations.

So with Jaques and Caliban: we are invited to do what we might not otherwise have done; to put these two together in our minds. Other Shakespearian characters with whom the Caliban 'image-cluster' is associated – Aaron the Moor, say, or Thersites – easily connect themselves thematically with their image-cousin of *The Tempest*. There the poet's psychology correlates well enough with certain palpable continuities in the *œuvre*. With Jaques and Caliban it would appear that some effort is required. But this must never become an effort to suppress. We need never deny the manifest differences as we hunt for latent similarities. After all, the differences are not such as logically to preclude any connection. Shakespeare is full of recurrence which is never mere repetition. Always there is variation, often outright reversal. His imagination was shamelessly promiscuous. Prince Hal himself speaks with the accents of Iago,[2] and the echo is, critically, no accident.

In terms of plot the connection between Jaques and Caliban is indeed tenuous. Jaques, like Antonio in *The Merchant of Venice* and Malvolio in *Twelfth Night*, is excluded from the ritual of coming together which marks the end of the comedy; Caliban, on the other hand, is filled with good resolutions and taken back to Milan. Jaques, it seems, could not be assimilated by the festive world, but Caliban could be domesticated. The best we can say is that they are both outsiders, opposed in some way to the proper harmony of society, which is to say very little.

One is sometimes tempted to assume that the notion of the outsider as a source of discord and possible evil begins with Shakespeare and ends with the decline of the Comic World-picture, say, with Miss Wade of *Little Dorrit* (for Miss Wade is already assuming the modern ambiguity). But this is too definite. Homer's Thersites is a social outsider, and Aeschylus' Aegisthus, with his illegitimacy and distinguishing 'low' style, is almost Shakespearian. Grendel is excluded from the mead-hall, *dreamum bedæled*, and even the Green Knight, before the bathetic dénouement, is noticeably *outré*. Nevertheless, it is in Shakespeare that the use of an outsider-figure becomes insistent, and in Milton an inherited cosmology is altered in such a way as to accommodate the consequent change in ethical imagination. The universe of *Paradise Lost* is geocentric; so far Milton follows Dante. But Dante's universe is, strictly speaking, not so much geocentric as a diabolocentric. At the centre of the earth, where Down becomes Up,[3] is the Devil; he is Hamlet's Old Mole, deeper than bedrock, the ultimate insider. But Milton's Satan comes from outside; the drop of light he sees suspended from the ramparts of Heaven at the end of Book II is not the Terrestrial Globe but the entire Ptolemaic universe, and he must penetrate the spheres before he can touch the top of Mount Niphates. To be sure, there may be a technical theological reason for this, and the curious reader can turn it up in *De Doctrina Christiana* (i. 33, *The Columbia Milton* (New York, 1934), vol. XVI, pp. 374–5). But whatever the motive of the change, the imaginative consequence is manifest: Satan comes from the other side of Chaos. Evil no longer threatens the soul from inside.

But the genre which pre-eminently concerns itself with people as composing a society is comedy; tragedy is about individuals as they fall away from the grand composition. Arguments about the comparative truth-value of tragedy and comedy are, so far, futile, for the following two sentences are both true. 1. People do fall in love, marry, and their children marry; life goes on. 2. Each of us, you who read and I who write, will die.[4] Hence comedy is an art of profile, of the third person, whereas in tragedy we are face to face. In Shakespeare we sometimes find a tragedy of individual(s) superimposed on a comic plot of social continuity. The thing is most clinically obvious in *Romeo and Juliet*, where the story of the families is comedy (at times almost farce) and only the lovers are tragic.

Because of the 'impurity' of Shakespearian genre, then, we need not be surprised to find that meditation on the idea of the outsider is possible even in a technical tragedy. The exotic Othello, who is honoured in the state of Venice for his soldiership, finds when he leaves the public, martial sphere for the private that he is not accepted, is not understood and cannot understand. The Venetian colour bar is sexual, not professional. Othello, coal-black among the glittering Venetians, is visibly the outsider, and in his bewilderment he looks for the man who is visibly the insider, the man who knows the ropes, the 'good chap' (or, as they said then, 'honest'). And he finds him.

But Iago has no friends, no loves, no positive desires. He, and not Othello, proves to be the true outsider in the play, for he is foreign to humanity itself. Othello comes from a remote clime, but Iago, in his simpler darkness, comes from the far side of chaos. Hence the pathos of Shakespeare's best departure from his source. In Cinthio's novel the Ensign, with a cunning affectation of reluctance, suggests that Desdemona is false and then, seeing his chance, remarks, 'Your blackness already displeases her.'[5] In Shakespeare we have instead a note of bar-room, masculine intimacy, an assumed complicity of sentiment; in effect, Iago says, 'Well, she went with a black man, you know . . . so what is one to think?' (see III. iii. 232–7). Othello's need to be accepted makes him an easy victim of this style.

Moreover, it may be that *Othello* can provide us with a clue to the labyrinth of the comedies. *Othello* itself is written against, rather than with, the grain of genre. Even more than *Romeo and Juliet*, it is Shakespeare's domestic tragedy, where 'domestic' is not merely a difference added to the genus 'tragedy' but is rather a mark of paradox. Othello leaves 'the big wars' and the windy seas for a little, dim world of unimaginable horror. 'War is no strife to the dark house and the detested wife' comes not from *Othello* but from a comedy, yet it will serve here. *Othello*, we might say, is the tragedy of a hero who went into a house. And the essense of the hero's humiliation is sexual.

Certainly, the outsiders of the comedies are variously connected with obscure sexual distress (and this too can be applied to Milton: Satan is sexually wretched, the voyeur in Eden). In *Twelfth Night* the baiting of Malvolio is sexual; his austere pride is founded on a Narcissism which his tormentors first stimulate and then snub. He is sexually only half-alive, but eager, clumsy and capable of being hurt. At the end of the comedy he finds no bride. Antonio in *The Merchant of Venice* is probably homosexual. The great love-feat of the play is performed, not by Bassanio for Portia, but by Antonio for Bassanio. The leaden casket bore the legend,

> Who chooseth me must give and hazard all he hath.
> (II. vii. 9)

W. H. Auden noticed that this line holds for two people in the play, neither of whom is Bassanio.[6] The real *agōn* of *The Merchant of Venice* is between Antonio and Shylock. At the end of the comedy there is no bride for Antonio. It begins to look as if the crucial unifying factor for outsiders in the comedies is exclusion from marriage. Angelo, in *Measure for Measure*, is an exception which proves this rule. He adds to personal asceticism an impersonalist theory of law, according to which judges are themselves subject to justice; only thus is law ethically practicable in a corrupt world. But Angelo's lust is awakened by the very purity of Isabella; the stimulation and baiting of Malvolio is re-enacted in a horribly intensified mode. At the end Angelo is presented with the bride he had previously rejected. Yet this, perhaps, is his final humiliation. He had affirmed that if ever he himself should break the law he ought in justice to suffer by the law. His precarious tenure of intellectual honour in the midst of his degradation before Isabella depends on the genuineness of his commitment to this view. But when the end comes he is not allowed to prove his honour. His importunate pleas for punishment are answered with forgiveness. Angelo has served his purpose; the Duke breathes forth again that uncharitable charity which will one day force him to hide his radiant face once more, while some detested substitute cleans up the mess. Thus, although Angelo is technically admitted to the festive conclusion of the comedy, his admission conceals an ingenious insult. By this marriage Angelo is finally emasculated. Yet forgiveness is forgiveness, and *Measure for Measure* is a real comedy.

II

The sexuality of Jaques is more problematical. It is likely that many who flinch from the association of Jaques with Caliban do so partly on the ground that Caliban is driven by undisguised lust whereas Jaques is donnish, neurotically self-frustrated – is, as we say, repressed. Yet this presentiment must be wrong since, as we have seen, the clearest connection between the two characters is at the point of sexuality. Jaques, with his mannered wretchedness, was of all things a libertine, or so says the Duke (and he must know). And, if we allow ourselves to reflect, it is even probable. It was never our sense of psychological reality that was offended, only of convention. I once met a Jaques, and he was not in a book.

Jaques, then, is in some ways a reversed Angelo. He is a tricky subject for psychoanalysis since he began with lust and ends with asceticism. His libidinal exterior concealed a rank hatred of the world. Of course, as we see him, he lacks the high principle of Angelo, and will probably never attain it, though at the end he goes to a monastery or hermitage. We have been told by social anthropologists[7] that in earlier ages social misfits were accommodated by the monastic system, so that there was a place even for the unplaceable. We may deceive ourselves for a moment into thinking that Jaques finds a home in this way, but not for long. Jaques goes to the religious order not to join but to watch. He will be to it as he was to Arden, *spectator haud particeps*, the everlasting looker-on. But in any case all this is mere typological doodling. Jaques, however often we listen, never sounds like Angelo, never feels like him. We had better follow where the echoes lead; we had better turn to Caliban.

Every cartoonist knows that the real point about desert islands is that they offer a sexually limited environment. The tiny mound of sand, topped by two palm trees, a voluptuous blonde and one or more others (male) has become part of our popular iconography. Shakespeare, variously prophetic in his last, futuristic production, foresaw this too. Part of the tension of *The Tempest* arises from our awareness of Miranda's situation. She is the only woman on the island; she is *tabu* to Prospero because she is his daughter, and to Caliban because she is white (and possibly of another species). Ferdinand on the other hand is both socially and mythically eligible. The anachronistic term 'colour bar' was applicable to *Othello* and it is still more applicable here. We saw how the Venetian colour bar was principally confined to sexual relations: 'Ah, but would you let your daughter marry one?' In *The Tempest* (which might have been called *America*) the primary sexual fear is extended and elaborated by the various tensions of colonisation. When Shakespeare pillaged the Bermuda pamphlets to write his play, he lifted not just incidental marvels but a fundamental theme. The black man (Caliban is perhaps an Indian) is now not just an exotic threat but the recalcitrant and ineducable serf. Nevertheless, the crisis of the relationship between native and newcomer remains sexual. It is when Caliban attempts to violate Miranda that the attempt to civilise him is dropped and the long vilification begins. Yet the island was Caliban's if it was anyone's.

But the clairvoyance of *The Tempest* is not exercised on the future only; it is audaciously retrospective. In the last phase of his writing life, Shakespeare seems to have been groping towards a kind of drama which was attained by Ancient Greece in the period which followed the age of the great tragedians. Some of the later tragedies of Euripides are almost comedies – the *Helen*, the *Iphigenia in Tauris* and, most vividly, the *Ion*. The idea of Shakespeare reaching out for a Euripides he cannot read and of whom he has scarcely heard may seem a subject for compassionate silence, but if we watch him at work any pity we may have felt is quickly forgotten. He had a nose for this business.

As early as *The Comedy of Errors* Shakespeare had known that what we may call the Stories of the Children Lost and Found were Greek, and that (because Menander still lay buried in the Egyptian sand) he must get what he needed from Plautus. It is instructive to compare Shakespeare's use of Roman Comedy with Jonson's. Jonson catches the ferocious energy, the intrigue, the cruel mirth – in a word the Roman-ness. Shakespeare catches the mythic resonance, the Greek behind the Roman. Already he was on the right path. The Greek Old Comedy we read at school – Aristophanes[8] – has nothing to do with Shakespeare. But in the fragments of that transitional and New Comedy which lie behind Plautus we find far more 'pre-echoes' of

Shakespeare than we could ever have hoped for: Falstaff and sack in Theopompus' *Nemeas*,[9] the miniscule fauna and flora, elves (σατυρίδια) and country dancing of *A Midsummer Night's Dream* in Strattis,[10] the awe-struck religious-tourist atmosphere of the Delphic scene in *The Winter's Tale* in Lysippus,[11] a meditative Duke Senior in Amphis,[12] and perhaps most striking of all, the Chorus of *Henry V* conjuring the vasty fields of France from a wooden O in Heniochus.[13] Less striking, but relevant, is the *Dyskolos* of Menander, which opens with the invitation, so foreign to the preceding age, to 'imagine that this place is Phylae in Attica'. It is sometimes assumed by historians of drama that a free allusion to the fact that something is being represented belongs naturally to the primitive phase. In Greek drama it comes late. In any case, the 'logical atmosphere' of a Menandrian prologue is subtle. The speaker does not say, 'I am acting the part of Pan'; he rather implies, 'I, the god Pan, have come down to tell you that this place is Phylae'. None of this material will be found in any textbook account of Shakespeare's sources, and it is quite proper that it should not, since (dare we say it?) he could not possibly have read it. It therefore stands as an uncanny example of mere likeness, of a latent reciprocity between Shakespearian drama and the Greek at the very period when it begins to slip from our knowledge. If it be unprofessional to entertain such analogies, then we must presumably censure Gilbert Norwood, who in his *Greek Comedy* (1931) noticed almost all the points of resemblance. But the myth was Shakespeare's proper quarry, and this directs us to Menander, the prince of New Comedy, the poet, above all, of ἀναγνώρισις, of the Recognition Scene (and now we should begin to think, not of *The Comedy of Errors*, but of *Pericles, Cymbeline* and *The Winter's Tale*).

Yet even Menander is not the true source. Though he has much more grace than Plautus or Terence he has only a little more enchantment. His world is not only socially exclusive; it is, as R. B. Braithwaite used to say, 'demythologised'. The nature of the New Comedy has been well summarised by T. B. L. Webster: 'Mythological comedy has little place; mythology travestied in the old way would be discordant, mythology untravestied belonged to tragedy.'[14] Thus in one respect Menander's historical position is the reverse of Shakespeare's. Menander was falling from myth into naturalism; but Shakespeare was aspiring from naturalism to myth. The English poet, it will be noticed, had the harder task. Nature is simply given; it is there to be observed. Myth is handed down, and in the process is subject to loss or diminution. Shakespeare knew that the real source was Greek and that the goods as they reached him had been damaged in passage. He could no longer trust the facile excesses of Renaissance iconography –

> Come, thou monarch of the vine,
> Plumpy Bacchus with pink eyne:
> (*Antony and Cleopatra*, II. vii. 111–12)

– but hungered for a deity more severe, more beautiful, more Greek:

> The gods themselves,
> Humbling their deities to love, have taken
> The shapes of beasts upon them: Jupiter
> Became a bull and bellow'd; the green Neptune
> A ram and bleated; and the fire-rob'd god,
> Golden Apollo, a poor humble swain,
> As I seem now.
>   (*The Winter's Tale*, IV, iv. 25–30)

Shakespeare tracked his myth as far as the Roman imitator of Menander and then went on alone. We, who know more than he could know, can judge how straight he ran.

Properly speaking, myth deals with the significant actions of gods and men, but Menander's gods are faded. The true object of Shakespeare's stylistic search therefore lies one stage further back. Now New Comedy is derived not, as many people think, from Old Comedy but from tragedy. The dramatist most parodied, most quoted and most revered by the poets of transitional and New Comedy is, of course, Euripides.[15] Satyrus wrote in his *Life* of Euripides:

> The quarrels that we remark in comedy between husband and wife, father and son, master and slave, or the climaxes brought about by rapes, suppositious children, recognitions by rings and necklaces . . . these of course are the framework of New Comedy, and were brought to perfection by Euripides.[16]

We must remember that it was not just any body of Greek myth that Shakespeare was seeking but one only: the Stories of the Children Lost and Found. The pattern of the story is comic as we have come to understand the term; but the divine dimension, which Shakespeare also needed, was, as the Greeks understood matters, tragic. It is likely that there was never more than one dramatist who fulfilled both these requirements, and that was Euripides. In the preface to his translation of the *Ion* Gilbert Murray wrote:

> The *Ion* belongs to a particular class of tragedy in which the hero is the Son of a God and a mortal princess. The birth is concealed, the babe is cast out or hidden and in danger of death from a cruel king, but in the end is recognised as a son of god and established as founder of a New Kingdom and ancestor of a royal house.[17]

Between Plautus and Shakespeare there is a demonstrable relation of influence; between Euripides and Shakespeare there is only the most tenuous and speculative historical connection. In the Temple Shakespeare of 1894 Sir Israel Gollancz suggested that Shakespeare read the *Alcestis*, perhaps in Pettie's Latin translation, and used his reading when he wrote *The Winter's Tale*. Today some scholars feel that the correspondences between the two plays are close enough to justify our naming *Alcestis* as an actual source. But the idea has never obtained universal assent. On the other hand, the objective similarity of certain passages (especially *Alcestis*, 1121–50, and *The Winter's Tale*, V. ii. 18–132) is beyond dispute. The *Alcestis* is early Euripides

(438 BC) but, with its comic episodes and solemn-happy ending it anticipates the manner of the late romantic tragedies. And it is the manner which is important. There is a sense in which the correspondences between the *Alcestis* and *The Winter's Tale* are in any case the *less* striking in virtue of the fact that the story of the *Alcestis* is the story of *The Winter's Tale*. But the congruity of atmosphere between late Shakespeare and late Euripides has a more persistent, if less tangible, interest. If we read, not as source-hunters but as critics, we shall see that late Euripides is *like* Shakespeare as no other dramatist is. We enter the world of the *Ion* and – as we watch an ἐγγενὴς φόνος (an 'in-the-family-murder') narrowly averted, the mutual recognition of mother and son in the sacred city, perhaps most of all as we listen to Creusa likening her fortune to that of a vessel lost in a storm (1502–7) – we feel that we have been here before. The reader who surveys the evolution of Greek tragedy from Aeschylus to Euripides and then turns to the parallel development of Shakespeare's work may begin to feel that some inner dialectical necessity is involved. After the abrupt catastrophes of tragedy the sweet intricacies of romantic comedy grow strong.

We are suggesting, then, that Shakespeare in seeking his myth recognised instinctively that the tradition was, precisely, a tradition, and not a set of terminal authorities. Plautus to him was not so much a model as a perspective glass through which he discerned new lands.

He seems in *The Tempest* to have used Virgil in exactly this way. This play is of course strewn with Virgilian allusions, ranging from mere names like Carthage, Dido and the Harpy to turns of phrase (e.g. 'lie there, my art', I. ii. 25, *artemque repono, Aeneid*, v. 484). Perhaps the most effective of these reminiscences occurs at I. ii. 421–7, where Ferdinand meets Miranda. These lines, the commentaries tell us, echo *Aeneid*, i. 328–9, *O quam te memorem, virgo?* Yet even here Shakespeare's true kinship is with the Greek behind the Roman. Virgil's lines describe the meeting of Aeneas and Venus, so that Aeneas' extravagant cry proves merely accurate; the woman before him is truly divine. Miranda, on the other hand, is the mortal daughter of the king of the island. This turns the sentiment into a mixture of erotic vision, lover's hyperbole and well-judged compliment. None of this is present in Virgil but all of it is present in Virgil's Greek source, Homer's description of the meeting of Odysseus and Nausicaa (*Odyssey*, vi. 149–52). Moreover, Nausicaa and her father, the King of the Phaeacians, live

> ἀπάνευθε πολυκλύστῳ ἐνὶ πόντῳ,
> ἔσχατοι
> apart, on the many-sounding sea, far away . . .
> (vi. 204–5)

And so did Miranda and Prospero. Think of the island, the magic, of Sycorax (the 'swine-raven'); this is the world of Calypso in her sea-girt isle, of Circe and her victims, of enchantment, sea-sorrow and bewilderment. Why do we pause on the *Aeneid* and on the laborious exodus from Troy when all this lies only a little further on? Shakespeare's play belongs far more firmly than does the *Aeneid* to the Odyssean genre of the νόστος, the 'journey home'.[18] It is the *Aeneid* which gets into the commentaries; the larger relevancies are more easily missed.

But what exactly are we claiming here? Not clairvoyance, this time. The correspondences are too close. Some of them, indeed, are fairly specific. Odysseus, just before his speech to Nausicaa, is worried about etiquette (vi. 142–4) and Ferdinand, within his speech, hopes to be instructed 'how I may bear me here' (I. ii. 425). Gonzalo's amazement that their clothes are not discoloured by the sea (II. i. 58–60) recalls the happiness of Odysseus when he washes away the sea-stains from his body and is made beautiful by Athene (vi. 224–37). No, Shakespeare has probably read a translation of at least the sixth book of the *Odyssey*. Homer was available to him in Latin, French or Italian, even if Chapman had not yet got so far with his English. But, in any case, with a source so celebrated it is in a manner idle to cite editions and translators; half an hour in a tavern with a learned friend could have supplied him with all he needed. The *Odyssey* has left fewer traces than the *Aeneid* in the verbal texture of the drama (perhaps it was read long before), but it is the Greek and not the Roman source which controls the *ethos* of the play.

III

One other channel of transmission remains: the Greek erotic romances. This has of course been dealt with pretty exhaustively by scholars.[19] The principal source of *The Winter's Tale* is Greene's *Pandosto*. In *Pandosto* Greene drew heavily on the *Daphnis and Chloe* of Longus, and less heavily on his more habitual favourite, Achilles Tatius. If we ask what element in Shakespeare's late plays was the peculiar contribution of this literature we might guess: the special sexual accent. Both Achilles Tatius and Longus are what Shakespeare is not, mildly pornographic. Only the rhetorical brilliance of the one and the lyric sweetness of the other remain to mark the contrast, in this sphere, between their age and ours. Most obviously, this sexual accent appears in Shakespeare in the preoccupation with virginity at risk which we find in all four of the late plays. But perhaps the most pervasively important of all the romance sources for Shakespeare's final period is the one he used for *Pericles*, namely the story of Apollonius of Tyre. *Pericles* was the first of the 'late plays' and set the new style. It is therefore not improbable that the story which gave Shakespeare the idea for *Pericles* also gave him the idea of a new kind of romance-comedy. But the sexual element in *Apollonius of Tyre* is very sinister.

We do not have the Greek original of the story of Apollonius. A Latin version exists, but Shakespeare used the medieval verse redaction of Gower. When Shakespeare had first essayed a Greek story, in *The Comedy of Errors*, he worked, as we saw, through Plautus. But he also made some use even then of Gower's version of the Apollonius story. When towards the end of his career he returned to Romance, Plautus was forgotten and *Apollonius* filled his mind.

Leslie Fiedler has argued in an unpublished paper that the motif of incest, which is strong in *Apollonius*, is importantly, if less obviously, present in other late plays. We begin to see that the root from which the late plays grew is older even than Euripides. Riddles, babies left to die in wild country, oracles, incest, royal children found and reared by shepherds – all these elements are present in the myth of Oedipus. Of course Sophocles is unequivocally the tragedian, and his plotting is centripetal whereas Shakespeare's (except for *The Tempest*) is romantically centrifugal. A summary of Sophocles' play does not sound in the least like a Shakespearian romance. But the article on Oedipus in any classical dictionary – which gives us, not the plot of a particular drama, but the prior myth – immediately suggests the story-pattern of *Pericles, Cymbeline, The Winter's Tale* and *The Tempest*.

In *Pericles*, of course, the incest motif is explicit. In *The Winter's Tale* Leontes is attracted to his own daughter (V. i. 223–8), a theatrically powerful moment based on a much longer incestuous episode in *Pandosto*. But it is only a moment; Leontes swiftly tells us that it was only because she reminded him of his lost wife, and we breathe easily again. And when the lost wife is restored, and given by Shakespeare an emphasis which tends to eclipse the restoration of Perdita, we may feel that the demons are safely under lock and key.

Thus, while the epilogue of *Pericles* sets the Prince of Tyre and Thaisa in antithesis to Antiochus and his incestuous paramour, in *The Winter's Tale* the incest motif occurs in the subject of redemption, Leontes. But the conclusion of either comedy provides the father figure with a lawful wife. In *The Tempest* this is not so. And yet we feel some need of it. There is of course no mention of possible incest between Prospero and Miranda, but the thought may be there. Prospero's rage at Caliban's attempted rape of Miranda is natural enough. It explains itself on political, social, ethical and perhaps even biological grounds. But his attitude to Ferdinand, the ideal son-in-law, is less perspicuous. Prospero's moments of real verbal energy are devoted to the prohibition of pre-marital sex. It is no good saying that in this he is merely the good father, protecting his daughter. It is not so much the presence of the paternal prohibition that is significant, but its violence, and together with its violence the absence of any other strong emotion. There is something deeply amiss in that final movement of *The Tempest* towards love and fruition. The very Masque breaks up in discord. Prospero has no real blessing to give. Further, his language to Ferdinand is edged with an excessive hostility, which Ferdinand can allay only by professing that long virginity has reduced his appetite (IV. i. 54–6)! Three men and a girl together on a desert island. The tensions are not really so obscure. The old Freudian myth revives in our minds; Prospero is not gaining a son but losing a female.

I have felt the need to explore the 'Greekness' of Shakespearian romance at some length partly to undermine the excessively Christian predisposition of many readers. Prospero belongs not in the ethically warm universe of Christianity but in the hard, bright, far-off world of Greek legend, with its demons, sun, sea and mortality.

After his strangely chill forgiveness of his enemies, Prospero goes home, not to marriage, nor even to resume the reins of government, but to think about death (V. i. 311). The ending of *The Tempest* is sick with ambiguity. Even the ostensibly idyllic discovery of the lovers playing chess is a discovery of possible cheating and proffered complicity (V. i. 172–4). Prospero's most memorable speech in the play ('Be cheerful, sir. Our revels now are ended . . .', IV. i. 147–8) begins as a word of comfort to Ferdinand and ends as an intuition of annihilation. We are told that in Jacobean times the old were encouraged to meditate on imminent death and that Prospero's resolve is healthy and proper to his circumstances. But Prospero is no saint out of Izaak Walton; we have small ground for confidence about his undiscovered country. The very epilogue of the play curiously combines the conventional appeal for applause at the end of a comedy with a plea for prayers to help one who is in danger of despair.

We are getting to know Prospero. Now look back at his relations with Caliban. Is there no residual, excessive anger there? When we imagine how a good duke should behave, and then listen to Prospero, do we feel no surprise? The abuse which Prospero pours out on Caliban is strangely copious; it implies an efficient rather than a final cause. Shakespeare's figures of authority, Henry V, the Lord Chief Justice, do not speak thus. Prospero's fierceness is not purely functional; it exceeds the object; it is pretty obviously epiphenomenal, the consequence of Prospero's psychological state rather than the instrument of his reasoned indignation.

But Caliban had really tried to ravish Miranda. What a rape was there! Glass-house innocence corrupted by – its shadow or its prototype? – outdoor ignorance. Prospero had arrived on Caliban's Eden and forthwith begun to act like God. In particular, he produced a marriageable girl, a kind of Eve. Remember Adamastor, the African giant in the fifth canto of the *Lusiads* (another epic of sea-sorrow) who poured out curses when he remembered how he had been promised a white bride, and found instead that he had lost his human nature.[20] It was Miranda, who hour by hour, took pains to teach Caliban language (I. ii. 353–8). The speech in which Miranda tells the story of this ill-advised tutorship has been ascribed by many editors to Prospero, but without warrant. It may seem curious that it was Dryden who began this dubious tradition – curious, because we might think that the author of *The Enchanted Island* knew well what *The Tempest* was about at the level of sex; indeed he laid on extra kicks. To meet the girl who had never seen a man he procured a man who had never seen a girl. But no, Dryden's instinct was coarse after all. There is already in *The Tempest* a man who has never seen a girl. His name is Caliban.

Perhaps Miranda found it easy to think of Caliban as a child. Not only is he taught to talk, but he is shown the man in the moon, and cries to dream again. Prospero let his daughter bring Caliban out of this dark infancy and yet professes to be astonished at the result. Diderot would not have been, for he wrote,

> Si le petit sauvage était abandonné à lui-même, qu'il conservât toute son imbécillité et qu'il réunît au peu de raison de l'enfant au berceau la violence des passions de l'homme de trente ans, il tordrait le col à son père et coucherait avec sa mère.[21]

The context of these famous words is a discussion of education. Moreover, it is the 'sound' *Moi* of the dialogue who speaks here, not the subversive *Lui*.

The Tempest, then, is about the complexities of innocence and civility. Foreigners come to an island, bringing science and a stronger magic, law and politics, courtesy and vulgarity, temperance and drunkenness – God-Prospero with his staff, God-Stefano with his bottle. Shakespeare's mind, nearing the end of its course, begins to race. His reach exceeds his grasp. In the story of Apollonius he glimpsed an antique literature still inaccessible: in the Bermuda pamphlets a continent still to be discovered. The genre of the play is not easily determined. It is surprisingly close to science-fiction (Ariel, unlike Puck, is a consistently imagined possibility for which no concept is already available) and is still closer to that Utopian fiction which is science fiction's rich relation (one of the most famous in this line has, appropriately, a title taken from *The Tempest*). When, in our own century, men reached the moon, the most beautiful thing they saw was earth-rise. The moon is blank, but from it can be seen something marvellous, huge, coloured, infinitely various and changing, and that is our own earth; so that if *per impossibile* a man had grown up on the moon there would be one place above all that he would long to reach. And we are already there. Remember Milton's Satan, looking in from outside. In a manner, Prospero too inhabits an island in the moon. Milan is home: corrupt, desirable, live. Hence Miranda's visionary cry, 'O brave new world, that has such people in it!' in part survives the undercutting cynicism of Prospero's reply, ''Tis new to thee' (V. i. 183–4).

The play looks forward, as I have hinted, to the idea of America (O brave new world!) and backward to the idea of Pastoral. The island is the green refuge, where wounds heal far from court or city, and it is the place of unredeemed brutality. Who then are the corruptors and who the corrupted? Prospero and Caliban live together in undissembled hatred. While Ferdinand and Miranda get on with the business of getting married, the real war is between master and slave. But the relationship, until Stefano and Trinculo come, is stable by its very asymmetry. Prospero is stronger than Caliban. He vilifies him for not working, but seems to need the vilification (and hence the idleness) more than he needs the work. Prospero is Caliban's keeper, and Caliban is Prospero's whipping-boy. Caliban is devoured by lust and Prospero is strangely shaken by his daughter's marriage. Neither gets a bride in the end (it will be said that Prospero is of the wrong generation, but Leontes got his Hermione and Pericles his Thaisa).

IV

Now that we have sketched in Caliban's setting, let us try to do the same for Jaques. *As You Like It* is true pastoral and an unequivocally happy play. But it is not serene. There is anti-pastoral scepticism, local unhappiness and, in the bloody napkin, the momentary thought of what death could do if it ever entered Arden.[22] Falstaff, old apple-John, the Silenus of the Histories, who died smiling on his fingers' ends and babbling of green fields, found himself in the middle of a real battle at Shrewsbury, and suddenly spoke like a small child: 'I would it were bed-time, Hal, and all well' (*1 Henry IV*, V. i. 125). Rosalind echoes him, 'I would I were at home' (*AYLI*, IV. iii. 159). But Rosalind is love triumphant, full of intelligence and sanity. Erotic security has made her strong. Only once does she mistake her path. Ardent herself, she sees Phebe frigid, and mistakes masochism (not, of course, the extreme variety) for narcissism (III. v. 35–63). By a delicious stroke of comedy, her joyous indignation, intended to arouse love for Silvius, draws an undesired devotion on Rosalind herself. But there is no satire on complacency here. Rosalind only wants for others the happiness she has attained herself, and the comedy plot finally ratifies her wish with power. Similarly, the down-to-earth scepticism which Rosalind loves to express – 'But these are all lies, men have died from time to time and worms have eaten them, but not for love, not for love' (IV. i. 92–4) – holds no destructive force, since it springs from a well-founded belief in the reality of Orlando's love.

Where loving health is joined with power, as it is in Rosalind, we might suppose that no shadow of perversion could ever cross the stage. But that is not quite true. First the very mechanism of the plot involves a sort of echo of sexual deviance. The lovers both look like boys. Further, the mere name 'Ganymede' is a homosexual allusion. Remember Marlowe's lines:

> Jove slily stealing from his sister's bed
> To dally with Idalian Ganymed[23]

Marlowe haunts this play as the 'dead shepherd' of III. v. 84 and perhaps as the source of the phrase 'a great reckoning in a little room' (III. iii. 11–12). But, in any case, what 'Ganymede' meant to the Elizabethan is clear in Richard Barnfield's *The Affectionate Shepherd, containing the Complaint of Daphnis for the love of Ganymede* (1593). All this, to be sure, is only there to be contradicted. Much of the comedy arises from the incongruity between Rosalind's appearance and her true sex. Nevertheless, we should concede that the joke is a little *risqué* (or even risky).

One can see very well why Shakespeare sustains this productive incongruity. But why does Rosalind sustain it? Why, in short, when she reaches Arden, does she not change her clothes? Her costume was chosen for its power to protect her from sexual importunity and was useful to her on her journey. But now that she has found her lover why does she continue to wear it?

Various answers can be given. Rosalind's disguise confers liberty. In a sense it permits her to be herself, in that it allows her natural energy to express itself in unrestricted movement. This release extends from the purely physical – skirts are cumbersome – to the psychological – women are conventionally expected to be passive. There is an irony here which goes a step beyond Miss Betty Friedan. Rosalind has found the conventional feminine *persona* restrictive, not just of her individuality as a human being, but of her very femaleness, of her proper sexual role. It is not Rosalind but convention which is awry.

Again, perhaps we were wrong a moment ago to distinguish so sharply between Shakespeare and Rosalind. Rosalind manipulates the rest, much as Shakespeare manipulates them all. She is the creator's ally in the camp of the creatures. She does the dramatist's work of coaxing the different strands of the plot to a proper solution. It is easy to feel that Prospero is an ectype of the poet himself, and the same is true, in a lesser degree, of Rosalind. Both of them have magical powers, and there is an old analogy between poetry and magic. It is with us still in Auden's epigraph to his *Collected Shorter Poems*:

> Although you be as I am, one of those
> Who feel a Christian ought to write in prose,
> For poetry is magic . . .

There is a related reason why Rosalind keeps her doublet and hose. Our earlier question was too banausically utilitarian in spirit. Of course, in the real business of life, she wishes to attract and marry Orlando. There will be a time for that. But now she is in Arden, and there is no clock in the forest, and she wants to *play*. The structure of the drama mirrors this suspension of the practical, for all the 'plot' is bundled into the first and last moments and the greater part of the play is a timeless meditation on the pastoral.

Lastly, Rosalind's disguise guarantees a certain objectivity in her relations with Orlando. If she were wearing her own clothes, he would recognise her and she could never afterwards quite trust a word he said. It would all be lover's rhetoric. But, as things are, she can eavesdrop on his thoughts. And yet, by a reversal of the usual routine, she hears nothing but good of herself – it is lover's rhetoric still (and she can afford to puncture it as often as she likes), but lover's rhetoric in the absence of the beloved has a different status. It is no longer tainted by a special hunger for results. Prince Hal was less lucky in his eavesdropping. No wonder Rosalind wants to prolong hers.

Yet there is something disquieting in this fission of erotic identity. There is a certain impropriety in any act of eavesdropping (and eavesdropping in an erotic situation can easily approach voyeurism) and the impropriety is not wholly cured if our own happiness forms the object of our surreptitious curiosity. Furthermore, this disquiet, almost imperceptible as long as we confine our attention to Rosalind, grows when we look elsewhere. The notion of a love which disregards the physical presence and prefers to feed on images recurs in the play. 'Am not I your Rosalind?' says Rosalind-Ganymede, and Orlando answers, 'I take some joy to say you are, because I would be talking of her' (IV. i. 79–80). Here, of course, the comedy lies in the buried propriety of the situation. But at III. v. 92–5 the situation is more perverse. There Phebe tells the suffering Silvius that since she has fallen in love herself she enjoys listening to his ardent language. In Arden we find everywhere a felicitously controlled promiscuity of the eye: 'The sight of lovers feedeth those in love' (III. iv. 52). But note the difference between Orlando and Phebe. Phebe, listening to Silvius, immediately attaches the emotion to Ganymede; Orlando listening to Ganymede cannot help seeing Rosalind – who is really there. But even the 'buried propriety' formula can generate a certain tension. In III. ii. 371–88 Rosalind-Ganymede says that she can cure love and replace it with monastic longings. Orlando replies that he does not want to be cured, but Rosalind-Ganymede insists that she will cure him nevertheless. Then comes the moment of strangeness: Orlando replies, 'Now, by the faith of my love, I will . . .' (III. ii. 392). Orlando, whose comradely kisses were too 'full of sanctity', of 'the very ice of chastity' for Rosalind-Ganymede (II. iv. 12–16) is now sexually attracted by that same Ganymede, and attracted moreover by an offer of *monastic instruction.* Yet all remains well. It is Rosalind who is attracting Orlando. But this time the propriety is more deeply buried. Orlando is not neglecting Ganymede and mooning after Rosalind; he is pursuing a Rosalind his conscious mind has temporarily forgotten in a youth he knows as Ganymede.

This, then, is the world of Arden, a place of love misplaced yet true. The chain of unrequited love so fundamental in ordinary comic suspense is here reserved for the lesser lovers. The truest love is reciprocal and the sort of plotting that normally turns on frustrated desire is supplied instead by disguise and ragging.

Thus far Arden would appear to be a kind of Eden, and the strongest kind too, for it can accommodate and absorb scepticism and psychological tension. Yet it cannot finally find a place for Jaques. Rosalind rejects hyperbole but is happy in the fact of love. Touchstone rejects the fact of love but is happy with its material accidents. But Jaques has rejected happiness itself. Because he is radically wretched he is a walking affront to the felicity of Arden. The Duke attempts to give him the secondary status of a player within the play by treating his eloquent acidity as if it were the performance of a professional fool. And, in a fashion, Jaques is content to let it be so. Yet it is a precarious complaisance. We know that Jaques himself views the Duke as an excessively extroverted, disputatious bore (II. v. 29–32). In any case, Jaques has his own way of spoiling the show.

The ideal pattern of the scene in which Orlando happens upon Duke Senior and the rest in the forest is clear enough. Orlando's drawing of his sword is to appear as a gesture of utterly misplaced aggression. Instead of the barbarous hostility he associates with wild regions he is to meet with nothing but civility and high courtesy. Such is the ideal of the scene, but what is the reality? It is no idyll of fellowship that Orlando interrupts but a peculiarly ugly quarrel between a high-born self-deluder and a sick spirit.

The scene is II. vii. It opens with the Duke musing, in terms which may seem excessive, on the subhuman nature of Jaques:

> I think he be transform'd into a beast;
> For I can nowhere find him like a man.
> (II. vii. 1–2)

His meditation is broken by the arrival of Jaques himself, in a mood of strange exhilaration. He has met Touchstone in the forest and is fired (though we feel no warmth) by the true fool's grave pronouncement on time and decay. 'Oh that I were a fool!' cries Jaques, 'I am ambitious for a motley coat' (II. vii. 42–3). The Duke, who ought to be delighted by this change in Jaques, is less than convivial: 'Thou shalt have one'. The tone of this, though muted, is strictly comparable with that of Hal's answer to Falstaff's 'Banish plump Jack and banish all the world' – 'I do, I will' (*1 Henry IV*, II. iv. 464). In both episodes a prince is addressing his dog; in both we find an exuberance from the 'butt' which is not reciprocated, in both a cunning manipulation of tempo whereby the naked encounter of two radically opposed natures is muffled by the sudden entry of another person. In *Henry IV* it all goes very fast. The interruption cuts across the crisis of understanding and Falstaff tries desperately to 'play out the play' over the heads of the interruptors. The result is an *overlapping* of plot-movements, an overlapping which crackles with life. In *As You Like It* we find instead a tamer consecutiveness, but otherwise the effect is similar. Jaques and the Duke have space for a brief exchange before Orlando runs in with drawn sword. Jaques pronounces himself content with the rank of fool, so long as he is given the full liberty of his wit; he asks that he be given leave to physic vice. Strangely, the Duke is enraged by this answer, and cries out that Jaques, being himself infected with the grossest lust, can never give physic to any man, but only 'embossed sores and headed evils' (II. vii. 67). Jaques has claimed fool's licence and the mere assertion of the claim has shaken Duke Senior. That the fool's freedom is a test of aristocratic confidence can be seen if we compare a moment in *Twelfth Night* with a parallel moment in *King Lear*. In *Twelfth Night* Feste offers to prove Olivia a fool. He completes his Erasmian catechism, convicts her of folly, and she turns, smiling, to her

neighbour: 'What think you of this fool, Malvolio? Doth he not mend?'
(I. v. 68–9). The fool in *King Lear* runs through the same basic routine with
the King, but, at the point where Olivia smiled, Lear cries out, 'Oh, let me
not be mad, sweet heaven, not mad' (I. v. 43). Duke Senior is far from Lear's
situation, yet Jaques has the power to enrage him.

What sort of man is the Duke? He has a genius for happiness, a genius
which involves a hint of mendacity. Translated to the forest, he preaches a
pastoral sermon. As we listen to the lulling music of his lines we may imagine
that we are being entertained with what Lovejoy and Boas called 'soft
primitivism'.[24] It will be remembered that soft primitivism commends
leisure and play –

Tityre tu patulae recubans sub tegmine fagi

– whereas hard primitivism commends work. But if we attend to the meaning
of Duke Senior's words we shall find that he is, after all, no soft primitive.
Nor, on the other hand, is he proposing the hard primitivism of the *Georgics*.
Strangely, and ironically, his pastoralism is epistemological. The life in
Arden is better, he says, because it replaces illusion with reality. Truth-
telling pain is better than mendacious ease. It is a startling doctrine but on
the Duke's lips it never causes us a moment's surprise – because we do not
begin to believe him. Amiens speaks for everyone when he compliments the
Duke at the end of his speech:

> Happy is your Grace,
> That can translate the stubbornness of fortune
> Into so quiet and so sweet a style.
> (II. i. 18–20)

The irony is intricate. The Duke preaches realism and is praised for his
power to transmute reality. Yet it does not occur to him to be annoyed at
Amiens' remark; he knows perfectly well that their situation is bad – after all,
he remarks at II. vii. 136 that he and his companions are not the only people
in the world who are unfortunate, and having affirmed that he would not
change his pastoral life,[25] he does just that at the first opportunity. No, it is
not Amiens who irritates the Duke, but Jaques. And that is because the Duke
is a fantasist ineffectively disguised as a realist, whereas Jaques is a realist
very effectively disguised as a fantasist.

Shakespeare's control of the ironies in this scene is breathtakingly sure and
shows, amongst other things, how he has matured since he wrote *Love's
Labour's Lost*. The earlier comedy was polemically intended. In it, if Frances
Yates was right.[26] Shakespeare backed the literary party of the realists, Eliot
and Nashe, against the conscious artists, Harvey, Chapman, Florio and
Vives; yet the play was pragmatically self-refuting, since it is itself a brilliant
specimen of artifice and stylistic virtuosity. In *Love's Labour's Lost* Shakespeare struggles with his own facility, is as little believed as Duke Senior and
is driven at the end to mortify the comic eucatastrophe with sudden death

and marriages deferred. It is interesting that Shakespeare's problem, at the beginning of his career, was his very fluency. But in *As You Like It* he has made the technical problem of *Love's Labour's Lost* into the stuff of human characterisation, in the figure of Duke Senior.

The contrast between the Duke and Jaques is pointed for us in a single scene. II. i. opens, as we have seen, with the Duke's sermon, where the style betrays the sentiment, but it continues with Jaques on the stricken deer. Jaques's moralising is presented in *oratio obliqua* and we therefore see it first as the Duke sees it – as a delicious performance. No doubt this does no great disservice to Jaques, who would have presented it himself in exactly that style. But now the relation between style and matter is reversed. With Jaques, the lightness of the style is betrayed by the importance of what is said. The Duke, according to Jaques, is no pilgrim at the shrine of the Real. He is instead a kind of criminal against the order of nature. He has usurped the place of the wild creatures just as surely as his brother had usurped *his* place. Against all the stylistic signals, we find that we must respect what Jaques says, and that is because the play as a whole confirms his words, just as it makes a mockery of Duke Senior's. For the play shows us, not a court made simple, but a simple place made courtly. Shakespeare makes sure that we feel the real degradation of rusticity in the opening scene, where Orlando complains, 'he keeps me rustically at home', and, lest we forget, includes in the opening part of his country pastoral the grim observation of Corin on the shepherd's continuing bond of villeinage (II. iv. 71–82).

Having noted the usurpation of the forest, Jaques turned his attention to one deer, singled out from the rest because it had been shot by the hunters. This passage is one of the strangest in the play. It is written as a specimen of preposterousness, as if it has to be either false sentiment or a deliberate parody of true feeling, yet it haunts the imagination with a strange directness. No doubt it is partly because we sense that Jaques's proclaimed kinship with the deer is not altogether playful. He, no less than Cowper, was a stricken deer that left the herd. Amiens left Jaques sobbing with the deer and we cannot tell (perhaps Jaques could not tell) whether the tears were real or feigned. At the heart of the Duke's pastoral idyll is the serio-comic killing of a wild creature –

> The wanton Troopers riding by
> Have shot my Faun and it will dye.

Thus Marvell's nymph; Shakespeare plays it as a brief ritual, to the tune of 'Who Killed Cock Robin?' Jaques, of course is for the prosecution:

> *Jaques*   Which is he that killed the deer?
> *First Lord* Sir it was I.
>
> (IV. ii. 1–2)

But the slayer is not punished; instead he is honoured with the dubious coronal of the deer's antlers. Jaques calls it a Roman triumph and indeed, where scurrility is mingled thus with celebration, the analogy is close. Did not Julius Caesar's soldiers sing at his triumph,

> Gallias Caesar subegit, Nicomedes Caesarem:
> Ecce Caesar nunc triumphat qui subegit Gallias
> Nicomedes non triumphat qui subegit Caesarem.[27]

> Caesar put down all of France
> (Nicomedes put down Caesar)
> Caesar, now in pride advance!
> As for Nicomedes, he's a
> Loser (though he put down Caesar).

But Jaques is dangerous only to the Duke, never to the pastoral idyll itself. All health and love is on its side, all the sickness on his. For pastoral is the most 'tough-minded' of genres, far tougher than tragedy. It achieves its strength by the paradoxical strategy of conceding, at the outset, the falsehood of its myth. The palpably artificial style of pastoral is a necessary element in the genre. Tragedy really pretends that death ennobles and suffering refines. Pastoral, by proclaiming itself a dream, rises above pretence. It says to us: learn the beauty, and hence the pathos, of this delusion. This is the third and last way in which the stylistic problem of *Love's Labour's Lost* is transcended. When pastoral drops its ostentatious artifice we find a poetry in which the highest lyric power is united with a kind of factual bleakness. Pastoral, even more than tragedy, is the genre of privacy. Bruno Snell accurately described the world of Virgil's *Eclogues* as a 'landscape of the mind'.[28] Truth and friendship fall away, leaving only a kind of joy in the kinship between wild nature and the interior mind:

> Blow, blow, thou winter wind,
> Thou art not so unkind
>   As man's ingratitude;
> Thy tooth is not so keen,
> Because thou art not seen,
>   Although thy breath be rude.
> Heigh-ho! sing heigh-ho! unto the green holly.
> Most friendship is feigning, most loving mere folly.
>   Then heigh-ho, the holly!
>   This life is most jolly.
>   (*AYLI*, II. vii. 174–82)

Or, in the more gentlemanly accents of Horace:

> Scis Lebedus quid sit; Gabiis desertior atque
> Fidenis vicus; tamen illic vivere vellem,
> Oblitusque meorum obliviscendus et illis
> Neptunum procul e terra spectare furentem.

> You know what *Lebedus* is like, I guess;
> A place more Godforsaken than *Caithness*.
> And yet, forgetting Friends, by them forgot
> I'd live there gladly; and from my snug Plot

Survey the wind-vex'd Sea in billows rise,
While *Neptune* raves, and *Jove* occludes the skies.
(*Epistles*, I. xi. 7–10)

Jaques can have no quarrel with Amiens' song. The first line echoes and transcends the Duke's thought and in its lyric impersonality exposes the too personal frailty of his affectation better than Jaques ever could.

As You Like It, though pastoral, is not Greek in character; at least it is not Greek as the late Romances are. Its immediate source is Lodge, not Greene, and, as S. L. Wolff wrote, 'Lodge's prose fiction on the whole is mediaeval, Euphuistic and Italianate rather than Hellenistic'.[29] In *As You Like It* we find no profound evocation of the pain of loss or the sweetness of restoration, no recognition-scene of power, no pre-moral impetus in the story (again it was Wolff who observed that the writers of Greek Romance seem positively to have avoided human causation and responsibility in the conduct of their plots)[30] – in short, no resonant myth. It might be said that Caliban is no more Greek that Jaques: but he is more fundamentally conceived. He is that of which Jaques is the social sophistication. And it may be that the Greek legends encourage such fundamentalism of mind, not just because they license us to explore the nature of such things as incest and lust (though it is important that they do that) but more importantly because they are themselves psychologically radical.

For example, it is curious that pastoral in post-classical times has seldom included sexual freedom in the catalogue of pleasures offered by the simple life. To be sure, this happens in the celebrated chorus in Tasso's *Aminta*, 'O bella età de l'oro' (565).[31] But the speech is not only untypical of Renaissance pastoral (it swiftly drew an answer from Guarini); it is also in a sense untypical of *Aminta*, since its function is to evoke an antithesis to what we see in the play, which is frustration and misunderstanding. It has been suggested[32] that the comparative chastity of Arcadia arises from the fact that the true, latent subject of all pastoral is childhood. It is easy to imagine the psychoanalyst's reaction to this insight: 'If you wish to delude yourself into believing that childhood is pre-sexual, please do.' But ancient pastoral was never so deluded. We might add, neither was the absurd hypothesis of a latency period ever among its illusions. The shepherd in Virgil was twelve when the sight of a little girl picking apples with her mother struck him to the heart (*Eclogues*, viii. 37–41). And, if we turn to the Greek pastoral of Longus we find, instead of the indefinite metaphor-mongering of the Renaissance, a hard clarity of vision; for *Daphnis and Chloe* is, quite simply, *about* immature sexuality. The differing instincts of later thinkers, some of whom have dwelt on the innocence of childhood, others of whom have stressed its passion, are all in a manner admitted. Daphnis and Chloe are innocent in that they know nothing of sexual behaviour; but they are full of desperate desires. Sexual behaviour, says Longus, is not instinctive but learned (and here, I understand, he has some support from quite recent research). *That* is why his

Arcadia is chaste. And, as we have seen, *Daphnis* plays an important part in the source-material of the Romances (affecting *The Winter's Tale* through Greene's *Pandosto*).

Now: has this nothing to do with Caliban? Caliban, as we have seen, resembles the *petit sauvage* of Diderot, in that he joins the passions of a grown man to the ignorance of a child. It may be that Greek Romance showed Shakespeare a way to resolve the main paradox of pastoral, which is that sexuality is natural, yet nature is pre-sexual. This paradox, submerged in the easy prose of Lodge, began to show again in the Hellenistic work of Greene. Caliban's lust is all his own yet he learned the use of it from the newcomers. Certainly *The Tempest* is structurally derived from unequivocally pastoral interludes in earlier comedies. But now we sense a fierce intelligence, less patient of concealment. In *The Tempest* pastoral feels curiously like a laboratory experiment.

V

But we have now assembled the materials we needed. We began with the strange coincidence of language applied to Jaques and Caliban, noted by Edward A. Armstrong. The scene of *As You Like It* in which all these anticipations of the later play occur is II. vii, the crucial scene in which the Duke quarrels with Jaques. It is the Duke, and only the Duke, who uses 'the Caliban language' to refer to Jaques. When we look at the relationship between Jaques and the Duke we can perhaps begin to see why this should be so. Both Jaques and Caliban are involved with a specifically sexual tension and sexual exclusion. But in both cases a conflict of sheer power seems to underlie the sexual conflict – the division between those who use and those who are used. Jaques, like Caliban, is kept in a situation of degrading servitude, though in Jaques's case it is largely a servitude of the spirit. Jaques, like Caliban, proves a recalcitrant serf. Highly educated as he is, he proves ineducable in the Duke's special mystery of happiness. Like Caliban, Jaques is sexually impeded, though in the case of Jaques the impediment appears to be internal. In either play, the anger of the governing figure assumes a strongly sexual form of expression. I think I know why this is so in *The Tempest* but I do not yet understand why it is so in *As You Like It*.

Moreover, the context of the quarrel, with its 'regress' of ill usage, prefigures *The Tempest*. Duke Frederick usurped Duke Senior's place; Duke Senior usurped the deer's; the deer themselves sweep on in 'fat and greasy' happiness, when one of their number is wounded to the death. And in *The Tempest* the usurpation of the Milanese dukedom is mirrored in the usurpation of Caliban's island. We noted before that *The Tempest* is founded on pastoral. We can now see in greater detail the significance of this foundation. The paradox of civility sequestered but unchanged is common to both plays. And in both there is one who marks the mendacity of this situation, in the one play by knowing and in the other play by being. In *As You Like It* all this is only a part of the drama, and largely exhausts itself in the relationship of two figures, Duke Senior and Jaques. In *The Tempest* it is the play's fundamental theme.

It has often been noticed that the plays of Shakespeare do not constitute a series so much as an indefinitely complex system. Each of the outsider-figures we have discussed is linked in some way with the rest. For example, Othello stands behind Caliban, not just because neither is white, but also because of particular words uttered in *The Tempest*. Sebastian says angrily to Alonso that he is to blame because he would not match his daughter with a European husband, but would rather 'loose her to an African' (II. i. 119).[33] This, as Dover Wilson has noted in another context,[34] is the language of the stud farm. Plainly, the suggestion is a deliberate echo of the situation of Miranda, Caliban and Prospero. Again, Jaques's famous speech beginning 'All the world's a stage' (*AYLI*, II. vii. 139) was prefigured in Antonio's speech which ends with the words 'A stage, where every man must play a part, and mine a sad one' (*The Merchant of Venice*, I. i. 78–9). Or again, the account given by the first and second lords of Jaques moralising the deer (*AYLI*, II. i. 44–65) is reminiscent in tone of Salerio's description of Antonio saying goodbye to Bassanio (*The Merchant of Venice*, II. viii. 45–9).

But none of these links is as strong as that which binds Jaques and Caliban. These two are held fast in the central paradox of pastoral. The coincidence of language with which we began proves, therefore, no freak of authorial psychology, but the clue to a thematic relation. I began this essay by conceding that Caliban was domesticated at the end of *The Tempest*, and this appeared to mark a difference between him and Jaques. But what if the process of domestication must produce, not an Amiens, but a Jaques? Perhaps this is the most remarkable instance of the pastoral paradox: the wild made courtly. Yet in Jaques courtliness never matured into true civility. Thus, if we indulge the fantasy and explore this Protean evolution which, for the fictitious character, serves instead of childhood, we shall find that if Jaques is Caliban, and Jaques is unassimilable, then Caliban too is, what we had always suspected, at bottom unredeemable. Which is why a good Shakespearian like Glynne Wickham against the bias of the text assumed that at the end of *The Tempest* Caliban was left on the island.[35]

Of course, since Shakespeare in all his reworkings never repeated himself, Jaques and Caliban are at least as different as chalk and cheese. Yet it is not a waste of imagination to consider Jaques as a Caliban who has been civilised. After all, Franz Kafka thought it worth his while to write about such another. In 'A Report to an Academy' we find, in all unconsciousness, a combination of the elements of Jaques and Caliban which is almost uncanny in its precision and suggests that the link between the two is more than accidental. Shakespeare, who led us back to Euripides, can propel us so far

forward. In this story an educated ape lectures on the process of his own
education. He tells how he was 'cabined and confined' in a sort of little-ease[36]
(remember Malvolio's darkness – the echoes will not still themselves); he
knew 'excellent mentors, good advice, applause and orchestral music'.[37]
Such was Arden. He is associated with cages and biting.[38] So was Caliban.
He is spellbound by the spectacle of a sailor with a bottle.[39] So was Caliban.
He ends by giving public entertainments at banquets and social occasions.[40]
So Jaques lived. Kafka's ape could never bear to look at the female they gave
him: '. . . she has the insane look of the bewildered half-broken animal in her
eyes; no-one else sees it, but I do.'[41] Did Jaques see this look in the face of his
fellow creatures? Swift's Gulliver saw the Yahoo in his own wife and
therefore removed himself from her proximity. Yet once more we smell
difference stronger than similarity. Perhaps Touchstone is in the end closer
than the Manichaean Jaques to Shakespeare himself. He could meet the gaze
of Audrey – a half-bewildered animal if ever there was one – mock it,
understand it and marry it.

Notes

1. All references to Shakespeare are to the text of Peter Alexander, 1951, except for
   the reference on page 23 to *The Tempest*, II. i. 119, where the line-numbering is
   Alexander's but the Folio reading is preferred. The translations, except where
   otherwise attributed, are my own.
2. See W. H. Auden, *The Dyer's Hand and Other Essays* (London, 1963), pp. 205–6.
3. *Inferno*, xxxiv. 74–81.
4. On this way of distinguishing tragedy from comedy, see Helen Gardner, '*As You
   Like It*', in *More Talking of Shakespeare*, ed. J. Garrett (London, 1959), p. 21.
5. See the Arden edition of M. R. Ridley (London, 1958), p. 241.
6. *The Dyer's Hand*, p. 235.
7. See e.g. David Riesman, Reuel Denney and Nathan Glazer, *The Lonely Crowd*
   (New Haven, Conn., 1950), p. 12.
8. With the exception of the *Ecclesiazusae* and the *Plutus*, which belong to a later
   genre.
9. Fr. 32, in *The Fragments of Greek Comedy*, ed. and trans. John Maxwell Edmonds
   (Leiden, 1957), vol. I. p. 860.
10. Fr. 66, Edmonds, op. cit., vol. I, p. 834. Norwood translates σατυρίδια 'elves' (in
    his *Greek Comedy* (London, 1931), p. 35) and has the backing of Liddell and Scott.
    Edmonds however suggests (loc. cit.) that the word may be either the name of a
    plant or of a kind of scarecrow, made in the shape of a little satyr. If Edmonds is
    right, the parallel with *A Midsummer Night's Dream* is not so close.
11. See Augustus Meineke, *Fragmenta Poetarum Comoediae Antiquae* (Berlin, 1840), vol.
    II, p. 746. This passage is excluded both from Kock's *Comicorum Atticorum
    Fragmenta* and from Edmonds.
12. Fr. 17, Edmonds, op. cit., vol. II (1959), p. 320.
13. Fr. 5, Edmonds, op. cit., vol. I, p. 916. Edmonds' free translation disguises the
    point at issue.
14. *Studies in Later Greek Comedy* (Manchester, 1953), p. 115.

15. Axionicus wrote a play called *Phileuripides* (*The Lover of Euripides*); a character in Philemon (fr. 130) says that if he believed in immortality he would hang himself to meet Euripides. Strattis (who, incidentally, wrote a play which sounds oddly like *The Winter's Tale* – about a man who fell in love with a picture – fr. 40) wrote a burlesque of Euripides called the *Phoenissae*. Quintilian (*Institutio Oratoria*, X. i. 69) says that Euripides' plays were greatly loved by Menander. See G. Norwood, op. cit., pp. 50f.; Katharine Lever, *The Art of Greek Comedy* (London, 1956), p. 189; A. S. Owen's edn of Euripides' *Ion* (Oxford, 1939), p. xvii.
16. *Oxyrhynchus Papyri*, 1176, ed. A. S. Hunt, Part IX (London, 1912), p. 149. See also Satiro, *Vita di Euripide*, ed. G. Arrhigetti (Pisa, 1964), p. 63. The translation is Norwood's.
17. (London, 1954): p. 5.
18. Nevill Coghill wrote, 'It is a play about going home' in his 'The basis of Shakespearean comedy', *Essays and Studies*, New Series, III (1950), p. 24.
19. See especially S. L. Wolff, *The Greek Romances in Elizabethan Prose Fiction* (New York, 1912); F. W. Moorman's Arden edition of *The Winter's Tale* (London, 1922), esp. pp. xixf.
20. Luis Vaz de Camoens, *Os Lusíadas*, V. xxxix–lx, in the edition of J. D. M. Ford (Cambridge, Mass., 1946), pp. 153–9; in Richard Burton's translation, 1880, vol. I, pp. 192–9.
21. From *Le Neveu de Rameau*, in Diderot, *Œuvres romanesques*, ed. H. Bénac (Paris, 1959), p. 479.
22. This observation is Laurence Lerner's. See his 'An essay on pastoral', *Essays in Criticism*, XX (1970), p. 292.
23. *Hero and Leander*, First Sestyad, 147–8, in *Marlowe's Poems*, ed. L. C. Martin (London, 1931), p. 35.
24. A. O. Lovejoy and G. Boas, *Primitivism and Related Ideas in Antiquity* (Baltimore, 1935), esp. pp. 9–11. This book was presented as the first volume of *A Documentary History of Primitivism and Related Ideas*, but no more volumes appeared.
25. The Folio gives II. i. 18, 'I would not change it', to Amiens. Dyce transferred it to the Duke, and has been followed by most editors. If Amiens is to deliver the speech he should cough politely, and assume an 'It-goes-without-saying' expression, as if he were merely completing the Duke's thought for him (Jeeves supplying Bertie Wooster with the needed phrase).
26. *A Study of Love's Labour's Lost* (London, 1936).
27. Suetonius, *De Vita Caesarum*, 'Divus Iulius', xlix, ed. H. E. Butler and M. Carey (Oxford, 1927), p. 23. The reference is of course to the rumoured seduction of Caesar by Nicomedes of Bithynia.
28. Bruno Snell, *The Discovery of Mind*, trans. T. G. Rosemeyer (Oxford, 1953).
29. *The Greek Romances in Elizabethan Prose Fiction*, p. 460.
30. *The Greek Romances in Elizabethan Prose Fiction* pp. 111f.
31. Torquato Tasso, *Poesie*, a cura di Francesco Flora, Riccardo Ricciardi (Milan, 1952), p. 632.
32. By Laurence Lerner in his *The Uses of Nostalgia*, Chatto and Windus (London, 1972), p. 61.
33. Have nothing to do with the reading 'lose'. It is Rowe's emendation of the superior 'loose'.
34. See his introduction to the New Cambridge Shakespeare *Hamlet* (1936), p. lviii.
35. *Shakespeare's Dramatic Heritage* (London, 1969), p. 53.
36. In *Selected Short Stories of Franz Kafka*, trans. Willa and Edwin Muir (New York, 1952), p. 171.
37. Ibid., p. 168.

38. E.g. ibid., p. 175.
39. Ibid., p. 176.
40. Ibid., p. 180.
41. Ibid., p. 180.

HAMLET

Conversations with the dead

'Who's there?' says Barnardo, bravely, in the cold darkness on the castle platform. These are the first words of the play, and it is hard to see how they could be bettered. They carry, as often in Shakespeare, both an immediate meaning and a larger meaning, which is not simultaneously present but can grow in the mind as the play unfolds. Barnardo means only, 'Who goes there?', the sentry's challenge. The larger meaning is, 'Who is there, in the darkness, among the dead?' As I struggle to paraphrase, I find myself in danger of opting too easily for the more usual phrases: 'Is there life beyond the grave?' 'Are there human existences on the far side of what we call death?' But these fail to take account of a certain grammatical peculiarity in Shakespeare's words; the sentry's challenge, though formally in the third person singular, is partly infiltrated by a sense of second person singular, arising from the fact that the question posed is addressed to its presumed subject. In which case we must modify our paraphrase, perhaps to 'Who, of you who are dead, is there?' The very awkwardness of the sentence is instructive. The English language naturally resists such a combination of second and third persons. Yet some such phrasing is needed, because *Hamlet* is not a cool treatise on death but is instead about an *encounter* with a dead person.

If Barnardo's words are to work at all, beyond their immediate sense, they must, so to speak, be set ticking, like a time bomb. All that is needed for this purpose is that the words be set slightly askew, so that the immediate meaning is felt to be in some degree unsatisfactory or incomplete. This is done, wonderfully, by Francisco's reply: 'Nay, answer me. Stand and unfold yourself!' Francisco means, '*I* am the sentry on duty, so I should be the one to issue the challenge. Now *you* tell me who *you* are.' This exchange, with its wrong-footing of Barnardo, is remotely linked to farce, as many things will prove to be as the play goes on (two comic sentries frighten each other). But here the sense of fear is of course much stronger than any intuition of the ridiculous. We may think that Barnardo should formally have taken over from Francisco before challenging strangers, but the whole point of the challenge is that friend and foe cannot be distinguished at first. Shakespeare for once holds back on the theatrical metaphor – he does not make Francisco say, as the Volscian says in *Coriolanus* (IV. iii. 48)[1] – 'You take my part from me, sir' – but some sort of self-reference seems nevertheless to be going on: the actor arriving pat upon his cue matches neatly with 'most carefully upon your hour' (I. i. 4) and 'Unfold yourself' is placed exactly to echo the other use of *unfold*: 'explain oneself to the audience; perform the exposition'. Thus we have fear, faintly absurd confusion and a question of identity, thrown out upon the dark. And all the while someone, or some thing – something other than Francisco – is there. At line 19 Horatio (if we follow the Second Quarto) or else Marcellus, shrewdly responding to the extra warmth of Barnardo's welcome, asks, 'What, has this thing appeared again tonight?'

Forty-six years ago in his Annual Shakespeare Lecture to the British Academy, C. S. Lewis said that the thing to remember about *Hamlet* is that it is about a man 'who has been given a task by a ghost'.[2] There is no ghost in Saxo Grammaticus's version of the Hamlet story, though there is in Belleforest's. We do not possess the Elizabethan *Hamlet* which preceded Shakespeare's, but we know from Lodge's reference to it that it contained a ghost. Curiously, we *do* possess Kyd's inverse *Hamlet* – for *The Spanish Tragedy* is about a father avenging his son – and there the whole action is watched by a dead man. In the *Ambales Saga* there are angels, and in remote Greek analogues there are, as we shall see, dreams, oracles and visions of a dead father. Hamlet, in Shakespeare's play, is beckoned into the shadows by something which may be his father, may be the Devil, may even be, since our disorientation is so great, negation itself. He is then made party to the dark world, is changed utterly, cut off from marriage and friendship, made an agent of death. The Ghost tells him to wreak vengeance, but Hamlet notoriously finds himself strangely impeded. It is as if, having joined the shades, he finds himself drained of substance. He savages Ophelia, because she is life, ready for procreation, but for the rest he is lost, suddenly adrift in the paralysing liberty of a kind of solopsism; bounded by a nutshell he could count himself king of infinite space, but for his bad dreams (II. ii. 244). Such reality as persists figures, we notice, as mere nightmare to Hamlet.

'There is nothing either good or bad but thinking makes it so', he tells Rosencrantz and Guildenstern (II. ii. 250–1). Professor Harold Jenkins in the New Arden edition robustly rejects the notion that ethical absolutes are here discarded, pointing out that the phrase is commonplace and has reference not to morals but to happiness or taste.[3] Certainly the same thought can be found (though not perhaps with precisely the same force) in Spenser and also in Montaigne, who knows it as a Stoic aphorism. But for all that, I sense that Professor Jenkins is here *too* robust. There was always a seed of epistemological relativism within Stoicism itself; the rational man is exhorted to rise above seeming misfortunes, bereavement, say, or exile, by exerting the power of reason, by reflecting that all must die, or that the good man is a citizen of the whole world and therefore cannot be exiled. One senses that reason is here being accorded, covertly, a fictive power to reconstruct reality according to the needs of the subject. Real reason, one feels, is an altogether more constrained affair. The Stoic philosopher in Johnson's *Rasselas*, when his daughter died, found the reality of loss simply insuperable: 'What comfort, said the mourner, can truth and reason afford me? of what effect are they now, but to tell me, that my daughter will not be restored?'[4] Of course it is true that in Stoicism the major constraint of a rationally ordered cosmos is always present. With this, reason must always accord, and so by implication keep relativism at bay. But what of *Hamlet*, a Post-Stoic text? Surely it is not only bad readers who sense that now this thought is in suspension, hanging between ancient and modern conceptions. The passage taken as a whole is so instinct with a vertiginous uncertainty as to what is real, what unreal, what is waking, what dream, that the relativism germinally present even in Senecan Stoicism grows suddenly stronger. Philip Edwards in the New Cambridge edition[5] accepts Professor Jenkins's note, but only after a concessive clause: 'While this phrase voices an uncertainty about absolutes which reverberates through the play, Jenkins makes it clear . . .' and so on. The wilder meaning, which is as much epistemological as it is ethical, cannot be entirely excluded.

I have argued so far in terms of mere metaphysical affinity: Hamlet, meeting the father who no longer is, becomes one with death and unbeing. Meanwhile, however, other lines of interpretation are open to us. William Empson in the 1950s offered a brilliant explanation[6] in terms of Shakespeare's orchestration of styles, now naturalistic, now theatrical. It is likely, he suggests, that Shakespeare was approached to do a rewrite of the immensely popular Ur-*Hamlet*. The audience which demanded this was not however quite like the audience which had been terrified in the 1580s by, as it might be, Kyd. The new audience was keen but it was also cool. Such audiences are, by a familiar paradox, notoriously 'tickle o' the sere', that is, a shade too ready to laugh. Meanwhile, the text of the old play, which Shakespeare had before him, was marred by a crippling improbability: the hero, simply in order that the dramatist might spin out the suspense, and for no other reason, continually delayed. Faced with this state of affairs Shakespeare had a choice. He could either render the delay ordinarily intelligible by interposing a series of practical obstacles, or else he could foreground the very oddity of the delay, make his hero comment musingly on his own inaction, and so transform an original error of construction into a psychological mystery. He chose the second course and in so doing solved his problem with the too-cheerful audience. They could now be given, to their great delight, serious pastiche of the old play, in those scenes in which Hamlet assumes his antic disposition, but at any moment the dramatist could wipe the smiles from their faces by showing that beneath the histrionics lay something which they just did not understand:

> I have that within which passeth show –
> These but the trappings and the suits of woe.
>   (I. ii. 85–6)

The play thus runs on a stylistic oscillation, between a histrionic seeming and a reality which is at first light and naturalistic but proves at last to be beyond our understanding. The melodramatic style, entirely appropriate to revenge tragedy, is disparaged by Hamlet in his advice to the players, but used by him to perplex the Court.

Empson's account is vigorous and elegant, yet finally somehow dispiriting. He dispatches centuries of laboured speculation on the sources of Hamlet's inaction through a single, meta-critical move: 'You are all puzzled because you were meant to be puzzled; Hamlet is constructed as a mystery, and there's an end on't.' In certain psychological experiments doggedly conscientious academics are made to struggle with problems which they are led to believe have solutions but in fact have none. It is so with the audience and readers of *Hamlet*. There is a sense, Empson implies, in which all that vivid adventurous thought was a waste of time.

Empson's thesis, in the simple form to which I have reduced it, resolves all difficulties by frankly placing sheer negation or absence in the centre. But this is too clear, too neat, and of course Empson knew that. Shakespeare may give us no ultimate answer but, equally, he refuses to make it unequivocally clear that no answer should be sought. The negative comfort is withheld as is the positive. Trails of suggestion are laid down, so that we can sense at once that certain interpretations, though they may indeed be irremediably speculative and insusceptible of a final determination, are manifestly more reasonable than others. With all his marvellous openness of mind, Empson brings to bear a spirit naturally and vigorously atheist, a robust confidence of absence. What is rather needed for *Hamlet* is, I would suggest, agnosticism.

Notice first how soon Hamlet's scheme of histrionic deception begins to go off the rails. At first indeed he out-Hamlets the Ur-*Hamlet* to bemuse the opposition. But, as he separates himself from the ordinary, truthful conversation with the living, his motivation decays. We sense, behind the feigned madness, a real disorder in his understanding. There is one moment, seldom picked up in the theatre, which shows this very exactly. In the play scene Hamlet says to Ophelia, 'What should a man do but be merry? For look you how cheerfully my mother looks, and my father died within's two hours.' Ophelia answers, 'Nay 'tis twice two months, my lord.' Hamlet answers, 'So long? Nay then, let the devil wear black, for I'll have a suit of sables. O heavens, die two months ago, and not forgotten yet!' (III. ii. 119–25) If we attend, as Empson taught us, to the shifting styles, we shall see that Hamlet speaks at first, not indeed in the ranting style, but in the 'wild and whirling' hyperbolical manner which is similarly, though less certainly, associated with the feigned madness. Ophelia is distressed by his flippant exaggeration and answers with what must be the truth, that 'twice two', that is, *four* months, have elapsed. Hamlet reacts at first with the same harsh jocularity – 'I'll have a suit of sables' – but then seems to drop into an ordinary speaking voice: 'Oh heavens, die two months ago and not forgotten yet?' But when at last he drops the false mannerisms, *he still gets the time wrong*; Ophelia said four months; Hamlet, thinking that he is agreeing, says two. Does he not know any more? To be sure, we could be dealing with an authorial slip, or just careless writing. But the moment can be very powerful and is in fact in principle quite easy to convey to an audience. A pause, and a frown from Ophelia will do it.

An interesting possible example of this subtle orchestration going wrong in performance is provided by the bad Quarto stage direction of V. ii. 252, directing Hamlet to leap into the grave after Laertes. The anonymous *Elegy* on the actor Richard Burbage[7] contains the line, 'Oft have I seen him leap into the grave'. This strongly suggests that the First Quarto stage direction is reflecting actor's practice rather than authorial intent (for the *writing* requires that Hamlet's demeanour be courteous at this point). It seems to me just possible that the *Elegy* is referring not to Shakespeare's play but to the old *Hamlet*, in which Burbage could conceivably have acted: the symmetrical structure of the line, 'No more young Hamlet, old Hieronymo' could be designed to mirror two inversely related plays by Kyd. If that were the case (since actors certainly leapt into the grave in later productions of Shakespeare's play[8]) it would mean that actors (themselves irremediably theatrical beings) could not resist carrying on in the manner of the old *Hamlet*, and ignored the subtler controls interposed by Shakespeare, all of which accords very well with Empson's perception of the psychology of the performance. But it remains more likely that Burbage behaved in this way in Shakespeare's plays, in which case, while we can make no inferences back to the Ur-*Hamlet*, we may still note the histrionic misfiring – the surviving sign of a now *ungovernable* theatricality in the principal actor.

Even our inner selves are nourished by relations with others. The contrast between a supposedly primary, inviolable self and outward relational behaviour can be sustained only for brief periods. Hamlet sees a real tear in the eye of the actor *playing* Aeneas but can find no emotion in himself, despite the fact that his father has actually been murdered. This prompts in him the thought that role-playing can be *used*, not to deceive others but (with infinite pathos) to reconstruct some sort of motivational core, from the outside in. That is why we find at III. ii. 379 the 'Now could I drink hot blood' speech, in language which imperiously requires the 'Kyd style' of acting, but is delivered *in soliloquy*. Hamlet is now working, not upon others, but on his own, ill-nourished self.

We have passed from a logical to a psychological negative: instead of 'There is no answer' we have 'The terminal self proves to be a kind of nothingness', so that role-playing can shift from being a means of deception to being a means of constituting that which was at first seen as its antithesis. For those who relish anachronistic terms I would add, it smells of Existentialism.

The critical formula 'This is constructed as a mystery, therefore do not search for a solution' is really very odd. The feeling one gets is like the sense of sudden triviality in a philosophical argument, when someone replaces a synthetic with an analytic account; for example, A says that all voluntary action can be shown to be fundamentally egoistic if one investigates the unconscious forces involved, and B says, as if in warm agreement, that this is certainly true, since a man who acts voluntarily does what pleases him – because that is what 'voluntary' *means*.

In fact, as I have suggested, drama resists this sort of collapse into logically pure circles of non-explanation. If the audience and the good reader are to think, they must be given some food for thought. The critic who austerely abstains from the entire process on the ground that ultimate certainty is not to be had will find himself or herself excluded from the vivid enjoyment of the rest, who are all thinking, imagining, guessing like mad.

It is curious how this sequence of critical moves recurs in history. If there is a modern Hamlet it is surely Dostoevsky's Raskolnikov. In a brilliant study Mikhail Bakhtin expressed disdain for those readers who are eager 'to philosophise with' the heroes of Dostoevsky.[9] L. C. Knights's rejection of motivational inference in 'How Many Children Had Lady Macbeth?' is in the same mode. The Empsonian example is, however, one stage further advanced: Empson does not argue that we should stop guessing because we are given images rather than people; instead he initially accepts the fact that audiences will make inferences, but declares those inferences contentless, on the (insufficient) ground that they fail to cohere in an unambiguous conclusion.

Let us, then, obey the play not the critics. If it helps us to wonder, let us do just that. It may seem that we have slid uncritically from the mystery of the Ghost to the mystery of Hamlet, but, if we have, the offence is venial. The embodied darkness without becomes a darkness within; in Act One the Ghost is visible to all who are present; in the closet scene he is visible to Hamlet alone. Together with the negatives of death, darkness, the unknown, we are offered possible positives. There seem to be shapes in this darkness and the good critic knows that such seeming must be respected. Hamlet's 'I know not "seems"' (I. ii. 76) is in a manner savagely ironic; there is a sense in which he knows nothing else. To put the matter with an almost idiotic simplicity, it would be false to say, 'Hamlet went out on the platform one night, but there was nothing there.' Hamlet met with something, which may have been a devil, may have been nothingness somehow concentrated into an inverse, palpable intensity . . . may have been his father. And it is this last thought that burns in his mind.

There is another poem in which the dispossessed leader of his people rejects the woman who loves him, visits his father in the world of the dead and returns, strangely dehumanised, with a mission. I mean the *Aeneid* of

Virgil. Virgil took the ancient episode, familiar in Homeric epic as the *nekuia* or Questioning of the Dead, and morally transformed it by causing Aeneas to meet old Anchises in the Underworld. The ghosts in Homer cry, as old Hamlet cries, for blood. Behind the dominant Shakespearian meaning, 'vengeance', an older thirst for life and substance may still, obscurely, persist (think of the special poignancy of the Ghost's references to the Queen). In particular, we find in Virgil a peculiar interpenetration of horror with good, arising from the introduction of the father-motif. The grim House of Hades becomes gradually a green world with a larger sky than ours (*Aeneid*, vi. 640) before the loved father meets his son again. In *Hamlet* the ghost comes from 'sulph'rous and tormenting flames' (I. v. 3). We learn later that the flames are purgatorial, but never quite lose the sense of a loved person, in the midst of damnation, obliging the hero to damnation, is certainly there. *Hamlet* is Shakespeare's *nekuia*.

But what if the loved father is also hated? This is the kind of remark to which Empson applies the epithet 'profound', as a term of abuse. It comes to us from the most famous post-Shakespearian theorist of father-figures, Freud. I ought to say now that I am unpersuaded, in general, by Freud's writings. I have never been convinced that adequate evidence exists for the theory that all male infants wish to murder their fathers and ravish their mothers. Nevertheless Shakespeare who thought of everything seems almost to have thought of this too. Hamlet, when he thinks of his father, seems unable to kill Claudius. But when he thinks of Gertrude's present relationship with Claudius, he can stab and kill. The first thing to reach us in III. iv is the setting. Traditionally, this is known as the bedroom scene, but it may be more correct to place it in the Queen's 'closet'. Either way the implication, more or less direct, is that the setting is intimate, not public; after all, closets normally open into bedrooms, are the place where one gets ready for bed. Moreover, before this scene is ended there will be talk of things that are done in bed. Indeed, to think of this as a kind of bedroom scene is not a peculiarly modern aberration. In the 1714 edition of Rowe's *Shakespeare* Du Guernier's drawing, illustrating III. iv. 97, 'Do you not come your tardy son to chide?', shows a sumptuous double bed in the background.[10] Of course such pictures do not always reflect theatrical practice. But they certainly do reflect what arose in the mind. Near the beginning of the scene Hamlet enters the curtained room, where Polonius is now hiding. He begins almost at once to bait his mother, and the baiting follows a swiftly rising sequence from 'You have my father much offended' (III. iv. 10) to 'You are the Queen, your husband's brother's wife, / And, would it were not so, you are my mother (III. iv. 15–16) (here I follow the Second Quarto reading). It is then that he adds, so menacingly that Gertrude thinks he is about to murder her, that he will set up a glass to show her her own inmost part. Gertrude's fear infects Polonius, who betrays his presence behind the arras. Hamlet – again, doubtless, because of the intimate setting – assumes that it is the King and strikes home without difficulty. The man who removed his father he cannot kill. The man who makes love to his mother he can kill.

In the dialogue which follows, the first rising sequence is re-enacted, more slowly. First we have the comparison of the two pictures in which Hamlet applies to his father the terms of classical mythology, Hyperion, Jove, Mars, Mercury, super-ego language to the Freudians. This is followed by the reappearance, to Hamlet only, of the Ghost and that in turn is followed by the violence of '. . . the rank sweat of an enseamèd bed,/Stewed in corruption, honeying and making love/Over the nasty sty' (III. iv. 82–4) which, equally clearly, is 'Id language'. The licentious movement in the listener's imagination from 'enseamèd' meaning 'greasy' to 'semen' is assisted both by the context and by the echoic character of the word chosen. Of course such a presumption is not rigorously demonstrable. But it is part of my point that in practice theatre-goers, if not dead from the neck up, habitually indulge in such culpably loose inferences. Moreover Shakespeare knows and in some degree relies on this fact. Even Empson says, 'Some kind of sex nausea about his mother is what is really poisoning him.'[11] We still have not reached the full Freudian thesis: the son who is sexually jealous of the father and sexually drawn to the mother. But it is a tolerably economical explanation of what confronts us. Occam – he of the famous razor – would be quite pleased with us.

We seem to be involved in an accelerating series of problems. If the Oedipal theory is itself baseless (as I suggested) how can such 'Oedipal' elements be present in *Hamlet* at all? Since Shakespeare cannot have derived these ideas from Freud must he not have derived them from life? But, if that is the case, can we continue to maintain that the Freudian theory is baseless? To this I offer two (less than adequate) answers. First, a theory which is implausibly asserted of all male infants is certainly much more credible if asserted of certain evidently disturbed adults. Secondly, Empson's abusive word 'profound' may provide us with a useful clue. Freud was a verbal artist as well as a psychologist, and he specialised in *depth* – in going deeper, stripping away more coverings than any predecessor; and Shakespeare did the same. It is not so very surprising that a similarity of method should produce at times similar structures of psychological paradox. But, once more, to follow this through we must be prepared to obey the poem's imperative to guess, to assume – even, if necessary, to make temporary fools of ourselves.

The truth is, however, that Greek tragedy has a much closer analogue to Hamlet than Oedipus. I mean Orestes. For this we must go back to a yet earlier British Academy Shakespeare lecture, Gilbert Murray's 'Hamlet and Oedipus',[12] given in 1914, some thirty-five years before Ernest Jones's psychoanalytic study, *Hamlet and Oedipus*.[13] Murray puts his case – at least until he mounts his hobby-horse, 'the Year Spirit' near the end – with disarming modesty. He uses, primarily, *Hamlet*, Saxo Grammaticus, the

Ambales Saga, Aeschylus' *Choephoroe,* Sophocles' *Electra* and Euripides' *Electra, Orestes, Iphigenia in Tauris* and *Andromache.* The case, at first unimpressive, becomes by gradual accumulation of detail overwhelming.

Murray begins with broad resemblances. The hero is the son of a King who has been murdered and succeeded by a younger kinsman; the dead King's wife marries this inferior successor; the hero, driven by supernatural commands, avenges his father. This gives us the vertebra, as it were, of our analogy. Murray conceded that Hamlet, unlike Orestes, dies on achieving his revenge, but observes that in the earlier Scandinavian version he succeeds to the kingdom. In all the versions there is some shyness about the mother-murder: in Saxo the mother is not killed, in Shakespeare she is killed by accident, in the Greek version she is indeed deliberately killed but the horror of the killing drives the hero mad. It is important that in all the versions the hero is under the shadow of madness (Orestes, Murray says, has that in him which makes us feel that 'it is easy for him to go mad').[14] Like Hamlet in his mother's room, Orestes sees visions which others cannot see. Orestes is remarkable in Greek drama for soliloquy and for hesitation. This last point is put briefly by Murray but seems to me to be of immense importance for the history of drama. John Jones in his *On Aristotle and Greek Tragedy* brings out the difference between Euripides' Orestes in the play of that name and Aeschylus'. In the older play the hero is as it were crucified by conflicting external imperatives, but in Euripides the conflict is internalised and the tragic hero becomes the locus of hesitation, of an interior indeterminacy.[15] It is remarkable that the figure of Orestes should evoke from Euripides this feat of dramaturgy and that Hamlet should have so similar an effect upon Shakespeare. In Euripides' *Electra* (979) Orestes suspects that the god commanding him to take vengeance may be an evil spirit in disguise and in the *Orestes* (288–93) says that his father would not have wished him to kill his mother (think here of old Hamlet's 'Nor let thy soul contrive/Against thy mother ought' (I. v. 85–6)). Orestes, like Hamlet, dissembles his true feelings, is thought to be dead, but returns. Like Hamlet (and Ambales) Orestes is given to cynically violent language against women. Indeed at *Orestes* 1590 he is given what Murray describes as 'the horrible, mad line'[16] in which he says that he could never weary of killing evil women. Both, Murray observes, bully any woman they are left alone with.

Finally Murray turns to odd details, some of which are very striking indeed. In both traditions the hero has been away when the action begins (Phocis, Wittenberg); in both he goes on a ship, is captured by enemies who try to murder him and escapes (*Iphigenia in Tauris*). In Saxo,[17] though not in *Hamlet,* the hero ties his dead soldiers to stakes to deceive the enemy, while in Euripides' *Electra* Orestes prays to his father to 'come, bringing every dead man as a fellow-fighter' (this, Murray concedes, may be just a weird coincidence). The father in both traditions dies without due religious observances. Hamlet has his friend Horatio as Orestes has Pylades. Hamlet in the Scandinavian versions is filthy, covered with ashes, and rolls on the ground. At the beginning of *Orestes* the hero is found with his sister, ghastly pale, his hair matted with dirt and in *Iphigenia in Tauris* he foams at the mouth and rolls on the ground (307). This is not prominent in Shakespeare's play, but Hamlet does appear before Ophelia with his doublet unbraced, his stockings fouled, 'pale as his shirt' (II. i. 79–82). Although there is no Ophelia in the Greek and no Electra in the northern story, there are signs that these two figures may themselves be analogically related. The pairing of the young woman with an old man who treats her as his daughter is present in Euripides' *Electra* (493, 563). Most telling of all, in all the Electra plays a peculiar effect is obtained by having Orestes first sight his sister in funeral garb or in a funeral procession (*Choephoroe*, 16; Sophocles, *Electra*, 80; Euripides, *Electra*, 107). Compare with this Hamlet's 'What, the fair Ophelia!' on seeing her carried to the burial.

But what can such an analogy, intricate as it is, mean? In these days of synchronic anthropology it is somehow bad form to worry about historical connection, about who read what or the mechanics of transmission. Yet I must confess to an unregenerate discomfort in the face of a resemblance so detailed and yet, at the same time, so signally short on visible causal links.[18] It is hard, indeed, to avoid the sense that we have an oddly coherent body of stories, probably having at some early date an extensive oral provenance. I do not know whether at some crucial point a Norse story-teller told the tale to a Greek or vice versa, and I imagine no one does. But some such transmission is inherently probable – much more probable than the freakish array of coincidences which otherwise confronts us.

Nor do I know whether it is fair to find in such materials corroboration of one's own interpretation of Shakespeare's unique play. I have suggested, a little nervously, that there is something odd about Hamlet's relation to his mother. When we learn that in Saxo[19] Hamlet remains always in his mother's house and that in the *Ambales Saga*[20] he actually slept in his mother's room, we may begin to feel that we were not after all merely imagining things. Later, when he came to write *Coriolanus*, Shakespeare read in Plutarch that his hero did not leave his mother's house even when he married,[21] and built wonderfully on the suggestion. Shakespeare certainly read Plutarch and probably did not read Saxo. But the author of the Ur-*Hamlet*, especially if it was indeed Kyd, is quite likely to have done so. Saxo is an important source, at one or two removes. It belongs quite clearly in the direct tradition of Shakespeare's story, as ancient Greek plays do not.

Yet the analogy expounded by Gilbert Murray nags at the mind. It can even, perhaps, be made to confirm our sense that behind the revenge story of *Hamlet*, blood for blood, lies a metaphysical drama of substance and unbeing. Earlier in this essay I saw the Ghost's persisting love for Gertrude as a kind of hunger for life in the midst of death, making him for a moment like the thirsting, bloodless shades in Homer's *Odyssey*. I suggested that Hamlet is paralysed partly because he has become one of them, a dead man walking among the living, opposite to life (which is Ophelia). Like the dead he cannot weep (tickle him and he might not laugh). All of this is grounded – but insecurely – in the text. Hamlet is dressed in black, in the garb of death; he talks to a ghost and later to skulls; his exchange with the grave-digger is a conversation of two persons expert in death. Thought to have been murdered, he returns, a lethal revenant, and kills others. Yet all these things could be turned, by an unsympathising critic, in another, more common-sensical direction.

In the Greek tradition, however, the notion that Orestes is himself a kind of ghost is explicit (here, again, I am guided by Murray): in *Orestes* (385–6), Menelaus, meeting with Orestes, says

ὦ θεοί, τί λεύσσω; τίνα δέδορκα νερτέρων;

Gods! What do I see? Whom, of those that live in this Underworld, am I looking at?

And Orestes answers

εὖ γ' εἶπας · οὐ γὰρ ζῶ κακοῖς, φάος δ' ὁρῶ.

You say well. By reason of the evils I have suffered, I live not, but I see the light of day.

Later in the same play the messenger tells of the citizen who alerted him to this sudden appearance of Orestes: 'He said to me, "Can't you see Orestes walking near, to run the race of death?" and I saw the unlooked for phantom' (877–8). As Murray observed, Hamlet's sudden advancing to meet Laertes, in the funeral scene, 'This is I,/Hamlet the Dane' (V. i. 254–5) is like *Andromache*, 884, 'It is I, Agamemnon's and Clytemnestra's son, Orestes'. *Iphigenia in Tauris*, 1361, has a similar ring: the self-announcing apparition. Moreover, this is the play in which Orestes interrupts his own funeral rites (at line 67). When Hamlet says, 'Horatio, I am dead/Thou liv'st' (V. ii. 289–90) the immediate meaning is, as at the opening, followed by a larger meaning which fills the play, this time retrospectively. Again a minor linguistic abnormality, the proleptic 'I am dead' for 'I am dying' (a little like the modern idiom, 'I am as good as dead') carries a potent charge. We are dealing, I surmise, with what must now be seen as an ancient European story, and that is public matter. Again – may we say? – the fear of a merely subjective reaction is less than it was. Presentiment looks more like intuition.

I have moved from a meta-critical insistence on the impossibility of explanation (Empson) to psychoanalysis and thence to ancient story patterns which, while they tend to confirm our sense of a certain strangeness in Hamlet's relation to his mother and Ophelia, push the range of reference further into the darkness, so to speak, forcing us to confront once more the embodied death and negation from which we began.

There has been much talk about this play because, I suggest, Shakespeare

has given us much to talk about. There is meat for the psychologically
minded and for the philosophically minded. The brilliant interplay of the
substantial with the artificially (theatrically) constituted self is answered at
another level by a disturbing displacement of sexual feeling. But the
beginning and end of the play is death. That is why the powerful, complex
analogy with Orestes is *critically* more fruitful than the looser analogy with
Oedipus. Wittgenstein said that death is not an event in life (*Tractatus*,
6.4311). It is a philosophically imaginative remark, and full of the
philosopher's contempt for the more usual uses of the imagination. It
respects the logical uniqueness of death, which is, in the words of another
philosopher, 'itself, and not another thing'. It reminds us of our confinement
to life; when we think we talk about death, we really talk about dying or else,
because of some natural intolerance of pure negation, we use our intelligence,
as Richard II did, to people a vacuity – with ghosts, machinery of
punishment – images, suitably darkened, drawn from our own order of
things. Faced with this philosophic challenge, *Hamlet* fares better than most
works of literature. Lewis was right to insist that it forces us to think not just
about dying, but about 'being dead'.[22] For every more or less palpable image
Shakespeare offers a correlative, undermining doubt. The ghost may not be a
ghost. Startlingly, the Christian scheme of after-life may be a delusion (the
play raises this possibility, though only at moments). Death is not the
metallically hard, systematic landscape of Dante nor is it plainly the
simplified scheme of the Reformers. It is an undiscovered country, or a
dream-invaded sleep. The days have passed when scholars could pretend
that agnostic thought was simply impossible in Elizabethan times. Indeed,
faced with the text of *Hamlet*, one wonders how they could ever have done so.

The drama, however, hinges upon you the initial encounter, and an
encounter must be with something. This element of the play, one supposes,
Wittgenstein would condemn as self-indulgence. I have argued that
inferences and associations which may appear under the searchlight of a
sceptical investigation to be less than rigorous are not only permissible but in
a way essential to a full critical response. It does not follow that any
comparison is as apposite as any other. The story of Hamlet is nothing like
the story of Jairus's daughter (Mark 5). But it is a little like that most
haunting of biblical narratives, which tells how Jacob met a man and
wrestled with him until the light came (Genesis 32). Traditionally the story is
known as 'Jacob and the Angel' but the Bible itself seems to say what
tradition dare not repeat: that Jacob wrestled with God. Gunkel in his
commentary on Genesis[23] assembles copious analogues, showing the pattern
of the ambiguous spirit who must depart when dawn breaks: 'It faded on the
crowing of the cock' (*Hamlet*, I. i. 138). I might have struggled to frame from
these materials some sort of bridge to the Hamlet story. But my own
licentious imagination, which is not perhaps so very unusual, made the step
long before I knew anything of Gunkel's work. Hamlet never engages in

physical combat with the majestic being he meets in the night, but there is a sense in which the rest of the play is taken up with his wrestling with the Ghost. We may think also of 'Loving Mad Tom' in which the world of darkness and death throws up an emissary and a challenge:

> With an host of furious fancies
> Whereof I am commander.
> With a burning spear and a horse of air
> To the wilderness I wander.
>
> By a Knight of ghosts and shadows
> I summoned am to tourney
> Ten leagues beyond the wide world's end.
> Me thinks it is no journey.[24]

Tom Stoppard's *Rosencrantz and Guildenstern Are Dead* is more than a *jeu d'esprit*. His question, 'Where do they go when they leave the drama?' is in profound accord with Shakespeare's play, though he is readier than Shakespeare could ever be to defuse primitive anxieties with logical jokes. In *Timon of Athens* Shakespeare was to dramatise negation in a manner more acceptable, I suspect, to such as Wittgenstein. There, no images are in the end allowed. Timon's epitaph is worn away by the sea and he himself is no more. The emptiness, in all its intellectual purity, is almost fatal to the drama.

The implied argument I have attached to the name of Wittgenstein works in this way: the very force of *Hamlet*, which must be at bottom a force of imagery, presupposes an intellectual softness, an impulse self-indulgently to tame the unimaginable with conventional pictures. This argument would, I suppose, have seemed strong to many philosophers in the 1950s and 1960s. But now philosophers seem less willing to dismiss as merely incoherent Hamlet's words 'There are more things in heaven and earth, Horatio, / Than are dreamt of in your philosophy' (I. v. 168–9). Perhaps it is the play, rather than twentieth-century philosophy, which perceives the full extent of our ignorance. If we do not know that death is any particular thing, equally we do not know that it excludes or is not any particular thing. If death is a sleep, there may be dreams in that sleep, and what kind of thing would that be . . . ? Even today, in 1988, in clear daylight, do we know with confidence the answer to Barnardo's question: 'Who's there?'

Notes

1. All quotations from Shakespeare, are, unless otherwise specified, from William Shakespeare, *The Complete Works*, edited by Stanley Wells and Gary Taylor (Oxford: Clarendon Press, 1986).
2. Proceedings of the British Academy, 28 (1942), pp. 139–54, p. 147. Also in C. S. Lewis, *Selected Literary Essays* (Cambridge: Cambridge University Press, 1969), pp. 88–105, p. 97.

3. The New Arden edition of *Hamlet* (London: Methuen, 1982), pp. 467–8.
4. *The History of Rasselas, Prince of Abyssinia*, ch. xviii, ed. Geoffrey Tillotson and Brian Jenkins (London: Oxford University Press, 1971), p. 51.
5. *Hamlet, Prince of Denmark*, the New Cambridge Shakespeare, ed. Philip Edwards (Cambridge: Cambridge University Press, 1985), p. 129.
6. 'Hamlet when new', *Sewanee Review*, 61 (1953), pp. 15–42, 185–242; reprinted as 'Hamlet' in William Empson, *Essays on Shakespeare* (Cambridge: Cambridge University Press, 1986), pp. 79–136.
7. Printed in *The Shakespeare Allusion Book: A Collection of Allusions to Shakespeare*, compiled by C. M. Ingleby, L. Toulmin-Smith and F. J. Furnivall, re-edited by John Munro (1909), reissued with a preface by E. K. Chambers, 2 vols (London: Oxford University Press, 1932), vol. I, p. 272.
8. See Arthur Colby Sprague, *Shakespeare and the Actors* (Cambridge, Mass.: Harvard University Press, 1948), p. 178.
9. *Problèmes de la poétique de Dostoevski*, traduit par Guy Verret (Lausanne: Éditions l'âge d'homme, 1970), pp. 314–16.
10. The drawing is reproduced in the New Cambridge edition of *Hamlet*, p. 65.
11. Op cit., *Sewanee Review*, p. 202; *Essays in Shakespeare*, p. 112.
12. 'Hamlet and Orestes: a study in traditional types', *Proceedings of the British Academy*, 6 (1913–14), pp. 389–412. A slightly modified version appears in Murray's Charles Eliot Norton Lectures under the title *The Classical Tradition in Poetry* (London: Oxford University Press, 1927), pp. 205–40.
13. Jones had embarked on the Hamlet-Oedipus theme earlier, in his *Essays in Applied Psychoanalysis* (London and Vienna: International Psychoanalytical Library, 1923).
14. *The Classical Tradition in Poetry*, p. 210.
15. London: Chatto and Windus, 1962, pp. 272–3.
16. *The Classical Tradition in Poetry*, p. 216.
17. See Saxo Grammaticus, *The History of the Danes*, 2 vols (Cambridge: D. S. Brewer; Totowa, New Jersey: Rowman and Littlefield, 1979–80), vol. I, p. 100.
18. William F. Hansen describes the link between Hamlet and Orestes as 'possible' but adds that certainty in this matter seems to be unattainable. See his *Saxo Grammaticus and the Life of Hamlet* (Lincoln, Nebraska and London: University of Nebraska Press, 1983), p. 16.
19. *History of the Danes*, vol. I, p. 84.
20. *Ambales Saga, capituli* xv, xvi and xviii, printed with a translation in Israel Gollancz's *Hamlet in Iceland* (London: David Hutt, 1898), pp. 98–9, 101–3, 109.
21. See the New Arden edition of *Coriolanus* by J. Philip Brockbank (London: Methuen, 1976), p. 317.
22. *Proceedings of the British Academy*, 28 (1942), p. 149; *Selected Literary Essays*, p. 99.
23. Hermann Gunkel, *Genesis: Übersetzt und Erklärt* (Gottingen: Vandenhoeck und Ruprecht, 1964), pp. 359–65. Cf. Gerhard von Rad, *Genesis*, trans. John Marks (London: SCM Press, 1972), p. 321.
24. *The New Oxford Book of English Verse, 1250–1950*, ed. Helen Gardner (Oxford: Clarendon Press, 1972), p. 371.

MEASURE FOR MEASURE
The bed-trick[1]

Helena won Bertram by a trick; in response he submitted formally to the contract, told his bride how he despised her and fled, preferring the grim visage of war to Helena's fair face; she pursued him and, by another trick, won him once more, and at last acquainted him with the felicity he seemed unable to perceive for himself.

Claudio got Juliet with child before their marriage contract had been solemnised, and so became liable to the biting laws of Vienna. Isabel conceded the viciousness of his act but interceded on his behalf to Angelo. Angelo in return made Isabel an offer: 'Submit to my lust and your brother lives.' The Duke suggested that Mariana, whose contract with Angelo had not been solemnised, should secretly take the place of Isabel in Angelo's bed. Isabel welcomed this suggestion. And so the knot of the comedy is untied.

Both of these stories, told thus in the barest language, are already tense and uncomfortable, *before* we endow the agents with any richness of character or psychological depth. I therefore reject the view that *all* our disgust in watching or reading these plays arises from an illicit, post-romantic urge to psychologise the agents. At the same time, it is equally clear that if we do allow the agents any richness of personality, the disgust becomes *more* acute.

First a confession of faith, or, rather, of conviction: I believe that it is in general surprisingly difficult to impart to any important Shakespearian figure a subtlety of character and psychology greater than that already given him by the dramatist. I allow exceptions to this rule: Lysander and Demetrius seem to me virtually without depth. But take Cordelia in the first scene of *King Lear*. The persons of the play tread before our eyes an ancient and beautiful measure of pre-personal fairy-tale: an old king and three daughters of whom two are wicked and the third good. And yet, as soon as Cordelia says, 'I cannot heave my heart into my mouth', she acquires inner complexity, and the situation implicitly assumes all the tensions which can impede relations between parents and even the best children.

In *Measure for Measure* the part of Isabel is given a sexual resonance which, though it may prepare us for her marriage to the Duke, is subliminally subversive of her status as virgin-martyr. The whole play, of course, unites an elegant intricacy of plot with the greatest possible inconsistency of ethical principle. I have described it elsewhere as a minuet performed to a sequence of discords.[2] But when Isabel in the splendid simplicity of her charity and the glimmering complexity of her desires, having denounced Claudio's vice, seems almost to *relish* the acting of a parallel offence by Mariana and Angelo – 'The acting of it gives me content already'[3] – our discomfort is made more vivid because we sense dimly that we have been offered a psychological explanation which we are nevertheless not authorised to accept.

But here I encounter a technical difficulty. I have assumed so far that this union of Claudio with Juliet on the one hand and that of Angelo with Mariana on the other are, morally and legally, parallel. However, it is sometimes suggested that Elizabethan law substantially distinguishes them. By far the best account I know of the legal background to *Measure for Measure* is Professor Schanzer's article in *Shakespeare Survey* for 1960. Professor Schanzer – Henry Swinburne *redivivus* – goes to work like an Elizabethan lawyer and offers us a legal analysis of great – perhaps too great – clarity: Claudio is joined to Isabel by what was called a *de praesenti* contract, Angelo to Mariana by a *de futuro* contract. This is a distinction of canon law and rests entirely on the tense used in affirming the contract: i.e. if one says, 'I take thee, Juliet' (present tense), that is a *de praesenti* contract, but if one says 'I shall take thee, Juliet' (future tense), that is a *de futuro* contract. The curious coexistence in Claudio's speeches of a sense of innocence with a sense of guilt is explained by the dual character in law of an unsolemnised *de praesenti* contract. It is both valid and illegal. That is to say, parties who have made a *de praesenti* affirmation are, even without any witnesses, without consummation and without solemnisation, validly and indissolubly married. Claudio is married to Juliet. At the same time it was laid down that to contract such a marriage without public solemnisation was illegal and contrary to the moral law.

A *de futuro* contract, on the other hand, is more like what we call 'engagement'. It does not constitute marriage but only an undertaking to marry. In certain circumstances it can be dissolved. If, however, the parties to a *de futuro* contract have sexual intercourse the relation between them is converted *ipso facto* into full and valid matrimony. Thus the Duke is a pious bawd: in bringing two together he creates lawful matrimony.

Such, according to Professor Schanzer, is the distinction between the two espousals in *Measure for Measure*. Claudio's is *de praesenti*, Angelo's is a sworn *de futuro* contract converted into matrimony by consummation. But I am not sure what weight Professor Schanzer attaches to the distinction. My own reaction falls into two parts. First, I have some doubt whether this technical distinction is discernibly present in Shakespeare's play. Secondly I think that even if we concede that it is present, the moral parallelism I assumed between the two contracts is unimpaired.

Let us take the first stage first. Neither of the phrases *de praesenti* and *de futuro*, nor any explicit contrasting of present and future contracts, occurs anywhere in the play.[4] The distinction, if it is to work in our responses, must therefore be supplied by the audience. But in that case the audience must be presumed to have a fairly vivid prior sense of the distinction since it must spontaneously apply it to the events of the play without any direct cue, so to speak, from the dramatist. The phrase *per verba de praesenti* does occur, of course, in *The Duchess of Malfi* (I. i. 478). But to my ear the tone of the Duchess's remark does not suggest that she is referring to matters so familiar as hardly to need mentioning. She says:

I have heard lawyers say a contract in a chamber
Per verba de praesenti is absolute marriage . . .

In fact the old distinction of the canonists proved too fine-grained for the courts and *a fortiori* that which magistrates and jurists had difficulty in applying clearly can hardly have been immediately perspicuous to the man in the street. Rudolph Sohm cites a number of cases in which practically the same form of contract was held at one time to constitute *sponsalia de praesenti* and at another *de futuro*.[5] In the *Liber Officialis*[6] of St Andrews we have a case for the year 1522 which by Ernest Schanzer's account ought to be unambiguously *de futuro* – the party concerned said, 'I promytt to yow Begis Abirnethy that I sall marry yow and that I sall never haiff ane uther wiff and thereto I giff yow my fayth.' But this case is described in the record as BOTH *de futuro* AND *de praesenti* (*tam verba de futuro quam de preasenti*). Martin Luther was sufficiently interested in the distinction to vent his ridicule on it on more than one occasion. He observed that in the German language the difference between future and present is often obscure.[7] The same point is made by Henry Swinburne in his *A Treatise of Spousals* (1686, but written a century before). He notes that to 'the vulgar sort' 'I will take thee, Mariana' can mean either 'I, in the future will take thee' *or* 'I willingly take thee here and now'. The matter is resolved, says Swinburne, by the intention of the speaker.[8] Meanwhile, in Shakespeare's play, a great and positive gulf is in any case opened at once between the legal practice of Vincentio's Vienna and James's England. The consummation of an espousal before matrimony may have been an offence in strict law but there was never any question of a death penalty. This is *story-book* law.

But, for the sake of argument, let us grant that Shakespeare's audience did draw the distinction Ernest Schanzer expounds; what then? In *All's Well That Ends Well* we can assert at once that every modern audience misunderstands the moment (II. iii. 171) when the King tells Bertram to take Helena by the hand and 'tell her she is thine'. He is ordering Bertram to marry Helena *on the spot*. By line 176 the King assumes that the two are married, though Bertram has in fact said only 'I take her hand', and not 'I take thee'. The tension is much greater than is usually supposed. But our main concern is with *Measure for Measure*. Professor Schanzer explains that the intercourse of Claudio and Juliet, though it occurs within marriage, is illegal and immoral because it precedes the solemnisation. Exactly the same thing is true of Angelo and Mariana. The union of Mariana and Angelo, like the union of Juliet and Claudio, is wrong because it is clandestine. Swinburne in his treatise is clear that this particular charge of irregularity is quite as applicable to *de futuro* parties as it is to *de praesenti*: 'The Law doth forbid all persons to make *secret* contracts of spousals or matrimony.'[9] An excellent account of the matter can be found in Francis Douce's *Illustrations of Shakespeare* (1807): speaking expressly of sworn espousals *de futuro* (that is, Angelo's situation) he observes that the parties 'were not permitted, at least by the church, to reside in the same house, but were nevertheless regarded as man and wife independently of the usual privileges'.[10] So now the Duke begins to look a little less pious and a little more of a bawd.

One part of Ernest Schanzer's article suggests to me that he also views the two acts of intercourse as morally parallel; that is, the place where he says that Isabel must be ignorant of the matrimonial bond between Claudio and Juliet, since otherwise it would be impossible to account for her censoriousness in the one case and her complaisance in the other. I agree as to the contradiction and reject the proffered resolution. It seems to me extraordinarily strained to say that Isabel, throughout her great debate with Angelo, argues from a false premise. *Nobody* in the play disputes the overwhelming strength of the *legal* case against Claudio. On all hands the plea is not for equity but mercy.

And so I reaffirm the first thesis of this paper, which is that the stories of *Measure for Measure* and *All's Well That Ends Well* are essentially and systematically disquieting, and that our disquiet is exacerbated by the presence in the plays of psychological complexity.

But now I come to my second thesis, which is that the plays are also fairy-tales; the endings are genuine eucatastrophes, the forgiveness is experienced as real forgiveness and the concluding matrimony as joy. Some years ago I wrote an essay on *Measure for Measure* in which I stressed the element of vertiginous scepticism which can be discerned behind the main movement of the play.[11] I was careful to insist, however, that it was an under-movement only, and – herein actually distressing some of my more iconoclastic friends – that the resolution, though threatened, was not overturned into cynicism by what had passed in the shadows behind the main action. This I think was always Shakespeare's way. He gave the dark gods their head, and yet love always remained love, forgiveness forgiveness (except perhaps in *The Tempest*) and marriage marriage.

My real quarry in this essay is the EITHER/OR thesis: the thesis that Shakespeare must be *either* a psycho-dramatist *or* a purveyor of folklore. It seems obvious to me that he brought the two modes together, quite deliberately, in a strange and quickening relationship. He could easily have smoothed the conclusion of *All's Well*. Remember how in Sidney's *Arcadia*, when Parthenia is restored under another name to Argalus, Argalus persists in fidelity to Parthenia's other, dead self.[12] Shakespeare could easily have shown Bertram as vowing, after the supposed death of Helena, that he could never marry again. Instead he went out of his way to show Bertram entirely willing to love another young woman altogether only minutes before he is joined indissolubly to Helena. What is the effect of this in the theatre?

Why, it makes the audience *smile*. I grow more and more convinced that the brilliant acceleration of the end of *All's Well* is entirely the product of deliberate art, and that the sense of joy against all expectation, against all sense, against everything and yet still joy, so far from being achieved *in spite of* the psychological depth of the drama, would actually have been impossible *without* it. Shakespeare was neither a medieval man nor a late Victorian but a great poet of the Renaissance. And at that word we may remember how often the greatest paintings and sculptures of the Renaissance work by uniting the new achievements in realism with what seem at first sight the least tractable iconographic subjects. The *pietàs* of Michelangelo derive from carvings in which the figure of Christ is made unrealistically tiny so as to fit on his mother's lap. 'If that were done realistically', they might have said, 'the figure of Christ would sag dreadfully to either side of the mother's knee.' 'Why then,' says Michelangelo, 'I will let it sag, and at the same time I will give you more majesty and pity than you ever saw before.'

The New Arden editor of *All's Well That Ends Well* is right when he says that the second half of the play is concerned with things working out under pressure of forces other than the personal.[13] But I add: Shakespeare wanted it to be felt as pre-personal. In straight fairy-tale the pre-personal character is not *awkwardly* vivid as in Shakespeare because it is uncontested; there is no tension between pre-personal and personal because there is no personal. No doubt the pre-personal factor isolated by Shakespeare is indeed something very ancient, a way of viewing the marriage contract which we are perhaps beginning to lose. Today we tend to think of marriage as drawing all its substance from the texture of personal relationship between the husband and the wife. For Shakespeare marriage has its own substantial reality. In *As You Like It* an unhappy personal relationship is actually promised[14] to Touchstone and Audrey, and yet their marriage also is marriage and matter for joy. I have said that today we think differently, but I am not sure that is true when one attends a wedding. To misquote Tolstoy, all married couples are different, but all weddings are the same. And if research into the history of law teaches us anything, it teaches us this same thing. There is a moment of mystery in the law of *de futuro* espousals. In spite of all the strictures against clandestine marriage, when the man lies with the woman sin is in a manner converted into virtue by the mere performance.

Dostoevsky has a fiercely negative parody of this strange logic – which one might describe as the anticipation of the ordinary serial order of *causality* by *entailment* in Smerdyakov's casuistry near the beginning of *The Brothers Karamazov*:

> Once I'm taken prisoner by the enemies of Christians who demand that I should curse the name of God and renounce holy baptism, I'm fully authorised to do so by my own reason, since there wouldn't be no sin in it at all. . . . For as soon as I says to my torturers 'No, I'm not a Christian and I curse my true God', I become, by God's high judgement, immediately and especially anathema, accursed and excommunicated from the Holy Church, just as if I was a heathen, so that at that very instant, Sir, not only when I says them words, but just as I thinks of saying them, so that before even a quarter of a second has passed, I'm excommunicated. Isn't that so, Mr. Kutuzov, Sir?' . . . Well Sir, if I'm no more a Christian, then I can't be telling no lies to my torturers when they ask me whether I'm a Christian or not, for God himself has stripped me of my Christianity on account of my intention alone . . .[15]

This to most men living before 1700 (and they would understand it very well) would sound like the logic of Hell, for it cuts man off pre-emptively from God. But the same logic, when in the very act of carnal intercourse it transforms Angelo and Mariana into man and wife before God, pre-emptively links man with God – and this, for all the worries about the lack of public solemnisation and so on, may have carried in some strange way the smell of Heaven about it.[16]

Marvellous sweet music. . . . But of course there are harsher chords, if we wish to listen for them. Elizabethan marriage held at its centre a high mystery, but at the same time it seems plain that the ease with which it could be contracted had trivialised it. The disparity between the absolute, indissoluble character of the bond and the casualness with which it could be formed must always have been too much to hold in one's head. Think what it must have been like for a man alone with a reminiscent conscience: 'Here am I, having lived with my Maudlin these fifteen years and three fine children, and my true wife is that wench whose name I have forgot, whom I married under a hayrick in my seventeenth year – and her with a man and eight children of her own, they tell me.' But this fellow is safe from everything but his conscience and the wrath to come. People would swear themselves married and then unswear themselves again.[17] In Act Three of *All's Well* Mariana warns Diana not to trust the oaths of soldiers.[18] We must understand that she is talking not of girls who think they are engaged, but girls who suppose themselves *married*, and may *be* married though the world and the husband will never after acknowledge the fact. The modern audience is at a loss; on the one hand we see old Capulet in *Romeo and Juliet* arranging a marriage for his daughter with a casual celerity which shocks us,[19] and on the other marriage itself is so absolute. The Jacobean sense of marriage must have been a curious compound: an imperative at once inescapable and muted by habit and expediency. Here we all are in merry Middle Earth and yet always, at the same time, we tread either in Heaven or in Hell.

To this infinite variety, to this illimitable divide Shakespeare is faithful. We must not take from him the humanity of his characters, the magic of their fortunes or the mysterious felicity of the end; we must not be ungrateful to that plenitude.

Notes

1. With regard to the legal questions discussed in this essay, I have deliberately chosen to address myself to Ernest Schanzer's interpretation ('The marriage-contracts in *Measure for Measure*', *Shakespeare Studies*, XIII (1960), pp. 81–9) rather than to S. Nagarajan's '*Measure for Measure* and Elizabethan Betrothals', *Shakespeare Quarterly*, XIV (1963), pp. 155–9).

2. '*Measure for Measure*: Quid pro quo?', *Shakespeare Studies*, IV (1968), pp. 231–51.

3. III. i. 250.

4. The word 'pre-contract' *does* occur, at IV. i. 70, where the Duke says that Angelo is Mariana's 'husband on a pre-contract', and at I. ii. 140 Claudio says that Juliet is 'fast my wife'; the space between these two passages, however, is too great for this to count as a 'contrasting'; moreover the possible clarifying force of 'pre-contract' is in any case dulled by the presence of the term 'husband' (not fully appropriate to a *de futuro* party) in the same phrase.

5. *Das Recht de Eheschliessung* (Weimar, 1875), p. 135, n. 51. See also G. E. Howard, *A History of Matrimonial Institutions* (Chicago, 1904), I, 344.

6. *Liber Officialis Sancti Andree: Curie Metropolitane Sancti Andree in Scotia Sententiarum in Causis Consistorialibus que Extant*, 'presented to the Abbotsford Club by Lord Medwyn' (Edinburgh, 1845), 'Johnsoune and Eldare, 5th May, 1522', p. 21. The case is cited in E. Friedberg, *Das Recht der Eheschliessung* (Leipzig, 1865), p. 58 and in Howard, *Matrimonial Institutions*, I, 344.

7. See Howard, *Matrimonial Institutions*, I, 340–1. He quotes: 'they have played a fool's game with their *verbis de praesenti vel futuro*. With it they have torn apart many marriages which were valid according to their own law, and those which were not valid they have bound up . . . Indeed, I should not myself know how a churl . . . would or could betroth himself *de futuro* in the German tongue; for the way one betroths himself means *per verba de praesenti*, and surely a clown knows nothing of such nimble grammar as the difference between *accipio* and *accipiam*; therefore he proceeds according to our way of speech and says: "I will have thee", "I will take thee", "Thou shalt be mine". Thereupon "Yes" is said once without more ado.' The passage, which is from *Von Ehesachen*, can be turned up in *Luther's works*, ed. J. Pelikan and H. T. Lehmann, vol. XLVI (Philadelphia, 1967), pp. 273–4, but the translation there provided is seriously misleading.

8. *Treatise of Spousals*, p. 62. He adds, more practically, that the most obvious sense must always be upheld for any words uttered.

9. *Treatise of Spousals*, p. 194. Swinburne uses *spousal* in contradistinction to *matrimony*; cf. p. 64 (where he is talking about rustics who are in doubt whether their contract was *de futuro* or *de praesenti*): 'If the one party should say, that he did intend to contract spousals and not matrimony. . . .'

10. *Illustrations of Shakespeare*, vol. I, p. 114.

11. See p. 51, n. 2.

12. In Ponsonby's Quarto of 1590, I. vi. p. 32 verso; in *The Prose Works of Sir Philip Sidney*, ed. A. Feuillerat (Cambridge, 1912), I, 50.
13. (1967), p. xxxii.
14. v. iv. 185–6.
15. *The Brothers Karamazov*, I. iii, 7, in the Penguin translation by David Magarshack (1958), I, 149–50.
16. Once more, however, the legal point seems not to have been generally known. In the eleventh chapter of Deloney's *Jacke of Newberie* (1626) a knight deludes a maidservant 'with hope of marriage', she becomes pregnant and reminds him of his 'promise' but he rejects her. At this, Jack, the good angel of the story, brings the two together, *not* by pointing out that they are married already (this is never mentioned) but by tricking the knight into a solemnised marriage with the girl he had wronged. See *The Works of Thomas Deloney*, ed. F. O. Mann (1912), pp. 64–8.
17. Compare the passage from Luther's *Tabletalk* quoted in Howard, *Matrimonial Institutions*, I, 344. 'Now the Pope and Jurists say that marriage can never be dissolved. What happens? The wedded people fall out and separate. So they come to me in the Cloister, or wherever an official can be found and swear themselves apart; then they marry again.' Luther goes on to explain how the parties later, smitten in their consciences, apply to 'swap back again'.
18. III. v. 17f.
19. III. v. 15–20.

SHALLOW'S ORCHARD,
ADAM'S GARDEN

I propose to talk about Shakespeare and one particular idea of his time – not a philosophical idea, rather an imaginative idea: the idea of the ruined garden. This use of *idea* may constitute a small affront to twentieth-century expectations, but (since *idea* and *image* were once more nearly equivalent terms than they are today) I comfort myself with the thought that it is good Elizabethan. Listen first to the voice of the gardener's man in *Richard II*:

> Why should we, in compass of a pale,
> Keep law and form and due proportion
> Showing, as in a model, our firm estate,
> When our sea-wall'd garden, this whole land,
> Is full of weeds, her fairest flowers chok'd up,
> Her fruit trees all unprun'd, her hedges ruin'd,
> Her knots disordered, and her wholesome herbs
> Swarming with caterpillars?
> (III. iv. 40–6)

And now hear the mingled voices of Justice Shallow and friends:

Shal. Nay, you shall see my orchard, where, in an arbour, we will eat a last year's pippin of mine own graffing, with a dish of carraways and so forth – come, cousin Silence – and then to bed.

Fal. Fore God, you have here a goodly dwelling, and a rich.

Shal. Barren, barren, barren; beggars all, beggars all, Sir John – marry, good air. Spread, Davy, spread, Davy, well said, Davy.
(*2 Henry IV*, V. iii. 1–9)

Davy, by the way, has said nothing.

Two years and a world of stylistic change separate the composition of these two passages. The first, by a trick of consciousness common in Shakespeare, describes itself; it keeps 'law and form and due proportion'. The language is rationally and rhetorically progressive, proceeding by due demonstration and immemorial analogy to a conclusion. The language of the second passage, on the other hand, is ultra-naturalistic, informal, non-progressive, discontinuous. One must travel far in time to find another poet who can write this kind of desultory alfresco dialogue, perhaps as far as Chekhov. I mention the outdoor setting because I suspect that it has a certain importance. Shakespeare had of course already written a great deal of outdoor dialogue, but it is usually energised by some violent action, present or impending. Here the absence of enclosing walls is permitted to assert its influence on the conversation. Anyone who has taken a seminar out of doors knows the effect of which I speak: rational continuities get lost, and the strongest argumentative voice is somehow dissipated in the air.

The difference between these two passages does not consist in a simple transition from allegorical to non-allegorical writing. The rhetorical development within the gardeners' scene is itself far from simple. The gardeners ('Old Adam's likeness' and his shadow) are not just allegorical but *self-allegorising*. At first, to be sure, they are given the status of *unwitting* actors by the fact that the queen and her lady withdraw into the darkness to watch them. Thus far they owe their special status to a purely external change of context. But this, as Andy Warhol showed, can be done to a soup can. The gardeners, however, instantly co-operate. They begin by discussing the jobs to be done in the garden. Then, as they talk, political metaphor creeps in:

> Go thou, and like an executioner
> Cut off the heads of two fast growing sprays,
> That look too lofty in our commonwealth . . .
> (III. iv. 33–5)

Then, alerted by the metaphor, they turn to the present and imminent state of the nation, and at last the tableau melts into shadows, and the gardeners actually advance the political *action* of the play by telling her that the king is in Bolingbroke's power. Thus the primary metaphor of the scene, gardening for politics, is formally treated by orators who actually *are* themselves both tenor and vehicle; they actually work in a garden and they actually convey the news of the king's humiliation; the transition from one practical function to the other by way of allegorical meditation is a small masterpiece.

Meanwhile, we cannot say that the Gloucestershire scenes in the Second Part of *Henry IV* are without allegorical reference. The metaphor of the garden in *Richard II* was partly elegiac in character; the garden, like the moated manor house in John of Gaunt's speech on England, is as it were something remembered from childhood, now ruined. So in the Gloucestershire scenes, with their glimpse of Shallow as King Arthur's fool ('I was then Sir Dagonet in Arthur's show' (III. ii. 275)), of withered apples, old men and with all a kind of sweetness in the air, we sense a reference to the state of England itself. It is still the ruined garden, and the meaning is the same.

Some directors feel obliged to *choose* between the orchard described by Falstaff – 'a goodly dwelling and a rich' (V. iii. 5–6) – and the orchard described by Shallow – 'barren, barren, barren' (V. iii. 7) – and deferring to

Falstaff, present a scene of gross abundance. In such a production (so long as the *text* survives) the notion of the garden ruined is relegated to the plane of allusion (where it will still exert its power). Meanwhile the director finds his antique Dingley Dell incongruously peopled with ghosts and scarecrows: 'this starved justice' Shallow, Master Silence, and the wretched recruits, Shadow and the rest.

Of course for most of the Second Part of *Henry IV* it is Falstaff who carries the weight of reference to a lost Arthurian England. In II. iv he enters singing 'When Arthur first in court' and in death (*Henry V* II. iii. 10) by the moving Malapropism of the Hostess he finds his resting place 'in Arthur's bosom'. It is Falstaff who is given the beautiful language of rural England ('come peascod time' and the like) and, far more than Shallow, it is Falstaff who conveys to our minds the Arcadian idea of infancy in age. In his death (if Theobald's guess was right) he 'smiled upon his finger's end and babbled of green fields') and he describes his own birth thus: 'I was born about three o'clock in the afternoon with a white head, and something a round belly' (*2 Henry IV* I. ii. 212). As we look at him, what do we see? A white head, and something a round belly. But in the Gloucestershire scenes it is Shallow who carries all, and Falstaff watches with a strangely bitter detachment.

So the difference between the two methods is not the difference between a metaphoric and literal mode, but rather between metaphor underlined and emphasised by a system of formal variations and metaphor almost suppressed. *Henry IV* draws on the special eloquence of inarticulacy. A criticism which confined itself to significance would miss this distinction altogether. The scene in *Richard II* is a kind of *texture*, almost, indeed, a tapestry. The Gloucestershire scenes in *2 Henry IV* make a kind of existential *hole* in the woven fabric of the play. In *Richard II* it is the majestic connections which speak to us; in *Henry IV* it is the silences. Indeed Master Silence is present in person and is given the wonderful line:

> By my troth, I was not there.
> (III. ii. 39)

What, then, prompted this great transformation? We might hazard the following answer: *Richard II* asserts the myth of the divinely ordained king while *Henry IV* stresses the falsification of that myth by the usurper; hence the one play is a poem of order while the other is all about the defeat of order – and to each Shakespeare has given the appropriate style. The mood of the later work is set in the opening words of *1 Henry IV*:

> So broken as we are . . .

This answer is partly right, but only partly. Once more the subtlety of Shakespeare's art forces us to refine our contrast. For if ever there was a play about the defeat of order it is surely *Richard II*. Twentieth-century critics may see in *Richard II* a celebration of the divine power of a king. In 1601 the Earl of Essex saw something else. It is in the early play that a king is deposed, and in the later that rebellion is crushed (even if Henry is a usurper).

It is convenient at this point to distinguish two myths which operate in Shakespeare's Histories, the first synchronic, the second diachronic. The synchronic myth simply asserts an ideal order: the king is divinely appointed, the gradations of society are divinely ordered. The diachronic myth on the other hand is more truly a myth in the original sense of the word, in that it tells a *story*, the story of how order was defeated. Arthur dead and gone, the garden ruined, Paradise lost. Since this second myth is clearly present in *Richard II* we must put our contrast in the following revised form: *Richard II* shows order being defeated; *Henry IV* shows order in defeat. Thus, the language of order is appropriate to Richard II, but it is not an appropriateness of simple logical correspondence. To stress, as many scholars did in the 1950s, the synchronic myth alone is a grave critical error, an error which can, for example, transform the dying Gaunt's speech on England into mere jingoism. But in *Henry IV* we no longer watch the desecration of the garden; indeed we can hardly remember exactly what it was that happened. Shakespeare enters the souls of the disinherited (as he was to enter the soul of a Roman Stoic or a black Venetian mercenary) and contrives for them a language of fitful reminiscence. A liberal use of outdated oaths assists the general impression of impotence. They are pre-Reformation oaths, redolent of that crepuscular England so well described by Keith Thomas, the England which clung to the sub-rational vestiges of Roman Catholicism: 'by the rood', 'by the Mass', 'by cock and pie', 'by God's liggens', 'by'r Lady'. Of course none of this makes any sense in special reference to the age of Henry IV. Shakespeare is rather working subliminally on the audience's sense of its own past. The sole exception is Shallow's use of the Puritan asseveration, 'by yea and no, Sir' (III. ii. 8), which Shakespeare seems to have thought very funny (he has Falstaff mock it at II. ii. 124), presumably because it seeks to present a prudent euphemism as forthright assertion. On Shallow's lips it assumes an added character of sheer indecision: 'yes and no'.

Silence prompts Shallow with the words, 'You were called lusty Shallow, then, cousin' (III. ii. 14), and at once Shallow's memory begins to work on him, with a kind of strengthless energy: 'By the mass, I was called anything, and I would have done anything indeed too, and roundly too' (III. ii. 16–17). Notice the joyous vagueness of this (he can't *really* remember). Shallow wildly enlarges the scope of his past reputation but betrays all with the hypothetical grammar of 'would have done'. Yes, Justice Shallow, but what did you *do*? And yet the past, thus dimmed by senility and distorted by self-regard, remains stronger for Shallow than the present. When Sir John Falstaff, weighing a good twenty stone, is all but standing on his threshold, Shallow can more easily summon recollections of Sir John at the Inns of Court than he can address himself to his guest's actual arrival. 'I see him', cries Shallow, but what he sees is not Sir John coming into view but the young Falstaff breaking the head of poor Scoggins at the court gate (III. ii. 29). Act Five Scene One opens with Shallow hurrying his servant to prepare a meal for Falstaff and in the middle of his hectoring Shallow forgets what he is about:

> *Shal.*   Why Davy!
> *Davy.*   Here, Sir.
> *Shal.*   Davy, Davy, Davy, Davy; let me see, Davy;
>   let me see –
>
> (V. i. 6–9)

Shallow's mode of attending to the present is largely confined to a sort of nervous tic, by which he periodically checks up on the current rate of inflation: 'How a good yoke of bullocks at Stamford fair?' 'How a score of ewes now?' (III. ii. 37, 49). But of course at the same time the lines evoke the immemorial life of the farmer, social instability together with social permanence. For the rest, the present is all ghosts, dead men:

> *Shal.*   Is old Double of your town living yet?
> *Sil.*   Dead, Sir.
> *Shal.*   Jesu, Jesu, dead! A drew a good bow, and dead!
>
> (III. ii. 40–3)

Falstaff is an uneasy companion to Shallow in all this, coldly dissociating himself from the grosser absurdities, but at last he gives the old man what he wants, says yes to the whole lost world with a line of great lyric power, a line which, even while it affirms the old happiness, sounds strangely like a death-knell:

> *Shal.* [*childishly eager to please*]. Ha, Sir John, said I well?
> *Fal.*   We have heard the chimes at midnight, master Shallow.
>
> (III. ii. 207–10)

It may seem that I have differed from the historicist critic on a question of fact only to agree with him at last on a point of principle. I have questioned the idea that Shakespeare's dramaturgy is governed by a belief in the universal *de facto* prevalence of a divinely ordained system of order, and have stressed instead the presence in the plays of a myth of loss. It might be said that the distinction is in practice unimportant, since the myth of loss presupposes an ideal order of things to which assent must first be given. Yet I insist upon the difference. The matter must be put very simply. We are told that the world of the Elizabethans was one miraculously ordered at all points. I say, no, it was not; the words of Shakespeare tell another story. Such is the factual disagreement. But here, it might be thought, I turn about and join hands once again with the historicist. So far from calling Shakespeare a modernist for his exploration of disorder I have instead set that very exploration in the context of a highly traditional myth, the myth of loss. Myths are suppler than people think. The world is not simply partitioned

into a period of order, expressed in myth, and a period of disorder, expressed
in an absurdist literature. Myth can express anything, including disorder
itself. Thus Shakespeare in his great poem of the ungoverned land remained
deeply obedient to traditional laws of the imagination.

Yet something is wrong. There remains a sense in which the Gloucestershire scenes are, if not modernist, then amazingly *avant-garde*. I have called
them Chekhovian, and the word, though it must seem fatuous to some, was
carefully chosen. Not the thing said, but the way of saying it, not the content
but the style is the astounding thing. *Non sequiturs* and brilliant mad dialogue,
to be sure, will be found within a few years in other dramatists. But for the
gentleness with which Shakespeare conveys Shallow's mental waywardness
(nothing so gross as madness) we must wait for a long time. And for that
marvellous, hesitant, free tempo of thought we must perhaps wait longer still.
Listen to it:

> *Shal.* Jesu, Jesu, the mad days that I have spent! And to see how many of my
> old acquaintances are dead!
> *Sil.* We shall all follow, cousin.
> *Shal.* Certain, 'tis certain, very sure, very sure. Death, as the Psalmist says, is
> certain to all, all shall die. How a good yoke of bullocks at Stamford fair?
> *Sil.* By my troth, I was not there.
> *Shal.* Death is certain. Is old Double of your town living yet?
>
> (III. ii. 32–41)

Fabula Docet. We look too much to content, too little to style when we seek
to describe revolutions in literature. Almost all the tenets which are noted in
textbooks as marking the significant innovation of Romanticism can be found
in older authors. Sometimes, indeed, we blind ourselves to preserve our
confidence. It is said, for example, that the God of Pope's *Essay on Man* is the
remote artificer of a gigantic machine and that it was left to Romanticism to
find God infused through organic nature. Yet Pope actually wrote of God
that he:

> Glows in the stars, and blossoms in the trees
> Lives through all life, extends through all extent
> (*Essay on Man,* ii. 272–3)

But of course this isn't romantic poetry; the style is wrong. It is said that the
essence of Wordsworth's romanticism lies in his finding in solitude a richer
society than the world of man could offer; in his own words:

> solitude
> More active, even, than 'best society'
> (*The Prelude,* 1805–6, 313–4)

But of course Marvell was there first with a rather neater version of the same
thought:

Society is all but rude
To that delicious solitude
('The Garden')

Of course neatness is the point. The musical celerity of the seventeenth-century poet is really unacceptable to the romantic. The same thought ('same' here refers to that which can fairly be elicited in identical paraphrases from more than one text) may be used, so long as it is delivered with some pain. So with the Gardeners' scene as against the Gloucestershire scenes. Both are ruled by a single ancient myth; but the Gardeners' scene parades its elegance while the Gloucestershire scenes parade their mental and spiritual disarray, and it is here that we must look for the profound innovation. New moments are hard to find in the history of ideas. Even Hume, I learn, followed unwittingly in the footsteps of Nicolas of Autrecourt. But the world of style renews itself miraculously over and over again. The parallels between Donne's ideas and those of his predecessors have been meticulously traced. But no one had ever written like *that* before.

So my conclusion is, yes, the Gloucestershire scenes are quasi-modernist, but I would found this assertion not on the thought but on, so to speak, the gaps in the thought. 'Shadow will serve for summer' (III. iii. 133). To say otherwise, to call the author of these scenes traditionalist, would be to commit the very fallacy of reduction to content of which I have accused others.

THE STOIC IN LOVE

Talibus orabat, talisque miserrima fletus
fertque refertque soror. sed nullis ille movetur
fletibus, aut voces ullas tractabilis audit;
fata obstant, placidasque viri deus obstruit auris.
ac velut annoso validam cum robore quercum
Alpini Boreae nunc hinc nunc flatibus illinc
eruere inter se certant; it stridor, et altae
consternunt terram concusso stipite frondes;
ipsa haeret scopulis et, quantum vertice ad auras
aetherias, tantum radice in Tartara tendit:
haud secus adsiduis hinc atque hinc vocibus heros
tunditur, et magno persentit pectore curas;
mens immota manet, lacrimae volvuntur inanes.

(iv. 437–49)

And Anna, most unhappy,
Over and over, told her heart, her pleading.
'No tears, no pleading, move him; no man can yield
When a god stops his ears. As northern winds
Sweep over Alpine mountains, in their fury
Fighting each other to uproot an oak-tree
Whose ancient strength endures against their roaring
And the trunk shudders and the leaves come down
Strewing the ground, but the old tree clings to the
    mountain,
Its roots as deep toward hell as its crest toward heaven,
And still holds on – even so, Aeneas, shaken
By storm-blasts of appeal, by voices calling
From every side, is tossed and torn, and steady.
His will stays motionless, and tears are vain.'[1]

The lines pose a famous critical question. Whose are the tears which flow in vain at the end? Most twentieth-century readers assume at once that the tears are Dido's. Let me say at once that they may be absolutely right. But St Augustine, who in time at least was a good deal nearer to Virgil than we are (he died in AD 430), assumed that the tears were Aeneas'. We know this from a passage in his great work *The City of God*, where he is talking about the way reason can subdue passion. He writes:

> Ita mens, ubi fixa est ista sententia, nullas perturbationes, etiamsi accidunt inferioribus animi partibus, in se contra rationem praevalere permittit; quin immo eis ipse dominatur, eisque non consentiendo, sed potius resistendo, regnum virtutis exercet. Talem describit Vergilius Aenean, ubi ait, mens immota manet, lacrimae volvuntur inanes.

> So the mind, once its resolution is fixed, allows no disturbances, even where they strike upon the lower parts of the mind itself, to prevail over it, against the force of reason. On the contrary, it dominates them, by refusing to consent – indeed by resisting – and so imposes the rule of virtue. Thus Virgil describes Aeneas when he says 'his will stays motionless, and tears are vain.'[2]

When we have read Augustine and look back at the original passage, we may notice various elements which tend to support his reading. For example, look at the great simile which immediately precedes it. Aeneas is compared not to a rock over which the waves break impotently, but to something more complex; to something in which both motion and resistance are dynamically joined; he is compared to a tree. When the northern wind blows the tree is not merely rigid. On the contrary, its extremities are tossed wildly and almost torn from it; but the *trunk*, the centre of the tree, remains strongly implanted. Perhaps most important of all,

Consternunt terram concusso stipite frondes;

the leaves are falling from the tree and strewing the ground. As Quinn has written, this image of the tree shaken yet holding firm with its falling leaves, if we take it in as truly analogous to Aeneas, perhaps suggests that Aeneas is not merely and simply obdurate to the tears of Dido, but is actually weeping himself, even as he resists.

I suppose one reason why modern readers assume that it *must* be Dido (I am here concerned only to suggest that it *might* be Aeneas) is because of a simple fact about our society. Women cry and men don't, or at least men cry much less. Now if we were talking about Homer one's answer to this would be very simple: ancient heroes were always bursting into tears. In many ways they seem to have been like gigantic, incredibly dangerous babies. When the hero falls out of the chariot in the race, 'his eyes fill with tears' (*Iliad*, XXIII. 390f.). But with this passage from Virgil such a brisk reply will hardly do. For Virgil's *Aeneid* is one of the great monuments of Stoicism, and what is Stoicism if it is not the Philosophy of Repressed Emotion? This passage especially, as E. V. Arnold says,[3] sums up Stoicism.

Now there can be no doubt that Stoic writers are firmly committed to the repression of all emotion, all passion. Stoicism belongs essentially to that post-philosophical period of Greek culture, when the thinkers gradually stopped asking 'What is really true?' and started asking instead 'How can I keep off terror, passion, how can I stop myself getting upset?' The watchword, both of Epicureanism and Stoicism, the great selling-point, so to speak, of either party, is ἀταραξία, or in Latin, *tranquillitas*, freedom from disturbance; in order words they were, to a small but clear extent, ceasing to be philosophers and becoming what we call psychiatrists, soul-doctors for a sick and terrified society. Thus the philosopher is ἀπαθής, without passion – one can almost say without feeling. Such at least is the ideal.

Now the first thing to point out about all this is that the ideal is one thing, reality another. It is a curious thought but it seems to me quite possible, that we with all our post-romantic talk of liberated feeling are actually more effectively repressed than many a Roman Stoic – for all *his* talk of rational control. Brutus himself may have wept more easily than William Blake. If this is true, it must, I suppose, be because of a sort of time-lag-between theory and the socio-psychological mechanisms which are gradually assembled to enforce it. The Stoics talked endlessly of mental control, but the myriad small inhibiting mechanisms were not yet built into the very psyche. After all, they were still constructing the theory. We meanwhile have elaborated a counter-theory while still carrying within us the potent repressive apparatus of the old culture. English men now actually find it very *hard* to cry.

So – first of all – I would suggest that your actual Stoic, if you met him, might strike you as far more extreme, more demonstrative in his emotional behaviour than half the people you meet at the pub or at the local flower show. As an inhibitor of male emotion, a stoic training is nothing to the accumulated power of the ethos of the stiff upper lip.

But secondly, I would want to argue that Stoic philosophy, even in terms of its professed ideal, has a somewhat more complex attitude to emotion that at first appears. And here I propose to employ a sort of chronological licence. That is, in order to understand Virgil I propose to use – with a sort of historical innocence – both texts which pre-date Virgil and texts which post-date him, not only Cicero but also Seneca (and even Epictetus and Plutarch). My excuse for this (and it is not perhaps *wholly* sufficient) is that Stoicism bears every sign of being almost from the outset a highly repetitious, not to say cliché-ridden, affair. I'd be willing to bet that most of the things Plutarch says could be paralleled in the lost books of Chrysippus.

Anyway here goes: Stoic ethics can take two forms, one involving a simple model of the ideal psyche, the other a complex or dynamic model. The simple model is of the philosopher free from all disturbance of mind, all passion, all emotion: in Cicero's words, the philosopher holds all external things in contempt (*rerum externarum despicientia, De Officiis* I. xx. 66) and is exempt from perturbation of mind – *omni animi perturbatione liber sis, De Officiis*, I. xx. 67).

The dynamic model suggests that the philosopher is the man who by an exercise of will triumphs over emotion. I might interject here that it has been suggested that Zeno used the term εὐπαθεία, not ἀπαθεία: see J. M. Rist, *Stoic Philosophy*, and J. M. Rist (ed.) *The Stoics* (Rist's article). Our knowledge of both Zeno and Chrysippus comes almost entirely from Diogenes Laertius. But in fact, whereas many recent commentators stress the fact that the Stoics allowed some sort of place for moderate emotion, *I* argue that there is a sense in which, after a while, they actually go looking for *violent* emotion.[4]

The truly emotionless man has no need to exert his *will* at all. Conversely, if you want to admire the moral heroism of your Stoic in controlling his passions, you have to grant him some passions, if only as the *material* of moral conquest. Thus Plutarch's οὐσία ἀσώματος καὶ ἀπαθής, 'bodiless passionless existence', soon gives place, one cannot say to a warmer ideal of humanity, but at least to a view in which coldness is at least temporarily contested by warmth. Passion, once more, figures in the picture.[5]

It is in fact almost funny how you can watch the simple idea being infiltrated by the dynamic in the writings of Seneca. For example, in his *De Constantia Sapientis*, he first praises tranquillity and constancy, then an *achieved* constancy, and then the *achieving* of constancy. That constancy is best which is achieved with *difficulty*. Thus he will start off saying that the tranquillity of the wise man is so perfect that he can be neither hurt nor helped by another person – *caret autem perturbatione vir ereptus erroribus, moderator sui, altae quietis et placidae* (ix. 3). 'The man rescued from errors is free from disturbance, is the moderator of himself, in a condition of profound peace'.[6] The only hint of difficulty there is the word *moderator*, which suggests there must be something which has to be controlled. But a little later this comes out much more strongly. Seneca tells us that the philosopher actually goes *looking* for troubles to test his virtue on – *adeo autem ad offensiones rerum hominumque non contrahitur ut ipsa illi iniuria usui sit per quam experimentum sui capit et virtutem temptat* (ix. 3). 'Accordingly, in order that the very injury might prove useful to him, he does not draw back from collisions with circumstances or other people. In this way he makes trial of himself and tests his virtue.' Not unnaturally we soon find Seneca actually *eager* to ascribe an emotional life to a Stoic hero: *Alia sunt quae sapientem feriunt etiamsi non pervertunt ut dolor corporis et debilitas aut amicorum liberorumque amissio et patriae bello flagrantis calamitas. haec non nego sentire sapientem nec enim lapidis ille duritiam ferrive adserimus, nulla virtus quae non sentias perpeti.* 'Some other things strike the wise man, though they may not shake his principles, such as bodily pain and weakness, the loss of friends and children, and the ruin of his country in war-time. I do not say that the wise man does not feel these, for we do not ascribe to him the hardness of stone or iron; *there is no virtue but is conscious of its own endurance.*'

At this point we may remember the remark of Augustine with which we began. Augustine said that reason may exert its rule over all perturbations of the soul and appealed to Virgil's picture of Aeneas weeping and yet constant. About this comment of Augustine's two things are clear. First that his picture is Stoical, second that he *assumed* that Aeneas was weeping. The personality, for Augustine, is not a single homogeneous thing. It is like a city, with a seat of government and at the same time suburbs where mutiny and rebellion may rage. Epictetus, the Greek Stoic thinker whom Augustine admired (he called the *Encheiridion liber Epicteti nobilissimi Stoici*), having affirmed the urgency of controlling all passion, says[7] 'yet I must not be passionless, like a statue, but maintain all relations natural and acquired' (an interesting passage, because I am sure that in popular Stoicism people actually *did* model themselves on Roman statues). There is a surviving fragment of Epictetus from the lost fifth book of the *Discourses* which comes very close indeed to Augustine's words:

> The appearance by which the mind of man is smitten with the first aspect of a thing as it approaches the soul, are not matters of the will, nor can we control them; but by a certain force of their own the objects which we have to comprehend are borne in upon us. [Now he begins to sound like Augustine.] But that ratification of them, which we name assent, whereby the appearances are comprehended and judged, these are voluntary and are done by human choice. Soon, however, the philosopher doth not approve the appearances to be truly objects of terror to his soul, – that is to say, he assents not to them nor ratifies them; but he rejects them, and casts them out. [This is very like Augustine's *eisque non consentiendo, sed potius resistendo*.]

Epictetus goes on:

> The Philosopher . . . though for a short time his colour and countenance have been changed, doth not then assent, but he retains in its steadfastness and vigour the opinion he ever had of these appearances, that they are in no wise to be feared, but affright only by a false show and empty threat.[8]

It is quite interesting to see Augustine bringing out this aspect of Stoicism. Interesting, but really unsurprising, since Augustine becomes himself almost the type of dynamic, contested virtue as against the tranquil unopposed virtue of an Aquinas. And it is among the adherents of the Augustinian revival in the sixteenth and seventeenth centuries that one finds the clearest examples of people who *need* the recalcitrant material of moral conquest, even to the point of courting sin. (Freud said of Dostoevsky and the Russian mystical tradition that they were men who deliberately sinned *in order to repent*.)

So – state of play so far – Virgil's Aeneas is a Stoic hero, according to the dynamic rather than the simple model. Such a conclusion would, I am sure, be agreeable to Cyril Bailey, who maintained, in his book on Religion in Virgil, that, more than any other, Stoicism was the dominant philosophy of the *Aeneid*. This would seem to be the time – before it is too late – to ask, in what ways is the *Aeneid not* a Stoic poem? For me the chief thing which divides Virgil from the great Stoics is that in the ethical scheme of his poem *iustitia* and *ratio* are replaced by something which would not have looked ethical *at all* to Chrysippus – *amor*. In Seneca the word is not prominent. Erotic love between the sexes he treats as a rudimentary physical need, a sort of trivial secretion of the body to be discharged when necessary and forthwith forgotten:

Libido, qua necesse est, fluat.
De Tranquillitate Animi. IX. 2.

(Ah, the bland brutality of Latin!) But in Virgil, love of the sexes, love of parents, love of country are all comprehended in the word *amor*, which becomes at once an ethical term. Ethical terms in Stoicism lack warmth. Virgil annexed for morality one of the warmest words of all.

The thing is immediately obvious in Aeneas' love of his home. This becomes, in the marvellously subtle tapestry of the *Aeneid*, a mysterious and shifting thing. Aeneas is expelled from Troy, the home he loved, and sent wandering over the seas in search of another home, one which is really more deeply his than Troy ever was. The first six books of the *Aeneid* are, like the *Odyssey*, a νόστος or home-coming, yet they are also a journey into the unknown. Little of this would be tolerated in a Stoic seminar. Love of individuals, even of individual places, is a threat to the unperturbed and tranquil rational soul. Love is psychically dangerous. You can get hurt. Thus the Stoic hero is a Citizen of the World and *cannot* be expelled or banished from his home:

Ego terras omnis tamquam meas,
meas tamquam omnium . . .

I regard all lands as my own,
my own as belonging to all.[9]

Patriam meam esse mundum sciam

I shall know that my country is the world.[10]

The mind is its own place and can at will conceptually modify external reality. (This is the dangerous relativism lurking in Stoic theory. Compare Hamlet's 'there is nothing either good or bad but thinking makes it so' (II. ii. 250). Thus Shakespeare's Coriolanus, a sort of unthinking Stoic hero (as against Brutus in *Julius Caesar* who is a *self-conscious* Stoic), when banished by the Romans turns his broad back, and says 'I banish you'.[11] But if ever there was a man sensitive to the pain, to the real evil of exile, it was Aeneas.

I have so far, with rather emotive words like 'warm' and 'cold', tended to disparage Stoicism, but I think I should make some effort to acknowledge the real philosophical force which still inheres in this 'post-philosophical therapeutic philosophy'. In this transition from an ethical philosophy which essentially sets personal love and devotion on one side to a philosophy which makes personal love the centre of the ethical life, something very mysterious is going on. It often used to be said that Virgil was an *anima naturaliter Christiana* – a man whose mind was on the very edge of Christianity – and I think there is a certain truth in this old critical superstition.

By the same token Christianity has happened, we are all now either Christian or post-Christian and it is almost impossible for us to look back on this transition without an immensely powerful – once again a *warm* – presumption that the Stoics must be wrong and Virgil must be right. Before we finally close the door we should make some attempt to see if there might be a real *moral* appeal in the older view.

The Stoic could say that there is a sense in which love is incompatible with perfect morality as long as justice or fairness is allowed a paramount importance. I am not thinking here of the conflict between mercy and justice, but of a deeper, less resolvable, less obvious conflict. Love is personal, and necessarily specific in its object. A mother may harbour her son and hide him from the police although she knows him to be a psychopathic killer. She does so because she loves him. We tend in this society to avert our minds from such cases – certainly we avoid condemning the mother's action – and we concentrate instead on cases where love and basic morality coincide – the man who loves his wife and saves her from the Gestapo. But cases of this (second) sort do not test the hypothesis: 'Love is basic in morality'. For that kind of testing we need instances of love isolated from merely coincidental ethical support. The Romans were much more willing to look at these than we are, and frankly admired Lucius Junius Brutus (the first Brutus), who as magistrate condemned his own sons to death.

If you want to look at the same problem in slightly cooler terms, take the notion of loyalty. Is loyalty a virtue? To be consistent the Stoic should say that it is not *of itself* virtuous, though it may be justified by service in a good cause. For Virgil, on the other hand, loyalty is quite obviously and immediately a virtue – 'loyal' is one of the possible translations of *pius*. As long as we confine ourselves to situations where loyalty is lavished upon some good cause we shall not have tested the proposition: 'Loyalty *itself* is virtuous'. Loyalty to the French Resistance was obviously a good thing, but then your rationally good men would have supported the French Resistance anyway, not out of loyalty, but simply because it was right. Ordinary general virtue would cover such actions without any need to invoke this special virtue. Loyalty is indeed isolated only in those situations where the cause to which it is attached is *not* obviously good: 'My country right or wrong'. But, surely, 'my country wrong' *must be* – is confessedly – immoral? What do we think of those who were loyal to the Nazis? In fact it is a consequence of our Christian, anti-Stoic training that we in a manner flinch from the thought.

Of course Christianity has in a way either transcended or evaded this problem by requiring that love should be universal. I'm never sure how far this is a sort of conceptual conjuring-trick. I said a few minutes ago that love was essentially personal and specific in its object. That is in pretty clear contradiction with Christian teaching. I find myself that when love is made *wholly* comprehensive and non-specific, it really is something else: something much more like Stoic rational benevolence after all. But this is a large question which I do not pretend to solve here. In Virgil it is I think clear that the moral world is *all* specific loves, specific loyalties.

Take Aeneas' reply to Dido of line 331:

ille Iovis monitis immota tenebat
lumina et obnixus curam sub corde premebat.
tandem pauca refert: 'ego te, quae plurima fando
enumerare vales, numquam, regina, negabo
promeritam, nec me meminisse pigebit Elissae,
dum memor ipse mei, dum spiritus hos regit artus.
pro re pauca loquar. neque ego hanc abscondere furto
speravi (ne finge) fugam, nec coniugis umquam
praetendi taedas aut haec in foedera veni.
me si fata meis paterentur ducere vitam
auspiciis et sponte mea componere curas,
urbem Troianam primum dulcisque meorum
reliquias colerem, Priami tecta alta manerent,
et recidiva manu posuissem Pergama victis.
sed nunc Italiam magnam Gryneus Apollo,
Italiam Lyciae iussere capessere sortes;
hic amor, haec patria est. si te Karthaginis arces
Phoenissam Libycaeque aspectus detinet urbis,
quae tandem Ausonia Teucros considere terra
invidia est? et nos fas extera quaerere regna.
me patris Anchisae, quotiens umentibus umbris
nox operit terras, quotiens astra ignea surgunt,
admonet in somnis et turbida terret imago;
me puer Ascanius capitisque iniuria cari,
quem regno Hesperiae fraudo et fatalibus arvis.
nunc etiam interpres divum, Iove missus ab ipso
(testor utrumque caput), celeris mandata per auras
detulit; ipse deum manifesto in lumine vidi
intrantem muros vocemque his auribus hausi.
desine meque tuis incendere teque querellis.
Italiam non sponte sequor.'

'There was nothing he could say. Jove bade him keep
Affection from his eyes, and grief in his heart
With never a sign. At last, he managed something: –
'Never, O Queen, will I deny you merit
Whatever you have strength to claim; I will not
Regret remembering Dido, while I have
Breath in my body, or consciousness of spirit.
I have a point or two to make. I did not,
Believe me, hope to hide my flight by cunning;
I did not, ever, claim to be a husband,
Made no such vows. If I had fate's permission
To live my life my way, to settle my troubles
At my own will, I would be watching over
The city of Troy, and caring for my people,
Those whom the Greeks had spared, and Priam's palace
Would still be standing; for the vanquished people
I would have built the town again. But now
It is Italy I must seek, great Italy,
Apollo orders, and his oracles
Call me to Italy. There is my love,

> There is my country. If the towers of Carthage,
> The Libyan citadels, can please a woman
> Who came from Tyre, why must you grudge the Trojans
> Ausonian land? It is proper for us also
> To seek a foreign kingdom. I am warned
> Of this in dreams: when the earth is veiled in shadow
> And the fiery stars are burning, I see my father,
> Anchises, or his ghost, and I am frightened,
> I am troubled for the wrong I do my son,
> Cheating him out of his kingdom in the west,
> And lands that fate assigns him. And a herald,
> Jove's messenger – I call them both to witness –
> Has brought me, through the rush of air, his orders;
> I saw the god myself, in the full daylight,
> Enter these walls, I heard the words he brought me.
> Cease to inflame us both with your complainings;
> I follow Italy not because I want to.'[12]

The tone of this speech is at first legalistic (Humphries misses the proper meaning of *pro re pauca loquar*, 'I have little to say *about this case*'). As he goes on he continues to sound careful – even repressed – until he at last says, very touchingly, that he does not want to follow Italy. Here one expects him to say, 'If I could do what I wanted, I'd stay here with you', but instead he says, 'What I want is Troy back again'. He wants neither Carthage nor Rome, and Troy is irretrievably gone. Nevertheless, one is led gradually to expect a Stoic conclusion: 'Reason tells me I must found Rome.' But instead we get:

> It is Italy I must seek, great Italy,
> Apollo orders, and his oracles
> Call me to Italy, *There is my love,*
> *There is my country.*

What is opposed to erotic love and nostalgic inclination is not reason, but another kind of love. This other kind of love is something infinitely mysterious, involved more with an effort of religious faith in the subject than with any sensuous apprehension of the object. Aeneas, by an effort of the spiritual will, already loves the place he does not know (yet it is more anciently his than Troy was). The word which commands this love in the *Aeneid* is, interestingly, not *Roma* but *Italia*. Remember the first glimpse of Italy at iii. 521:

> iamque rubescebat stellis Aurora fugatis,
> cum procul obscuros collis humilemque videmus
> Italiam. Italiam primus conclamat Achates,
> Italiam laeto socii clamore salutant.

> As day reddened
> and the stars faded, we saw a coast, low-lying,
> And made out hills. 'Italy', cried Achates,
> 'Italy!' all the happy sailors shouted.[13]

At first the place is merely hinted through the refracting medium of Greek:

Est locus, Hesperium Grai cognomine dicunt
(iii. 163)

There is a place, the Greeks call it 'Hesperia'.

Then there is the strange image of Italy as something which flies from the pursuer, as when Dido says (almost as if she were speaking of a rival):

I, sequere Italiam ventis, pete regna per undas
(iv. 381)

So, chase Italy down the winds, seek your kingdom
through the waves.

Many critics have felt that this love-of-the-thing-unknown which in Virgil replaces Stoic *ratio* as the moral heart of this poem is fundamentally *religious*. And yet the object of this love – Italy and future Rome – though unknown to Aeneas, is crushingly familiar to Virgil's listeners, who are sitting there in the middle of this vast monument of power and vulgar cruelty.

Arising from this is a sort of unease and moral tension, even desperation, in the poem. Italy eludes Aeneas' grasp because, if she did not, her real visage would be seen. The pageant in Book vi ends with the death of Marcellus, the last book ends with the death of an unconsenting Turnus. This element of half-articulated dissent can be partly dealt with by the poet in two possible ways. First he can make the 'love of the unknown' into love of the *radically* unknown – that is, he can turn the poem into a sort of instinctive allegory of a religious quest – so that we intuit in the poem a vision of the City of God beyond the earthly. Thus Dante read the poem and was no fool to do so. Certainly the Olympian Homeric apparatus is no adequate object for the longing of Aeneas and his dispossessed followers.

The other way is to draw on what is empirically known in order to give substance to the love – without conjuring up Rome itself. This accounts for the emphasis on Italy and a pastoral remote past rather than on the city.

Yet the poem itself fights these palliatives, in the running imagery of pastoral opposed to Aeneas. The Roman gifts of law and government which Aeneas brings are scarcely needed by the Latins, who as Latinus explains (vii. 203) are a simple people, righteous *sponte sua*, and have no need of sanctions. The first thing Aeneas does in the poem is to kill a deer (i. 190). The war in Italy is precipitated when Iulus, the son of Aeneas, kills the pet deer of Silvia, the woodland girl. Above all, Dido is likened to a stricken deer (iv. 2–4, 69. 550–1):

volnus alit venis et caeco carpitur igni.
multa viri virtus animo multusque recursat
gentis honos; haerent infixi pectore voltus

. . . qualis coniecta cerva sagitta,

non licuit thalami expertem sine crimine vitam
degere, more ferae, . . .

Deep in her veins
The wound is fed; she burns with hidden fire.
His manhood and the glory of his race,
Are an obsession with her, like his voice
Gesture and countenance.

. . . a deer
With a hunter's careless arrow in her flank . . .

It was not permitted,
It seems for me to live apart from wedlock,
A blameless life. An animal does better.

Remember the simile with which I began. I observed in passing that the tree stretched between Heaven and Hell seemed almost medieval – an allegorical tree between Good and Evil. Earlier in the talk I asked you to take seriously the detail of the analogy between the tree and a possibly weeping Aeneas. But what of these branches in Heaven and roots in Hell? Surely Virgil should have avoided this awkward collision of values (since it is the roots of the tree which are displaying Stoic virtue and tenacity, and the wayward branches which are swayed by passionate love). Why then are the roots of Hell and the branches akin to Heaven? It's a rather unfashionable suggestion, but I'll make it: *could* Virgil's unconscious be breaking through, *against* the Stoic tenor of the passage, in the opposite tenor of the imagery?

Notes

1. Trans. R. Humphries, *The Aeneid of Virgil* (New York, 1951), p. 103.
2. *City of God*, ix, 4.
3. *Roman Stoicism* (Oxford, 1911), p. 391.
4. There was a highly technical but interested counter-movement carried out within Stoicism by Posidonius, who said Chrysippus was wrong to insist on the unitary rational character of the soul; the soul includes emotions. See I. G. Kidd, 'Posidonius on emotions', in A. A. Long (ed.) *Problems in Stoicism* (London, 1971), especially p. 203. Posidonius further insisted that emotions are both irrational and
   integral to the human spirit.
5. Throughout this discussion I lump together emotion/passion/disturbance as comprehended under the word πάθη. Many modern soothing commentators (most notably Rist) stress that the Stoics were happy to admit decent emotions and by πάθη meant only perturbations of a strongly irrational character. But, if that is so, why did they feel that they were in disagreement with the Peripatetics who believed in μετριοπαθεία – the cultivation of decent and the exclusion of violent emotion? Rist says it was a cross-purpose conversation – the Peripatetics happened to use πάθος to connote emotion, the Stoics not. Dubious?
6. Aubrey Stewart's Bohn translation.
7. Dissertation, III. ii. 1–10 in Schweighaüser's edition (Leipzig, 1799), vol. I, p. 359.
8. Fragment (180) in Schweighaüser, translated by T. W. Rolleston, *The Teaching of*

Epictetus, being the Encheiridion of Epictetus, with Selections from the 'Dissertations' and the 'Fragments' (London, 1886), p. 59.

9. Seneca, *Dialogorum Lib. VII, De Vita Beata, xx. 3.*
10. Ibid., XX. 5.
11. *Coriolanus,* III. iii. 121.
12. Humphries, pp. 98–101.
13. Humphries, p. 79.

FISHES IN THE TREES

I

We all know now that tradition can as easily confer life as death. We do not censure El Greco because his work derives from Tintoretto's. The old romantic idea that the derivative is bad is now tacitly limited to examples of *passive* derivation, to poets whose writing is not only drawn from but is also reducible to the work of predecessors. It seems that we must distinguish between, on the one hand, active traditions, like that of seventeenth-century English verse with its endless innovation, its chronic impetus, and on the other, passive, retrospective traditions. After all, it might be said, the romantics never really wished to deny the excellence of Webster (who is clearly in the tradition of Shakespeare); they were rather concerned with the frigid 'rule-dominated' art of neo-classicism – and here, surely, tradition was truly a kind of mortification. But this generalisation, too, is over-confident. We never really know whence life may come. The repetition of even the most barren and jejune classical motif can result in a scarcely foreseeable enrichment of our literature.

At the beginning of his *Ars Poetica* Horace tells us what the bad artist is like. He is a person who grotesquely misdescribes the world, who paints scenes which have no place in reality:

> qui variare cupit rem prodigialiter unam,
> delphinum silvis appingit, fluctibus aprum . . .

> The man who is keen to vary his subject in the
> most marvellous way paints the dolphin in the woods,
> the boar in the waves of the sea.

> (29–30)

As a means of distinguishing bad poets from good this is, of course, useless. The greatest poets in the world have again and again shown us prodigies, not, indeed, because they thought them normal, but precisely because the abnormal was, for the moment, their concern. Only a bad poet, says Horace, would ever give us fishes in the trees. Was it a bad poet, then, who wrote these lines?

> . . . terruit gentis, grave ne rediret
> saeculum Pyrrhae nova monstra questae,
> omne cum Proteus pecus egit altos
>   visere montes,
>
> piscium et summa genus haesit ulmo
> nota quae sedes fuerat columbis,
> et superiecto pavidae natarunt
>   aequore dammae.
>   (*Odes*, I. ii. 5–12)

He has filled the nations with fear, lest the age
of Pyrrha should come back, replete with new
prodigies, the time when Proteus led out his marine
flock to gaze upon the high mountains and fishes
clung to the elm-tree tops, where formerly pigeons
had nested, while the scared deer went swimming on
the flood.

Horace the poet had, it seems, a healthy contempt for Horace the critic.

It will be said that all this depends on a naïvely literal reading of the *Ars Poetica*; that when Horace tells us not to set human heads on equine bodies (as he does in the Heads, Bodies and Legs opening section of the poem) his language is gnomic, pithy, with the special laconic extravagance of good conversation, so that it is absurd to collect actual examples of centaurs and prodigies: all he means is, 'Don't put the cart before the horse, don't give us a fish out of water.' But we have only to reread Horace's lines to see that this particular escape route is cut off. He is too circumstantial by half. With some care he describes a painting of a creature half woman half fish and asks, 'Who can forbear to smile?' The answer rises in our minds with a swiftness which is almost embarrassing (for we do not want Horace to be a fool): 'Anyone'. Mermaids are not funny, nor was Virgil's Scylla. C. O. Brink[1] has another expedient to rescue Horace; he points out that the line

> qui variare cupit rem prodigialiter unam
>   (29)

implies that a certain degree of variation is proper, since the next line

> delphinum silvis appingit, fluctibus aprum

is in antithesis to its predecessor: 'the man who is essaying the legitimate end of variation ends by producing a monster.' From this and some other passages Brink concludes that Horace is moving in a tensely dialectical suspension between the polar ideals of unity and variety. But 'dialectical' is not appropriate. There is no real theoretical tension here. Horace unequivocally and repeatedly attacks extreme incongruity. The word *prodigialiter* –

probably used pejoratively here – effectively embarrasses Brink's reading. Modest variation Horace is of course willing to admit, since it is compatible both with unity of tone and ordinary verisimilitude. But he has inadvertently outlawed conscious paradox, which neither he nor any other great poet after Homer can afford to do.

Moreover, we cannot help noticing that, as soon as Horace in the *Ars Poetica* begins to give examples of what good poets don't do, at that very point his verse becomes poetry. Horace is parasitic upon his imagined victims. Had not Virgil himself written:

> Ante leves ergo pascentur in aethere cervi
> et freta destituent nudos in litore piscis . . .
> (*Eclogues*, i. 59–60)

> The light deer shall graze in the air first, and
> the seas shall abandon the fishes, naked on the
> shore . . . ?

This is, after all, the ancient trope of the ἀδύνατα, the *Impossibilia*, descending from Archilochus. Horace's audience knew this, and so we might be tempted for a moment to construe the passage as, after all, a sophisticated joke. In fact, Horace's lines are really both elegantly turned and intellectually inchoate. In this complex world of literary discourse this rustic simplicity (however urbanely expressed) can only be very unfortunate.

Or so we may have thought. But in seventeenth-century France we find a kind of echo of the Horatian sally in *L'Art Poétique* of Boileau:

> N'imitez pas ce Fou, qui décrivant les mers
> Et peignant au milieu de leur flots entrouverts
> L'Hebreu sauvé du joug de ses injustes Maistres,
> Met pour le voir passer les poissons aux fenestres,
> Peint le petit Enfant, qui *va, saute, revient*,
> *Et joyeux à sa mère offre un caillou qu'il tient.*
> Sur de trop vains objets c'est arrester la veuë.
> Donnez à vostre ouvrage une juste étenduë.
> (iii. 261–8)

What looked like mere confusion in Horace has sorted itself out into a systematically polemical literary situation. The Horatian use of the *Impossibilia* has become a repeatable motif in its own right, a *topos* within a *topos*. Horace, it might be said, did not know what he meant, and so history had to work it out for him. With Boileau we no longer pretend that incongruity has never found a place in serious art; we grant that it has, and are thus enabled to pronounce an intelligible condemnation on an identifiable criminal. 'Identifiable' is not too strong, for Boileau's readers knew that by 'ce Fou' Boileau meant Marc-Antoine de Gérard de Saint-Amant, author of the Biblical epic *Moyse Sauvé*.

The poetry of Saint-Amant is full of birds and fishes. Baroque to his finger-tips, he neglects the heavy element of earth and prefers the heady rarefaction of water and air. Moreover, as Gérard Genette points out,[2] he is never so happy as when the birds swim and the fishes take to the air. It was a matter of no small delight to him that in the southern hemisphere (where the world really is reversed) there really are flying fishes.[3] Children know that in Australia everybody is upside down; Baroque poets, in some ways so unchildlike, are like children in their sense of Up and Down. Andrew Marvell wrote:

> But now the *Salmon-Fishers* moist
> Their *Leathern Boats* begin to hoist;
> And, like *Antipodes* in Shoes,
> Have shod their *Heads* in their *Canoos.*
> How *Tortoise like*, but not so slow,
> These rational *Amphibii* go?
> Let's in: for the dark *Hemisphere*
> Does now like one of them appear.
> (*Upon Appleton House*, 769–76)

Saint-Amant's poetry can be tedious, but he has his moments of sublimity, and these moments commonly involve a kind of vertigo. I have myself always been strongly affected by any poetry which expresses the unfathomable magnitude of the sky, by, say, Romeo's upward-gazing lines –

> thou art
> As glorious to this night being o'er my head,
> As is a winged messenger of heaven
> Unto the white-upturned wond'ring eyes
> Of mortals that fall back to gaze on him,
> When he bestrides the lazy-pacing clouds
> And sails upon the bosom of the air.
> (*Romeo and Juliet*, II. ii. 25–32)

or by Dante's comparison of the Giant Antaeus to the leaning Torre Garisenda at Bologna (if you stand under the tower and look up as a cloud passes over, the tower seems to begin to fall – *Inferno*, xxxi. 136–9). Or, again, by the marvellous passage in *The Merchant of Venice* when Lorenzo turns the world over and sets the sky under our feet with

> Look how the floor of heaven
> Is thick inlaid with patines of bright gold;
> (V. i. 57–8)

Saint-Amant has lines which can rank with these. In one place he has the marvellous phrase 'les abismes du ciel',[4] and in another speaks of water as a fluent mirror in which the sun can see himself in an explosion of light, a second sunburst in the nether sky.[5] This, then, is Boileau's chosen butt. The lines of battle are clearly drawn. On the one side stands Boileau, with detestation of the low, the capricious, the incongruous, the startling. On the other side, Saint-Amant has his counter-theory, which is in essence

Marino's: 'The poet's business is to astonish'.[6] Moreover, Saint-Amant had
his followers in the Baroque poets Marie de Pech, Coras, Desmarets.

But this clarity of antithesis is not sustained when we follow the dispute to
England. There, caprice proved irrepressible. Dryden purged his style but
not his mind; Pope, who revered Boileau, continually deviates into miracle
and paradox. And yet somehow no one could be quite as wayward, as
footlingly ornate, as Saint-Amant. Nevertheless England for a time caught
what we may without too much impertinence call the French disease.
Neo-classical theory was easy to understand and travelled well, and if
men were unwilling to apply the new canons to Shakespeare and Spenser
(always better loved than the Baroque poetry of France) there were the
Metaphysicals, and there was that veritable conduit by which Gallic
curiosity flowed into English literature, Du Bartas, translated by Sylvester. It
has been alleged, notably by Harry Ashton,[7] that Du Bartas's influence had
come to an end by 1616, but the allegation has been sufficiently refuted by
Sayce.[8] Both in England and in France Du Bartas's hold upon men's minds
continued. He is manifestly the father of the Baroque poets. Saint-Amant
echoes him again and again, and it is no accident that the echoes cluster most
thickly in the passage on which Boileau seized, the crossing of the Red Sea.
In particular, Du Bartas's 'estourgeon' who 's'esmerveille de voir tant de
toits sous les eaux' may have suggested Saint-Amant's notorious 'poissons
ébahis'.[9] But in England Du Bartas was more than influential; he remained
the supreme, representative name. When Sir William Soames translated
L'Art Poétique he considered Boileau's gibe at Saint-Amant at i. 21–6 too
recondite to be translated as it stood, but by a happy accident Du Bartas had
also described the crossing of the Red Sea and Soames was able smoothly to
substitute the master's name for the disciple's. Moreover, in the translation
at i. 101–2 we find (though there is no shadow of this in the French original):

> Nor, with Du Bartas, bridle up the Floods
> And periwig with Wool the bald-pate Woods.

The same lines of Sylvester (Du Bartas himself is altogether tamer) are
quoted, somewhat less accurately, in Dryden's dedication of his *The Spanish
Friar* (1681):

> I remember, when I was a boy, I thought inimitable Spenser a mean poet, in
> comparison of Sylvester's *Dubartas*, and was rapt into an ecstasy when I read
> these lines: –
>
> > *Now, when the Winter's keener breath began*
> > *To chrystallize the Baltick Ocean;*
> > *To glaze the Lakes, to bridle up the Floods,*
> > *And periwig with Snow the bald-pate Woods.*
>
> I am much deceived if this be not abominable fustian, that is, thoughts and
> words ill sorted, and without the least relation to each other. . . .[10]

One is tempted to conclude that Soames is a mere ape of fashion; docile even in his contempt, he takes his very sneers from Dryden. But this may not be just. According to Tonson's note prefixed to the 1708 edition of Soames's translation, Soames wrote his version in 1680 and then passed it to Dryden, who made various improvements.[11] Thus it could be that Dryden wrote both passages, though the world knows him as the author of the second only.

But the real question is: what kind of pleasure had the young Dryden derived from this stuff? If such poetry is to thrill, it must do so by a kind of surrealism. This, ultimately, is the 'proper pleasure' of Saint-Amant's fishes at the windows. And the pleasure was never quite lost. Geoffrey Tillotson has described[12] how the lessons learned from Du Bartas continued to exert a special power in Augustan verse; Sylvester's lines on the going back of the sun in the time of Ezekias –

> Thy Coach turn'd back, and thy swift sweating Horse
> Full ten degrees lengthned their wonted course:
> *Dials* went false, and Forrests (gloomy black)
> Wondred to see their mighty shades go back.[13]

– are recognisably akin to Pope's description in *Windsor Forest* of the natural miracle of the spread of agriculture:

> O'er sandy wilds were yellow harvests spred,
> The forests wonder'd at th'unusual grain . . .
> (88–9)

L'estourgeon . . . s'esmerveille' . . . 'les poissons ébahis' . . . 'The forests wondered . . .' . We are still far indeed from the *nil admirari* of Boileau's aesthetic.

Yet Pope is willing to tread peaceably enough in the track of Horace and Boileau (for fools admire but men of sense approve). In the *Dunciad* (1742) he wrote of Dullness, surveying her realm:

> She sees a Mob of Metaphors advance,
> Pleas'd with the madness of the mazy dance:
> How Tragedy and Comedy embrace;
> How Farce and Epic get a jumbled race;
> How Time himself stands still at her command,
> Realms shift their place, and Ocean turns to land.
> Here gay Description Ægypt glads with show'rs,
> Or gives to Zembla fruits, to Barca flow'rs;
> Glitt'ring with ice here hoary hills are seen,
> There painted vallies of eternal green,
> In cold December fragrant chaplets blow,
> And heavy harvests nod beneath the snow.
> (i, 67–78)

These lines are justly famous, but what does their excellence consist in? Not, surely, in their cogency as argument, for the polemical impetus of Boileau is here quite lost. Boileau, however, had nothing to lose by clarity of definition. He was a great man, and Saint-Amant, Faret, Scudéry – these were little men. But who was the writer in whom Tragedy and Comedy embraced, in whom Time stood still, realms changed their place and oceans turned to land? Remember the sea-coast of Bohemia. Remember *The Winter's Tale.* Pope had better not tell us too clearly what he has in mind or he will find his argument in ruins.

Yet how much does the argument matter, when his language betrays love in the very place of hate? Even a satirist cannot be sneering always – affection keeps breaking in. So much of the imagery here has pleasant associations. Tragedy and Comedy are not shown in some perverse coupling; instead, they embrace. The lines on time and place stir us more easily to delight than contempt, for they are a description of the poetic imagination. Pope, in his examples of ineptitude, has chosen to send rain on the desert, fruits and flowers on waste places, when he might have visited drought on Kent or hailstorms on Tuscany. As for the icy hills and green vallies, this (if the hills are high enough) is mere sweetness and sanity, to which the Gallic Aristarch himself could scarcely object. Pope's intelligence has by this point surrendered to some profounder source of delight. After this the last couplet becomes an explosion, not of absurdity, but of wild, lyric joy.

Thus Pope is, like Horace, unlike Boileau, confused. But such confusion, we begin to see, is in a manner salutary. The real blasphemy against the generosity of human imagination, committed by the Frenchman, is really refused by both the Latin and the English writers. Readers have quite rightly taken these lines of Pope to their hearts. The 'heavy' of the last line clinches the case. In a satiric couplet it has no function. In a lyric line it has great power. Who wishes it away?

The English poets really knew what they were doing, even if they could not explain it. Much was at stake. We may try to persuade ourselves that 'the Dryden revolution' in England was a rational reaction against a very precise and local reality; the corrupt style, say of Dryden's own early verses on the death of Lord Hastings (so strangely different from the poetry of the Metaphysicals), but the attempt is mistaken. Neo-classical theory moved forward on a broader front. Implicit in it is a kind of escalation to tautology. It begins by commending truth, proceeds by excluding the unusual (even if true) and ends by exalting a poetry in which fish are always scaly, streams for ever purling. This kind of mind is skilled in finding

> Sermons in books, stones in the running brooks.

That Dryden knew this road led to poetic extinction is proved by a single line, which transfixes *L'Art Poétique*:

> So just, like tautology, they fell
> (*Mac Flecknoe*, 56)

To turn to Pope after Boileau is to have one's mind and spirit stretched. There is so much happening in Pope, so much more than one can easily

comprehend. It is instructive to compare Pope on Timon's villa with Boileau
on the ostentatious house. Here, first, is Pope:

> The suff'ring eye inverted Nature sees,
> Trees cut to Statues, Statues thick as trees,
> With here a Fountain, never to be play'd,
> And there a Summer-house, that knows no shade;
> Here Amphitrite sails thro' myrtle bow'rs;
> There Gladiators fight, or die, in flow'rs;
> Un-water'd see the drooping sea-horse mourne,
> And swallows roost in Nilus' dusty Urn.
>
> (*Epistle to Burlington*, 119–26)

Note that the fishes in the trees are still, spectrally, with us in this passage,
for while the sea-horse thirsts and dust chokes the River Nile, the daughters
of the sea sail on flowers. Moreover, the target, as in the *Ars Poetica*, is
absurdity in taste. But now Boileau:

> Un Auteur quelquefois trop plein de son objet
> Jamais sans l'épuiser n'abandonne un sujet.
> S'il rencontre un Palais, il m'en dépeint la face:
> Il me promène aprés de terrasse en terrasse.
> Icy s'offre un perron; là regne un corridor,
> Là ce balcon s'enferme en un balustre d'or:
> Il compte des plafonds les rondes et les ovales.
> '*Ce ne sont que Festons, ce ne sont qu'Astragales.*'
> Je saute vingt feüillets pour en trouver la fin,
> Et je me sauve à peine au travers du jardin.
> Fuyez de ces Auteurs l'abondance sterile,
> Et ne vous chargez point d'un détail inutile.
>
> (i. 49–60)

How thin the French is compared with the English. Boileau, having made
use of the Horatian trope (holding it, as it were, at arm's length in a silver
tongs) has now discarded it, and even his specimens are now free – not from
excess, indeed, but at least from paradox. The underlying plan of the passage
is full of promise: the baroque Scudéry described a house which was itself an
extravaganza; let Boileau send up this balloon of redoubled absurdity with
full satiric afflatus, and we shall see some fun. But Boileau knows he cannot
jazz up his account of Scudéry without committing the very vice he is most
concerned to rebuke, hyperbole. As a result his lines are merely limp. The
Horatian *Impossibilia*, even as a weapon of censure, is too corrupting to be
used. Boileau remains aloof, and his style, alas, never begins to betray him.

Pope, in contrast, is utterly corrupt. The trope, the *Impossibilia*, is given its
head, to generate fresh structures, foreseen or unforeseen. To be sure, there is
no reason to doubt the sincerity of Pope's aesthetic disapproval of garden
statuary. But descend lower in the artist's consciousness and you will find a
very different state of affairs. For, if Pope disapproves of statues, he also likes
them, for in unbuttoned mood (that is to say, in his garden at Twickenham)

Pope crowded his small domain with what Horace Walpole called 'mimic representations of the excluded sons of men'[14] – in fact, in addition to four lead urns, sixteen stone urns and the obelisk to his mother's memory, a Venus, a Mercury, 'a Stone Statue with a Wood Pedestall', and four 'Bustos Antike'.[15] Descend still lower and our intuition is only confirmed. If Pope's Twickenham Garden is the landscape of his unguarded affections, the Grotto (that strange Holy of Holies) shows us the heart of the man. And the Grotto was full, not merely of images, but of grotesques. Of course a kind of decorum rules here too (in the etymological link between *grotto* and *grotesque*) but it is far indeed from the bland pieties of Boileau. It is here, rather than in any literalist doctrine of *vraisemblance*, that the root of Pope's art is to be found. Maynard Mack rightly observes[16] that Pope's grotto was 'a shrine to poetry's transforming power'. Likewise Timon (remember how the lines from the *Dunciad* conjured up Shakespeare before us) with his reckless coupling of drought and inundation, of flowers and death, may seem (in the momentary climax of the 'gladiators' line) a better emblem of poetry than of bad taste. Does not the very concept of 'taste' seem friable and irrelevant whenever we turn from a minor to a major poet?

But Pope has not yet finished. The delicious absurdity of Timon must in the end be eclipsed by a madness more sublime. Timon's villa will decay, Nature will return – and reassert her own surrealism:

> Another age shall see the golden Ear
> Imbrown the Slope, and nod on the Parterre,
> Deep Harvests bury all his pride has plann'd,
> And laughing Ceres re-assume the land.
> (*Epistle to Burlington*, 173–6)

II

So far I have artificially arrested the stream of literary tradition at three points: at Horace (where we found a venial confusion); at Boileau (where we found a clarity less easy to forgive); and at Pope (where venial confusion returned and made sport to mock itself). We must not forget that the motif before us – the use of the *Impossibilia* as an instrument of critical censure – is a curiously partial phenomenon; it is, as I have said, a *topos* within a *topos*. The major *topos* itself, the *Impossibilia*, with its long genealogy from Archilochus, holds almost all the real motive power. Our subject ought not to be left therefore without a glance at its proper context.

The *Impossibilia* is, from the start, a systematically ambiguous motif. It can be to the poet either a way of talking about what could never happen, the absurd, or else (in formal contradiction with its traditional name) a way of describing miracles. Thus the lines I quoted from Horace's *Ode* at the beginning of this essay were written at a time of political anxiety to describe

how the world had once before been overwhelmed by a disaster at once
absurd and catastrophic. On the other hand, when Horace returns to the
topic in the *Epodes* (xvi. 34) the context is one of deliberately extravagant
conjuration: 'To be sure, let us move to another city, but only on condition
that pigs grow wings first.' The slave in Lycophron's *Alexandra* who sought to
apprise King Priam of his danger by telling him how once before the dolphin
browsed on the oat, the acorn and the grape (83–5) is clearly closer to the
solemnity of *Odes*, I. ii than to the hyperbole of *Epodes*, xvi. Ovid, who visits
this *topos* in his elegant creation myth (*Metamorphoses*, i. 299), moves in his
wonted Ovidian Limbo, somewhere between the two. Nisbet and Hubbard,
commenting on *Odes*, I. ii, say, 'This topic starts as a proverbial
impossibility.'[17] But it is hard to be certain that it did. True, in the speech of
Soficles the Corinthian in Herodotus (v. 92a) the rhetorical context makes
his words a trope to convey wild absurdity. But in Archilochus (the earliest of
all our sources) the situation is less simple. There the poet upbraids the
people for their superstitious reaction to a perfectly genuine prodigy, an
eclipse of the sun (either that of 711 or of 648 BC). In Virgil we find, as we
might have expected, a subtle system of echoes by which one term of the
antithesis is made to mirror the other. In 1865 John Conington observed[18] of
the *Eclogues* that to an ear retentive of Virgilian music all those passages in
which the shepherd envisages a world gone grazy (e.g. i. 59; viii. 53) are
strangely like all those other passages in which the Golden Age was brought
before us (iii. 89; iv. 30; v. 50).

This tension between paradox and miracle has an important bearing on
the Boileau stage of our comparison. In France the opposition took the
special form of an antithesis between *le merveilleux païen* (a tissue of
intemperate falsehood) and *le merveilleux chrétien* (the real prodigies wrought
by the hand of God). Boileau, who in his old age described himself,[19] with
proud humility, as the 'ami de la verité' might have been expected to
condemn the first and commend the second. The links which join Boileau-
Despréaux and Jean-Paul Sartre must be few indeed, but at least both of
them have written that the business of literature is to call a spade a spade
('appeler un chat un chat').[20] But what if not spades but miracles be our
subject? Surely the Friend of Truth, if he is a Christian, should not flinch
from these. Yet Boileau does exactly this, and in doing so betrays the fact
that in literature it was never really truth he loved but only a certain style.
Saint-Amant dealt, precisely, in *le merveilleux chrétien*. Both he and Boileau
were obliged to believe, as a matter of blunt fact, that the Israelites had
passed dryshod over the Red Sea. When God stretches forth his hand the
fishes actually do get into the trees, and Holy Scripture has a curious
tendency to dwell on these occasions. Skilled to repress anomaly in art,
Boileau is somewhat at a loss when confronted with anomaly in nature.
Literature must be true, but some truths are truer than others and are better
left alone. In other hands, in another age, such a doctrine might have
attained some sort of sublimity; but not in Boileau's.

Boileau believed in *vraisemblance*, a thesis which rapidly reduces itself to a preference for the commonplace: 'lifelike' comes to mean 'like most of life', and, hence, 'typical'. According to this sense of the word, miracles, though verities, lack verisimilitude. They may be truth, but they do not *look like* truth. Boileau in his *Sixième Réflexion* struggled to apply this enervate doctrine to the *Moyse Sauvé*: the fishes in the Red Sea would not, he says, have been able to see as Saint-Amant says they did; a watery wall gives poor visibility; moreover, even if they were to stick their heads out their eyes are wrongly placed for seeing properly. Clearly, something is amiss. Can a man really accept the crossing of the Red Sea and then cavil on a point like this? Boileau, having swallowed his mackerel (the miracle) now chokes on a sprat (les poissons).

But what is really troubling Boileau is something very simple, nothing to do with truth, verisimilitude or probability; it is the *triviality* of Saint-Amant's account. This Plain Man, this *ami de la vérité*, is really on rather better terms with decorum than with truth. He sought to present himself as the enemy of empty grandiloquence, when his most heartfelt objection was to the opposite vice: to the tiny, the detailed, the distinctive, autonomous particular. It was not the magniloquence of Saint-Amant which offended him; it was rather, so to speak, his miniloquence. It is only the unperceptive critic who sees Boileau as the deflator of tumid eloquence. He was, of course, the Great Inflator. Even in his satires, as Cotin noted,[21] his style with its polished pseudo-colloquialism was too pompous for the genre. As time went by it grew clearer still. His association with the Lamoignon group after 1667, his consequent declaration of allegiance to 'la magnificence des paroles',[22] his final failure to distinguish that fierce sublimity of nature which Fleury, Bossuet and Rapin had found in the Bible from the majestic diction of his own over-polished age – all this tells the same tale. Moreover, the argument will bear conversion. For not only is Boileau intolerant of *le merveilleux chrétien* as long as it is expressed in the wrong style, he is also perfectly tolerant of any sort of prodigy, Christian or pagan, if only the style be right:

> Il ne'est point de Serpent, ni de Monstre odieux,
> Qui par l'art imité ne puisse plaire aux yeux.
>
> (iii. 1–2)

Not truth, then, but style.

III

Under the canopy of this *topos* various issues find themselves conjoined. It is this power of conjoining ideas, rather than any originative force, which gives its special fruitfulness. Is the preposterous always the absurd? Do great poets play? How are we to distinguish lawful from unlawful metaphor? Or is metaphor itself always at bottom a mode of lying, a kind of truancy from the object? But what then of language? To utter a thing we must be willing for a moment to loose our material hold upon it, to trust ourselves to the other, fluid medium of symbolic representation (unless, like Balnibarbian professors, we are to converse not with words but with things). It is easy enough to show how the dream of total literalness is unfounded. The story of how in the seventeenth century men hoped that the number of ideas in their heads could be brought into exact correspondence with the number of things in the world, and the number of words then adjusted accordingly – this story has been told often and need not be dilated here. The idea of a one-to-one language of nature – 'Words, which are but Pictures of the Thought' as Cowley put it[23] – has foundered on three rocks, the real nature of thought, language and the world.

And so we grow willing to say that metaphor is as much a means of grasping as of fleeing truth. But even as we theorise the *Impossibilia* begins to laugh behind our backs. Look for a moment at its wilder children: Theóphile de Viau with his oxen on church steeples, his bleeding rocks, or Bishop Corbett –

> *Saturne* crauls much like an *Iron Catt*
> To see the naked Moone in a slipshott hatt.
>   Thunder-thumping toadstools crock the pots
>   To see the meremaids tumble.
>   Leather catt-a-mountaines shake their Heeles
>   To heare the gosh-hawke grumble.
>   The rustic threed
>   Begins to bleed,
>   And cobwebs elbows itches;
>   The putrid skyes
>   Eat mulsacke pies,
>   Backed up in logicke breches.[24]

– or, latest born and craziest far, the Reverend C. L. Dodgson. Perhaps metaphor can bring us to reality, but manifestly it has other uses. No one knew this better than W. H. Auden, who wrote:

> Be subtle, various, ornamental, clever,
> And do not listen to those critics ever
> Whose crude provincial gullets crave in books
> Plain cooking made still plainer by plain cooks,
> As though the Muse preferred her half-wit sons;
> Good poets have a weakness for bad puns.[25]

Auden in this brilliant poem offered another solution. If man is everywhere consumed with the instincts of the mountebank, a creature

> With no more nature in his loving smile
> Than in his theories of a natural style,

then perhaps the only honest course left him is to proclaim his artifice. Truth can never survive the presumptuous rape of the literalist; but by modest hyperbole and undeluded fancy her springs are untouched. Truth cannot be uttered, only acknowledged in a tacit confession, a confession to be found in every golden line of *A Midsummer Night's Dream*, and nowhere, perhaps, in *L'Art Poétique*:

> What but tall tales, the luck of verbal playing,
> Can trick his lying nature into saying
> That love, or truth in any serious sense,
> Like orthodoxy, is a reticence?

But yet . . . are those last lines themselves obliquely fanciful, or has the poet essayed the last blasphemy of literal utterance? Plainly, he has tried to *tell* us the answer, contradicted his own precept and left us with a marvellous poem. And so the argument begins to revolve once more.

The function, then, of the literary motif with which I began has been to bring together with a special force certain issues, of which the most radical concerns the tension between a literalist and a figurative view of language. Auden apart, I have followed this story no further than the eighteenth century. The nineteenth century, of course, had its versions; Coleridge grappled with it more ably than most. In comparison our own times have seen only the most sluggish and inarticulate version of the tension. But, I predict, it will all arise again.

Notes

1. See his *Horace on Poetry*, vol. II, *The Ars Poetica*, 1971, pp. 80f. (esp. p. 81).
2. 'L'univers réversible', in his *Figures*, Paris, 1966, pp. 9–20.
3. *Moyse Sauvé*, Septiesme Partie, in *Œuvres Complètes de Saint-Amant*, ed. M.Ch.-L. Livet, vol. II, p. 252.
4. Ibid., Troisiesme Partie, p. 190. The expression is perhaps less startling in a French context than it would be in English.
5. Ibid., Sixiesme Partie, p. 238.
6. *La Murtoleide*, Fischiata, xxxiii, quoted in Brian Nicholas, *A Critical Study of the Works of Saint-Amant*, a Thesis for the Degree of Bachelor of Letters, Oxford, October 1958, p. 45. Nicholas notes (op. cit., p. 45) that Saint-Amant called his *Moyse* not an epic but an *Idyle Héroique*, while Marino called his fables *Idilii*, the word being then rare in both French and Italian. But Saint-Amant in any case proclaims his debt to Marino in his Preface to *Moyse Sauvé* (i. 12). See R. A. Sayce, *The French Biblical Epic in the Seventeenth Century*, 1955, pp. 92–7.
7. See his *Du Bartas en Angleterre*, Paris, 1908.
8. Sayce, op. cit., pp. 42, 44, 92, 95.
9. Du Bartas, *La Muse Chrestienne*, Part II, *Première Semaine*, ii. 1103–4, in the edition of U. T. Holmes, J. C. Lyons and R. W. Linker, Chapel Hill, N.C., 1938, vol. 11, p. 264; Saint-Amant, 11. 214.
10. In *Essays of John Dryden*, selected and edited by W. P. Ker, 1900, vol. I, p. 247.
11. See Hugh Macdonald, *A Bibliography of Early Editions and of Drydeniana*, 1966, p. 36. Ironically enough, when Soames's translation was reissued in 1715 the

gentleman-reviser adjusted these lines to agree not with Sylvester but with Dryden's celebrated allusion in the dedication of *The Spanish Friar*. The case thus resembles that of Mr Davies who had the temerity to attack the scholarship of Gibbon. Gibbon in his crushing reply made only one mistake, which was to misspell his victim's name; such was Gibbon's authority that Mr Davies has gone down in history as Mr Davis. The very errors of a Dryden or a Gibbon become, ineluctably, part of the fabric of reality.

12. In his *On the Poetry of Pope*, 2nd edn, 1950, pp. 87–9.
13. *Du Bartas, his Divine Weekes and Workes*, translated by Joshua Sylvester, 1641, I. iv, p. 38.
14. Horace Walpole, 'On modern gardening', in his *Anecdotes of Painting in England*, 1827, vol. IV, p. 243.
15. See the inventory printed in Maynard Mack's *The Garden and the City*, 1969, p. 258.
16. Ibid., p. 76.
17. R. G. M. Nisbet and Margaret Hubbard, *A Commentary on Horace Odes Book I*, 1970, p. 23.
18. *P. Vergilius Maronis Opera*, edited with a commentary by John Conington, vol. I, 1865, p. 89.
19. Boileau, *Odes etc.*, ed. C.-H. Boudhors, Paris, 1960, p. 66.
20. Boileau, 'Satyre contre les moeurs de la ville de Paris, 52, in *Les Premières Satires de Boileau*, ed. A. Adam, Lille, 1941, p. 159; Sartre, 'Qu'est-ce que la littérature?' in *Situations*, vol. II, Gallimard, Paris, 1948, p. 304.
21. See Peter France, *Rhetoric and Truth in France, Descartes to Diderot*, 1972, p. 158.
22. Reflexion, xii, in *Les Reflexions sur Longin*, ed. M. Bonfantini and S. Zoppi, Turin, 1965, p. 140.
23. 'To the Royal Society', prefixed to Thomas Sprat's *History of the Royal Society*, ed. J. I. Cope and H. W. Jones, 1959.
24. 'A non sequitur', one of the *dubia* in *The Poems of Richard Corbett*, ed. J. A. W. Bennett and H. R. Trevor-Roper, 1955, p. 96.
25. 'The truest poetry is the most feigning', *Collected Shorter Poems, 1927–1957*, 1966, p. 315.

CAUSAL *DUM*

A note on Aeneid, *vi. 585–6*[1]

Vidi et crudelis dantem Salmonea poenas,
dum flammas Iovis et sonitus imitatur Olympi.

I wish to draw attention to these verses in order to show how much of major critical importance can turn upon a point of syntax.

The opinion that philology and literary criticism are unrelated seems to have gained ground in recent years. Undergraduates are not easily persuaded that the minute analysis of syntax can have anything important to tell us as humane readers. No doubt fifteen years ago the scholars were prone to overstate their case; they would say, for example, that in order to understand the whole one must first understand the part, that sound literary criticism could be founded only on sound linguistic understanding, that it is a contradiction for a man to claim critical authority if he does not also lay claim to the prerequisite knowledge. This austere doctrine has proved too rigid to survive; the variety of human nature, the proleptic nature of intelligence (which always runs ahead of its data), the fluidity of the 'hardest' linguistic scholarship – these have conspired to overwhelm it. I believe that the man who taught me Latin at school knew far more than T. S. Eliot about the language of Virgil. But I am certain that Eliot was the better critic of Virgil. The notion, then, that minute linguistic scholarship is an essential prerequisite of critical understanding proves false.

But must we therefore fly at once to the converse thesis? It may be that there is a strong and a weak form of the scholars' position, and we have so far considered only the strong form. The weak thesis may be expressed as follows: although the linguistically ignorant critic may succeed, his success is always at risk; any critical judgement of his may at any moment be undermined by the scholar who can demonstrate a new meaning for a given word; conversely, we can never be certain that the analysis of linguistic elements may not modify our understanding of a poem's nature. Thus, linguistic scholarship, though not an essential prerequisite of criticism, remains, naggingly, relevant.

But to show this clearly we need, if possible, a spectacular example, of which two things must be true; first, that it should initially present a problem of the utmost 'aridity', the utmost technicality; second, that it should have consequences of the utmost generality. If such an example can be found the unlearned critic can never again enjoy completely untroubled dreams.

At line 585 of *Aeneid vi* the Sibyl is describing to Aeneas those tortures of the damned which he is not himself allowed to see. Just as Aeneas was guided through the world of the dead by the Sibyl, so the Sibyl herself was once guided through the Hell-within-the-Underworld by Hecate (565). Aeneas' journey, terrible enough in itself, is briefly mirrored by one more terrible still. This device of replication and regression sets up a rhythm of apprehension in the reader's (or, better, the listener's) mind. The Sibyl tells how she saw the Titans writhing in the Pit, and the Aloidae who had tried to tear down Heaven itself. She continues:

> vidi et crudelis dantem Salmonea poenas,
> dum flammas Iovis et sonitus imitatur Olympi.

The most natural way to translate this sentence is as follows: 'I saw too Salmoneus being cruelly punished while he imitated the fires of Jupiter and the din of Olympus.'

But this is obviously absurd. We are not in Elis but in Tartarus; Salmoneus is not bragging but is the victim of humiliating torment for things done long ago. And so editors invoke the comparatively rare linguistic usage known as 'causal *dum*'. This, it is suggested, makes possible the much more satisfactory translation: 'I saw too Salmoneus being cruelly punished *because he had imitated* etc.'

But this in its turn is a little too easy. If we look at the commonly offered examples of 'causal *dum*' we find fairly quickly that they have a distinctive flavour. One of the more famous is from Plautus:

> Certa mittimus dum incerta petimus . . .
> (*Pseudolus*, 685)

To translate this 'Because we go chasing after uncertainties we let slip certainties' is to translate very coarsely. 'In chasing after uncertainties we let slip certainties' is better. In other words, although we may concede that a causal implication is present, we distort the proper effect of the sentence if we make the causal element explicit. English, too, avoids the frontal assertiveness of 'because' in such situations (cf. 'For we bid this be done,/When evil deeds have their permissive pass/And not the punishment', Shakespeare, *Measure for Measure*, I. iii. 37). Many other examples simply refuse any translation with 'because', e.g.

> dum 'mihi' volui, 'huic' dixi . . .
> (Plautus, *Casina*, 367)

or the celebrated

... dum Cyri et Alexandri similis esse voluit ... et L. Crassi et multorum
Crassorum inventus est dissimillimus

(Cicero, *Brutus*, 282)

It appears that 'causal *dum*' is typically used to express the ironically
unforeseen consequence of an action. Commonly there is some antithesis
between an agent's expectation and what he does or suffers. Some grammar-
ians have tried to take account of this in their characterisation of this usage;
for example, Ernout and Thomas say that *dum* so used denotes '*la cause
involontaire d'une action*'[2] and Kuehner-Stegmann call it '*kausal-adversative*'.[3]
What then prevents us from translating the verses on Salmoneus as follows:
'I saw too Salmoneus undergoing a cruel punishment he had scarcely looked
for when he imitated etc.'? What prevents us is that awkward time-lag as
against the force of *imitatur*.

In example after example of 'causal *dum*' we can trace the persistence of the
notion of *simultaneity* (presumably strongly associated with *dum* from its use to
mean 'while'). It is this sense of simultaneity or overlapping of actions which
is responsible for the 'ironic' effect already noted. Phrases like '*in doing* so and
so he actually did . . .' or 'and all the while . . .' repeatedly occur to the
translator of these examples. It may be said that in so far as it can be shown
that a *dum* clause expresses a *consequence* the notion of simultaneity is removed.
But 'causal *dum*' is commonly used to refer to actions which are interpreted in
one way by the agent and in another by fate. It is indeed afterwards that the
real tendency of the action becomes evident, but the action was moving
towards that result even *while* the agent thought otherwise:

... dum ex honoribus continuis familiae maiorumque suorum unum ascendere
gradum dignitatis conatus est, venit in periculum ne et ea quae ei relicta, et
haec quae ab ipso parta sunt amittat.

(Cicero, *Pro Murena*, 55)

And so the notion of simultaneity is preserved.

But does not this leave us little better off than when we started? The causal
use of *dum* was invoked in the first place in the hope that it would remove the
awkward implication that Salmoneus' crime overlaps with his punishment.
We needed in fact a sense of *dum imitatur* (present indicative) which would
make the phrase equivalent to *quod imitatus erat* (pluperfect indicative). This
has not proved forthcoming.

The verse, then, is still not perspicuous. The notion that Salmoneus was,
even as the Sibyl watched his punishment, bragging his way through Elis
continues to distract us. Wild analogies arise in our minds: we may think of
the saints in Italian paintings, exalted in beatitude yet with the butchers'
cleavers by which they were martyred still stuck in their heads. But all this
seems a long way from Virgil. Yet *the idea of a picture,* or a relief sculpture, may
be relevant. Certainly, Sir Frank Fletcher thought so, for in his comment he
wrote, 'The two verses read as if Virgil had originally intended to describe a

picture or bas-relief, such as those on the doors of the Sibyl's temple referred to in the beginning of this book.'[4]

The very confusions and errors of the greatest poets are commonly the product of some coherent imaginative pressure. Shakespeare's mangled lines in *Othello* (I. iii. 261–4, the Folio reading) –

> ... I therefore beg it not
> To please the pallate of my Appetite:
> Nor to comply with heat the yong affects
> In my defunct, and proper satisfaction

– contain the thought of Othello's impaired sexual powers, and the thought is important to the drama as a whole. So here in *Aeneid vi* the sense, if only as a subaudition (for I think we must concede that the dominant sense of the passage is causal), that we are looking not at a man but at his picture proves to be part of a larger preoccupation.

It is obvious that the loving Homeric description of artefacts fascinated Virgil. The passages he wrote in creative imitation, at once formal and haunting, lie very near the centre of his art. Literary history produced a technical name for this sort of writing – *ecphrasis* – only in the sixth century AD. But Book *vi* of the *Aeneid* is remarkable in possessing, not just an ecphrastic passage (20–33), but a certain overspill of 'ecphrastic atmosphere'. If in reading poetry, we are right to attend not just to univocal meaning but also to implication and ambiguity, we shall find this shadowy sense of the dead as pictures of themselves at several points. There is for example a hint of it in the description of Idaeus at 485:

> Idaeumque etiam currus, etiam arma tenentem.

Or, again, when the shades of the *ultima arva* see Aeneas approaching, they instantly compose a weird tableau of passion and terror, a ghostly re-enactment of the Trojan War:

> Ut videre virum fulgentiaque arma per umbras, ingenti trepidare metu; pars vertere terga, ceu quondam petiere rates, pars tollere vocem exiguam: inceptus clamor frustratur hiantis.
>
> (490–3)
>
> When they saw the hero and his arms gleaming through the shadows, some turned their backs and fled, as long before when they fled to the ships, some raise a cry, but it is faint; the mere beginning of a clamour mocks their gaping mouths.

Sir Frank Fletcher's conjecture concerning 585–6 seems a little stronger to one who has just read these lines.

Why should Virgil have thought of the dead as images, or pictures of their former selves? There is, no doubt, a certain eeeriness about portraits, statues, tapestries, which can be put to good use by a poet concerned to convey a general effect of uncanny half-reality. Such things are between life and not-life. A statue, especially if encountered by night, is a man and yet not a man. Miss Annie Moberley, who in 1911 sought to convince the world that she had seen ghosts in the gardens of Versailles, made skilful use of the device: '. . . even the trees behind the building seemed to have become flat and lifeless, *like a wood worked in tapestry*'.[5] But perhaps the Romans were in any case more statue-haunted than we (I am told that there was a period when the statue-population of Rome exceeded the human). Cicero in his *Somnium Scipionis* describes how the younger Africanus saw the elder's ghost in a dream, and was able to recognise it only from its resemblance to the dead man's statue: *Africanus se ostendit ea forma quae mihi ex imagine eius quam ex ipso erat notior* (*De Republica*, VI. x).

To see the dead as mere images is to see the dead as less real than the living. If Virgil did so, it might be said, we should not be surprised, since the great difference between ancient and Christian conceptions of the next world lay precisely in this; that the ancients saw the next world as a place of attenuated half-beings, mere echoes of their former selves, whereas Christianity teaches that in the next world we are more fully and richly ourselves than we ever are in this. When we talk of the dead, *self, ipse,* αὐτός – these are the words to watch. It has often been observed that, whereas the Christian will say, 'His body lies on the battlefield but he himself is in Heaven', Homer says that Achilles sent the ψυχάς ('ghosts'?) of many heroes down into the house of Hades, but left *the men themselves* (αὐτούς) for the dogs and birds of the air to eat (*Iliad*, i. 4). It is as if Homer did not believe in immortality at all, since what survives is not the man himself. Thus in classical epic the νεκυία is normally a sort of aberration from the main movement of the story, but in Dante (in the *Commedia* it is *we* who are the *umbrae*, the *figurae*[6]) the νεκυία swallows all the rest and becomes the whole poem. So we may wish to say that Virgil intermittently thinks of the dead as pictures because, like Homer, unlike Dante, he thinks of the dead as not fully real.

But we must acknowledge that Virgil himself creates in the reader a certain resistance to this view before it is finally ratified by Anchises. Most readers feel a bathetic discrepancy between the prayers offered by Aeneas for his homeless followers and the moral triviality of Olympus. The inherited Pantheon of epic is somehow not the proper object of such piety. But when we come to Book *vi*, with its distinctively Italian *religio*, its journey beyond the grave which is also (in typically Virgilian fashion) a journey back to the source, to the dead father who makes good in Aeneas the spiritual destruction wrought by Dido – here, we may think, we have the true focus of Virgilian *pietas*. It is therefore in a way shocking to discover that in the Underworld Aeneas' religious hunger can receive no final satisfaction; even Elysium proves a sort of spectral auditorium in which the spirits watch the really absorbing thing: the future history of Rome.

Some hints of the opposite sentiment remain. The words,

desine fata deum flecti sperare precando
(*vi.* 376)

are, contrary to popular belief, addressed not to a man who would evade
mortality but to one who cannot, fully, die. Again, the phrase

clausae tenebris et carcere caeco
(*vi.* 734)

refers not to the souls in Hell but to those on earth; the conventional imagery
of Tartarus is finely inverted. But when Aeneas asks the crucial question,

quae lucis miseris tam dira cupido?
(*vi.* 721)

Anchises tells him that once it is washed in the waters of oblivion the soul is
willing to go where it must go, back into the body. Elysium, for all its *largior
aether, solem suum, sua sidera*, VI. 640–1, is really only 'a place of transit where
the dreams cross'.

In Virgil's use of his sources for Anchises' philosophical sermon (724–51) a
certain direction can be discerned. It is to deny the substantial ultimacy of
life in the next world. The implication of the strange *dum* clause with which
we began could be expressed in similar terms. Apart from its specifically
Stoic elements, Anchises' speech relies heavily on the tradition of the mystery
religions. In this tradition two strands can be distinguished which we may
call for convenience Transcendentalist and Cyclical. And we must at once
concede that the Transcendentalist strand constitutes an important challenge to our blanket thesis: 'Ancients place reality in this world, Christians in
that.' According to Transcendentalism man can attain to the divine; our
present condition gives place to one more intense involving punishment,
purgation and perhaps bliss beyond the grave. According to the Cyclic
conception (strong in Pythagoreanism) we return again and again to this
world and so enjoy at best a sublunary immortality. Evidently, these two
doctrines, though endlessly confused and combined, are implicitly opposed.
After all, if *vita mors est*,[7] as the Transcendentalists say, a recurrent return to
this life is a pretty poor sort of immortality (more like mortality, in fact). It is
generally agreed that Virgil learned this ontosophy from such sources as
Pindar's second Olympian Ode and Plato's *Phaedo, Republic, Gorgias* and
Phaedrus. What he made of this material has been dismissed as an
indiscriminate farrago; in fact Anchises' speech issues in a clear acceptance
of the Cyclic conception and a rejection of the Transcendentalist.

Pindar in his second Olympian Ode gives us the Cyclic view transcended
by the Transcendentalist: after three virtuous lives the soul may find felicity,
in the company of Peleus and Cadmus, Achilles and the Aethiopian King,
child of the morning. Fragment 114 in the Oxford text looks like a description
of this felicity. Certainly Plutarch so understood it in his consolatory letter to

Apollonius (we owe this fragment to his quotation bug – *citandi cacoethes*). On the other hand the Cyclic conception prevails, perhaps, in the Pindaric fragment quoted by Plato in the *Meno*. Here it seems that reincarnation is itself the reward of righteousness, and that the best eternity we can hope for is the perpetuation of our fame. In Plato himself we find a similar diversity. The myths in the *Gorgias* and the *Phaedrus* both make a return to earthly life the ultimate term of the series. The myth of Er in the *Republic* seems to say the same, but is preceded by a conversation in which ultimate reconciliation with the divine is hinted:

> Being akin to the divine and immortal, to that which
> exists forever . . . and disengaged from rocks and shells . . .
>   (611e–612a)

In the *Phaedo*, on the other hand, an ineffable, transcendent heaven is reserved for the especially righteous (114c). Doubtless, Virgil had access to other writings, now lost. But enough survives to show that both theories were available to him, and thus that his poem represents an act of choice, conscious or unconscious. It is curious that of the two major Latin accounts of life after death, Cicero's is the more other-worldly; the *Somnium Scipionis*, crucial as it is in the process of Romanisation, offers a non-Roman terminal heaven for those released from the body.

The *Aeneid* is built on the principle of systematic frustration. Long before Dante's Ulisse the Odyssean νόστος was turned inside out; Aeneas is looking for a home he does not know, which is yet anciently his. His journey to Elysium itself shows him only figures who point elsewhere, backwards to the world of men, onwards in time. Italy itself is not a fixed but a flying thing. We should not miss the verbal audacity of such phrases as these:

> Italiam non sponte sequor
> I do not follow Italy freely
>
> i, sequere Italiam ventis, pete regna per undas
> Go, chase Italy down the winds, seek your kingdom through the seas
>
> Italiam sequimur fugientem et volvimur undis
> We pursue a fleeing Italy, and are rolled on the waves
>   (*iv*. 361, 381; v. 629)

The intangible fluidity of Virgil's poetry suggest that his very art is that of the hand not grasping but outstretched, his love essentially the love of a further shore.

We can, however, name the object of Aeneas' religious hunger; not Olympus, not Elysium but Rome itself. But Rome, as we all know (and Virgil, I imagine, knew it too) was a place of vulgarly material power. Which is perhaps why Rome too is withheld from us. The note of *ter conatus . . . ter frustra*, 'three times he tried . . . three times in vain', pervades the poem. At those moments when triumph is within our grasp Virgil fills his foreground with a doomed Marcellus or a dying, unconverted Turnus. No doubt he saw the ideal City of Justice interpenetrating the real city of Augustus. But, lacking the Miltonic effrontery, he never risked a direct account of the thing Aeneas laboured to create.

I have argued that the *dum* clause at 586 betrays Virgil's attitude to life after death, betrays, that is, the fact that he sees it not as autonomous but as ancillary, existing essentially for the sake of this life. The Beatrice whom Dante met in Florence was only the *figura* of the Beatrice he met in Purgatory; the Salmoneus whom the Sibyl saw in Tartarus is only a picture of the Salmoneus who provoked the wrath of Jupiter. Thus the ecphrastic colouring of the descriptions and the urgent (*nunc age* . . . !) disclosures of Anchises tell the same tale. It may be objected that my comparison with Dante is misleading since he would regard the epic as represented only in his *Inferno*, and in the *Inferno* the characters are nothing if not hungry for news of earth. But although Dante's religion would have led him to reject the pretensions of an Orphic Elysium, it can scarcely be denied that Virgil's *seclusum nemus* corresponds, in terms of structure, more closely with the *Purgatorio* than with the *Inferno*; and in any case the characters in the *Inferno* are presented (as Anchises is not) as persons depraved in judgement. Last, the this-worldly preoccupations of the *dannati* are almost exclusively retrospective; in the *Purgatorio* the prospective note of religious aspiration takes over. But in Virgil the attention of the spirits is at once prospective and this-worldly.

Notes

1. The discussion of 'causal *dum*' in this essay owes much to a letter I received from Mr. R. G. C. Levens in which he compared certain uses of *dum* with what he described as 'the one-time novelist cliché, "Little did he know that . . .".'
2. A. Ernout and F. Thomas, *Syntaxe Latine*, Paris, 1959, pp. 349–50.
3. R. Kuehner and C. Stegmann, *Ausfuhrliche Grammatik der Lateinischen Sprache*, Hanover, 1912–14, Part II, p. 377.
4. In his 1941 edition of *Aeneid vi* (the 1955 impression), p. 75.
5. *An Adventure*, 1911, p. 5. The book was first published pseudonymously as the work of 'Elizabeth Morison and Francis Lamont'. Later the authors' true names were revealed: Annie Moberley and Eleanor Frances Jourdain.
6. See Erich Auerbach, 'Figura', in his *Scenes from the Drama of European Literature*, New York, 1959, pp. 11–76.
7. Cicero, *De Republica*, vi. xiv.

OVID IMMORALISED

The method of wit in Marvell's 'The Garden'

Marvell's 'The Garden' is not for the literal-minded. For what is the unilinear intelligence to do with a poem which is evidently ascetic in its commendation of withdrawal from social and sexual relations to a private place of contemplation even while, equally clearly, it celebrates voluptuous gratification? At the precise moment at which the literalist begins to knit his brow, the good reader begins to smile, since he knows that what strikes the literalist as contradiction is really wit. The Flatlander who can conceive only of two dimensions, though he lives in fact on a very small globe, is dumbfounded when, having begun to lay paving stones in broadening circles round his polar house, he finds in due course that the stone rings are growing smaller until at last (for he is now at the opposite pole) they encircle his feet. But if we suddenly endow our Flatlander with awareness of a third dimension, he smiles, relaxes, understands. So the literalist, it might be said, were he admitted to the third dimension of metaphoric discourse, might come to understand and so to enjoy the wit of 'The Garden'.

What is this wit and how does it work?

> Not white nor red was ever seen
> So am'rous as this lovely green.
> (17–18)[1]

The first thing to reach the mind's eye is a strange contest of colours, white and red on one side challenged by green on the other. Then we become aware that white and red are the colours of ladies' complexions while green (which wins the contest) is the colour of plants. Thus these lines must be disparaging love and preferring instead solitary communion with the plants. But for what reason? Because the lovely green is 'am'rous', that is not less but more erotic than women can ever be.

Pierre Legouis in his revision (1971) of Margoliouth's edition does his best to flatten the paradox, suggesting that 'am'rous' be taken in 'the passive obsolete sense of "lovely"'.[2] In other words the line is merely an elegantly

dissembled tautology: 'so lovely as this lovely green'. Legouis has in effect
withdrawn its sting; if we did not owe so much to his scholarship one might
be tempted to borrow Blake's words, 'This man was hired to depress art.'[3]
The word 'am'rous' is obviously a challenge; notice how it is thrown into
metrical prominence by the lack of a strong syllable in the strong position
('as') immediately following.

The concept of actively amorous plants is relatively familiar. (Thus John
Guillim, in his *A Display of Heraldrie*, 1611, writes,

> The *woodbine* is a loving and amarous plant, which embraceth al that it grows
> neere unto, but without hurting of that which it loveth: and is therein contrarie
> to the *Ivie* (which is a *type* of *Lust* rather than of *Love*).[4]

Within a few lines we are to be offered the extravagant conception of an
Apollo who is not so much frustrated as gratified by a Daphne who turns into
a laurel and then, as if to clinch the extraordinary suggestion of a real sexual
responsiveness (or more than that), the most famous lines of the poem:

> the Luscious Clusters of the Vine
> Upon my Mouth do crush their Wine;
> The Nectaren, and curious Peach,
> Unto my hands themselves do reach;
> Stumbling on Melons, as I pass,
> Insnar'd with Flowr's, I fall on Grass.
> (35–40)

The trick, therefore, is to daze the conventionally-minded reader by drawing
one's criterion of preference from the disparaged party. Retreat is preferred
to sexual gratification because it gives more erotic pleasure. If we reduce the
line to 'Green plants are more beautiful than women' we lose the wit.
Marvell is exploiting an ancient ambiguity in the very notion of a garden: the
place of innocence as against the arbour for dalliance.[5] Milton in his picture
of Eden strove to harmonise the two with the high-minded Protestant
sexuality of Adam and Eve. Marvell, though he will gesture towards
Paradise before his poem is over, prefers to sustain an ingenious dissonance.
Indeed, he treats classical myth (as we shall see) and Genesis with the same
freedom: he wickedly reverses the Christian story by suggesting that God
created Eve to mitigate the otherwise excessive happiness of Adam (57–64).

It is possible that the sexual paradox is already in train before the third
stanza. The second ends with the words,

> Society is all but rude,
> To this delicious solitude.
> (15–16)

It might seem that, although the device of the borrowed criterion is quite
clearly employed here, the meaning is exclusively social and not sexual:
'Society, normally the paradigm of civility, is in itself uncivil (barbarous)
compared with the exquisite social solitude enjoyed by one who is alone with

plants.' But there is also the provocative adjective 'delicious'. In a responsive reader the effect of this word is proleptic, so that the sexual paradox is already hinted within the social. We may try to render the poetry inert by glossing 'delicious' as merely 'delightful', as the Dictionary permits. But if we drop our defences we may become aware of a group of associated words, *delicious, luscious, luxurious, lecherous*. *Luxurious* and *lecherous* are different forms of the same word. Otherwise these words seem not to be etymologically cognate, though there is a theory that *luscious*, a word of obscure origin, may be connected with *delicious*. The point is rather that they are *imaginatively* cognate. If we admit such associations we may sense that the light, trisyllabic 'delicious' at line 16 begets in due course the full weight of 'luscious' which actually appears at line 35. *Luxurious* appears nowhere in 'The Garden' but lovers of Marvell will easily think of the beginning of 'The Mower against Gardens':

> Luxurious Man, to bring his Vice in use,
> Did after him the World seduce:
> And from the fields the Flow'rs and Plants allure . . .

In fact the English word *delicious* has from medieval times carried a connotation of sensuous indulgence. It can even in seventeenth-century usage be virtually equivalent to *lecherous*. Thus William Lithgow in his *Rare Adventures and Painefull Peregrinations* (1632) speaks of Aeneas and his followers 'forsaking the delicious lives of the effeminate *Affricans*'[6] (where 'effeminate' means either 'self-indulgent' or 'unduly devoted to women'). A mind alert to the structure of Marvellian paradox will admit such echoes, just as it will sense an opposite, monastic connotation in 'retreat' at line 26, even before it comes upon the secondary confirmation of this sense provided by *crepidatus inambulat*, 'walks to and fro, sandalled' at the equivalent point in Marvell's Latin version of 'The Garden'. Here, notice, although *inambulat* has impeccable Classical credentials, it assumes a monkish resonance from the later development of *ambulatory* and associated words.

Marvell then chooses to subject ancient myth to the controlled indiscipline of transposed criteria:

> The *Gods*, that mortal Beauty chase,
> Stil in a Tree did end their race.
> *Apollo* hunted *Daphne* so,
> Only that She might Laurel grow.
> And *Pan* did after *Syrinx* speed,
> Not as a Nymph, but for a reed.
> (27–32)

It is likely that Marvell was here thinking, as often, partly in Latin. Every schoolboy used to know that '*ut* final' is easily confused with but nevertheless quite distinct from '*ut* consecutive'. The first means 'in order that', the second 'with the result that'. The familiar form of the myth evoked in this stanza leads the reader to expect a quasi-ironic *consequence*: 'Apollo pursued Daphne, only to find that she turned into a laurel.' Marvell keeps this expectation alive to the last possible instant with the word 'only', but then the little word 'that' is unmistakably *purposive* (*ut* final): 'Apollo pursued Daphne with the express design that she should turn into a laurel.'

Once again Marvell has wickedly changed the terms of the argument. Stories of desire frustrated (when girl becomes plant) are, with breathtaking cleverness – and minimal linguistic interference – transformed into stories of desire kindled *less* by the girl than by the plant she becomes. The mythic metamorphosis is thus arrogantly appropriated and is itself metamorphosed, in an extravagantly idiosyncratic manner.

Ovidians may wish to say at this point that I exaggerate the originality of Marvell. Ovid's version of the Daphne myth is certainly the principal classical source and in that version, by a typically Ovidian twist, the god is actually made to persist in his love-making *after* Daphne has been changed:

> Vix prece finita torpor gravis occupat artus:
> Mollia cinguntur tenui praecordia libro:
> In frondem crines, in ramos brachia crescunt:
> Pes modo tam velox pigris radicibus haeret:
> Ora cacumen habet: ramanet nitor unus in illa
> Hanc quoque Phoebus amat, positaque in stipite dextra.
> Sensit adhuc trepidare novo sub cortice pectus.
> Oscula dat ligno, refugit tamen oscula lignum.
> Cui Deus: At quoniam conius mea non potes esse,
> Arbor eris certe, dixit, mea . . .[7]
>
> (*Metamorphoses*, i. 475–85)

In George Sandy's translation (1632):

> Forthwith a numnesse all her lims possesst
> And slender filmes her softer sides invest.
> Haire into leaves, her Armes to branches grow:
> And late swift feet, now rootes, are lesse than slow.
> Her gracefull head a leavy top sustaynes:
> One beauty throughout all her forme remaines.
> Still *Phoebus* loves. He handles the new Plant;
> And feeles her heart within the barke to pant.
> Imbrac't the bole, as he would her have done;
> And kist the boughs: the boughs his kisses shun.
> To whom the God: Although thou canst not bee
> The wife I wisht, yet shalt thou be my Tree . . .[8]

Clearly there are elements here which may have prompted Marvell's conceit, more especially the perverse hint of what we may call phytophilia. Also, when Apollo says, 'If you can't be my wife, you shall be my tree' the rustic simplicity of the sentence together with the wildness of the thought may have led to the bizarre notion, earlier in 'The Garden', of carving, 'Andrew Marvell loves Beech' on the appropriate tree, like some deranged Orlando, strayed from *As You Like It*:

> Fair Trees! where s'eer your barkes I wound,
> No Name shall but your own be found.
>   (23–4)

It has been pointed out[9] that whereas the general effect of Marvell's English poem, 'The Garden', is Horatian, *Hortus*, the Latin version, is noticeably Ovidian.

Yet the Ovidian passage does not constitute a conceit. Certainly it invites all the terms of praise currently in vogue: it is aberrant, unstable, dynamic, transgressive. It discovers in the ancient myth of frustrated desire an opening for a purely narrative moment of deviance. But it stops short of moral and conceptual restructuring. Marvell on the other hand transmutes piquant accident into joyously perverse intent and, because the whole is set within a rhetorical set argument for retreat, the mild erotic perversity becomes at the same time an intellectual perversity. When Marvell writes,

> And *Pan* did after *Syrinx* speed,
> Not as a Nymph, but for a Reed.
>   (31–2)

'for', like 'that' earlier, is cleverly shifted from a neutral to a purposive sense. It is likely that 'for' directly represents '*pro*' in Ovid's account of Syrinx; but Ovid's *pro* means, unequivocally and unexcitingly, 'instead of', with no hint of deviant desire:

> . . . cum prensam sibi iam Syringa putaret,
> Corpore pro nymphae calamos tenuisse palustres[10]
>   (*Metamorphoses* I, 599–600)

In Sandy's:

> . . . when he thought he had his *Syrinx* claspt,
> Betweene his arms, Reeds for her body graspt.[11]

The *direction* of the substitution is clear in Ovid: 'instead of the girl's body, reeds'; in Marvell, in so far as the neutral sense 'instead of' persists, it seems to work in reverse: 'Pan pursued Syrinx instead of (the more truly desirable) reed.' It is always said that the Middle Ages and the Renaissance moralised Ovid by ascribing intellectual and ethical meanings to the stories. Marvell chose (surely with a better ear for the poetry) to *im*moralise him.

It remains true, therefore, that, although Marvell may have received a strong hint from a passing moment in Ovid's narrative, he may still be said to have produced a fundamental transformation of an anciently familiar story. Ask most informed people whether Apollo was pleased or sorry when Daphne turned into a laurel, and you will receive the answer, 'Sorry'. This means that his method is, in a manner, the extreme opposite of that characterised by Erich Auerbach as *figura*. Auerbach, in a famous essay,[12] contrasted two medieval traditions of biblical exegesis, under the Latin terms *allegoria* (the ancestor of our 'allegory') and *figura* ('figure'). According to the method of *allegoria* we suppose that first Scripture and then literary texts propose *fictions* by means of which a given meaning is conveyed to the reader (in due course the Scriptural application of this method, associated with the name of Origen, was condemned as heretical; meanwhile in literature, where fiction is, so to speak, positively encouraged, there is of course no such problem). According to the method of *figura* we deem the persons or events presented in a text to be real, though at the same time they carry a meaning beyond themselves. Thus, although the Exodus of the Israelites from Egypt may indeed signify the passage of the soul from terrestrial corruption, that does not mean that the Exodus itself is a mere illustrative fiction: there really was an Exodus and the meaning it bears is *in rebus*, objectively built into it.

In later literature examples appropriate to *allegoria* naturally far out-number those appropriate to *figura*, since as we have already suggested, in poetry fiction is, as it were, authorised and wholly proper. Nevertheless certain major poets seem to belong naturally to the world of *figura*: Dante, whose persons, unlike those of the *Roman de la Rose*, are obstinately historical and Wordsworth, whose most significant figures must, we feel, have been encountered, not feigned by the poet. It is noticeable that, as we move into the Romantic period, the signification of the *figura* becomes less and less clearly formulated; instead we find an effect of incorporation and (while vaguer resonances are freed) closure of separate meaning; the figure *has* meaning (we continue to affirm) but the meaning is increasingly fused with the given, resonant fact, until we reach the curious metaphoric tremor of Modernism in which objects are said to signify themselves. To all of this, Marvell's lines may stand as an ultra-opposite. It is not just that, as in *allegoria*, the vehicle is fiction: Marvell goes further in that he takes a great received story, of which the meaning is known, and wantonly reverses its most immediate and basic significance. For all except, perhaps, the early Greeks themselves the story of Daphne and Apollo is already *allegoria*, in so far as it is myth (one part aetiological, say, to three parts sheer fun). But the *allegoria* has, by the gradual accretion of tradition, undergone what we may call a process of secondary objectification. The story, even if untrue, is *the* story. Thus, to reopen, by a sheerly rapacious act of individualism, the significance of the story is to reassert with conscious violence the original freedom of *allegoria*. In this way Marvell can be seen as contriving a kind of poetry which is as different from that of Dante, as profoundly *opposite* to *figura* as poetry can well be. So far from showing us a world of compacted significance in which meanings are locked into certain resonant truths or facts, Marvell shows the degree to which the 'facts' or the great objective stories themselves can be manipulated by the fictive imagination.

We are now in a position to see that the easy contrast between two- and three-dimensional vision with which we began is in fact an inadequate instrument for the task in hand. When Donne writes in the Holy Sonnets

Nor ever chast except you ravish mee

we may indeed 'cure' the collision of erotic and religious reference by invoking our 'third dimension' of metaphor: Donne refers indeed to ravishing but does so metaphorically; he describes a hoped-for spiritual conquest in erotic terms, but there is no problem (though there may be a certain shock effect) because we know what is metaphorical and what is not. A trickier example is Isabel's speech in *Measure for Measure*:

> The impression of keen whips I'ld wear as rubies,
> And strip myself to death, as to a bed
> That longing have been sick for, e'er I'd yield
> My body up to shame.[13]

Here Isabel, newly entered on her novitiate, scorns the vile proposal of Angelo. She reasserts her chastity, but in violently erotic – even sado-masochistic – language. The tenor of her speech is, 'I'd rather die than submit to you', but meanwhile the vehicle invests her converse eagerness for death with a libidinal intensity which seems more appropriate to Angelo's hated suggestion. Rhetorically the whole can function as an imperiously deliberate castigation of Angelo; he is lashed with his own imagery. But at the same time there is nothing here to prevent the psychoanalytic reader from inferring in Isabel an unconscious which really desires that which the super-ego reprehends. The language is so strong that it suggests that the rhetorical control may after all be less than absolute. Nevertheless the original problem of apparent contradiction can be formally or provisionally resolved by pointing out that Isabel's erotic references are all at one remove (metaphor, simile, comparison). In 'The Garden' this way of resolving contradictions through distinction of levels, metaphor and letter, is formally forbidden, since the two are joined, explicitly, in an ostensibly logical relation of ground and consequent. Marvell is not content to suggest that retreat is, by metaphor, a blissful consummation; rather he insists that solitude is to be preferred *because*, as we say in the 1980s, it is sexier than society; the proposition is presented and then supported with a reason but – lo – the reason is borrowed from the opponent's armoury. Marvell's use of 'so . . . as' ('so am'rous as'), like his use of 'that' ('only that she might Laurel grow'), logically enmeshes the erotic with the meditational and forces the reader after all to literalise – or try to literalise – what would otherwise have been comfortably figurative.

   Imagery thus enjoyed in argument produces in the poem a distinctive, double effect. First, because the criteria are so systematically crossed, the intelligent reader perceives the proposition *as a joke*. Reasoning so perverse cannot be seriously intended and human psychology provided in laughter another path of response. We have learned in this century not to read metaphysical poetry as if it were real metaphysics, not to expect the arguments offered to have the status of philosophy. Rather we expect what

Emanuele Tesauro[14] called 'arguments urbanely fallacious'. Thus the extravagance is itself the point, the absurdity integral to the art. By this mode of reading the argument becomes a pseudo-argument and, because the rational challenge is then dropped, the sense that what we have is after all equivalent to a fundamentally harmless metaphor can have some force.

But that is only one element in the double effect. The other is that the mind, once hooked by the admittedly frivolous, hyperbolical reasoning, cannot quite get free. That is because the *thought* offered is, even while it is manifestly extravagant, haunting enough, novel enough, cogent enough to continue to work upon our deeper responses. Thus our reading is in a manner stratified; on encountering Marvell's preposterous version of the Daphne myth, the learned reader smiles, but the smile can then give place to a simpler joy, to an intuition of a Nature perceived so intensely as really to vie with the libidinal. It is as if the poem erects a series of successively destroyed defences. First we may think, 'it is only metaphor', then, having registered the argument, 'it is only a pseudo-argument', before at last we bow to a conception of nature which destroys the convention of discourse and thought. To write poetry of this kind requires a combination of intellectual 'cool' with an equal capacity for intellectual surrender rarely found. Indeed I will call it distinctively Marvellian.

For the whole strategy of 'The Garden' is to show, in a way which eerily anticipates the subsequent development of Romanticism, conventions dying or quickening into nature. 'The Palm, the Oke, or Bayes' of the first stanza are in a minimal sense natural images; all are plants but, first and foremost, they are their stock meanings; military, civic, literary victory. They are consciously frigid, as if carved in stone by some Roman hand. What Marvell then does is to turn the tables on this received priority of conventional significance and to bring forward, as primary, the plants themselves. It is as if the marble turns green and comes to life (we may think here of the ecphrastic tradition and the process of colouring and coming to life which unfolds in Keats's 'Ode on a Grecian Urn'). Romanticism increasingly privileged nature, where 'nature' was seen in antithesis to that which is manipulated by human intellect, the green, living world against the 'fixities and definites'[15] proposed by the ratiocinative mind. All this is enacted in the sequence of 'The Garden'. The conventions of culture are gravely displayed and then overwhelmed by a nature which is other and greater than they. That is why readers cannot resist the sense that, while the carefully poised opening is classical, at the heart of the poem the language really has become Keatsian:

> The Luscious Clusters of the Vine
> Upon my Mouth do crush their Wine.
> (35–6)

The speaker is no longer the arrogant manipulator of meaning, but instead falls back, supine, under the soft assault of fruits and flowers. In like manner the mind, which can in its ingenious fecundity of images outdo even the buzzing plurality of the objective world, fuses at last with simplicity:

> Annihilating all that's made
> To a green Thought in a green Shade.
>
> (47–8)

'The Garden' is not a Romantic poem because it admits as poetically usable the intellectual elements so gloriously defeated within its sequence. But it is also the one metaphysical poem in which the conceit itself is made to fail and die before a Nature which literary history in the two following centuries will increasingly present as primary. There is no structure and therefore no wit in a green thought; it is therefore not a conceit – scarcely indeed a concept (as distinct from a percept). But of course it is placed in the sequence of the poem with consummate, intelligent art.

The lines about Daphne and Apollo are, I have said, explosively anti-figural in their wanton inversion of a received story. But now we see that this very wilfulness of intellect is made to serve an end in which, through a yet deeper stroke of wit, intellect is silenced by – what can we say? – sheer 'greenness'. This means, in Auerbachian terms, that the anti-figural virtuoso display is prelude to a converse movement: the foregrounding of a pre-conventional sheer presence, a resonance which is *in rebus*, not feigned – and *this*, as my argument has suggested, actually looks forward to the Wordsworthian-figural.

Yet all the while Marvell, like the great pastoral poets, unlike the Romantics, is always conscious of a poignant absurdity in his project. I have in this essay suggested that the wit in 'The Garden' is miraculously eclipsed by a proto-Romantic Nature only *half* ironically presented. I am uneasily conscious that I could have reversed the procedure in order to show, beginning from the Romantic element, how all these haunting intuitions of a perhaps impossible unmediated experience are everywhere guarded with an unsleeping intelligence. Indeed Marvell does all these things, holding them in a suspense which never allows the reader to relax. That Marvell should be writing in this way in the early 1650s presumably makes him (for those who are interested in such things) a mildly old-fashioned figure. Waller and Denham had by this time already begun to shift English poetry towards Augustan simplicity and polish. Yet for us, some three centuries later, it is Marvell who continues to challenge and defeat the intelligence, to delight and extend the spirit.

Notes

1. All quotations from Marvell are from *The Poems and Letters of Andrew Marvell*, ed. H. M. Margoliouth, 3rd edn revised by Pierre Legouis with the collaboration of E. E. Duncan-Jones (Oxford: Clarendon Press, 1971).

2. *Poems and Letters of Andrew Marvell*, p. 267.
3. Written by Blake on the title page of Sir Joshua Reynolds's *Works* (1798); in *William Blake's Writings*, ed. G. E. Bentley, Jr. (Oxford: Clarendon Press, 1978), vol. II, p. 1450.
4. Sect. III, ch. vii, p. 107. This work is available in facsimile (Amsterdam: Walter J. Johnson, 1979). Cited in *NED sub* 'amorous'.
5. See Frank Kermode, *Shakespeare, Spenser, Donne* (London: Routledge & Kegan Paul, 1971), esp. pp. 285–7.
6. *The Totall Discourse, Of the Rare Adventures, and painefull Peregrinations of long nineteene Yeares Travayles* (London: Nicholas Okes, 1632), p. 22. Cited in *NED sub* 'delicious'.
7. The text is that of *Metamorphoseon*, ed. Jacobus Pontanus (Antwerp: 'apud heredes M. Nutii', 1618), p. 60; available in a facsimile edn (New York and London: Garland Publishing, 1976).
8. *Ovid's Metamorphosis English'd, Mythologiz'd and Represented in Figures by G. S.* (Oxford: J. Lichfield, 1632), pp. 12–13: also available in facsimile (New York and London: Garland Publishing, 1976).
9. See C. A. Martindale, 'Paradise metamorphosed: Ovid in Milton', *Comparative Literature*, XXXVII, no. 4 (1985) pp. 301–33; p. 301 n.
10. *Metamorphoseon* (Pontanus), p. 68.
11. *Ovid's Metamorphosis English'd*, p. 16.
12. 'Figura', in his *Scenes from the Drama of European Literature* (New York: Meridian Books, 1959) pp. 11–76. This essay first appeared in Istanbul in 1944.
13. II. iv. 101–4; in *The Riverside Shakespeare* (Boston: Houghton Mifflin, 1974), p. 564.
14. 'Argomenti urbanamente fallaci', *Il Cannocchiale Aristotelico* (Turin: Gio. Sinibaldo, 1654), p. 583.
15. S. T. Coleridge, *Biographia Literaria*, ch. xiii, in the edn by George Watson (London: J. M. Dent, 1965), p. 167.

GULLIVER AMONG THE HORSES

Gulliver, newly landed on unknown soil, some leagues south of Nuyts Land, sees in a field a group of repulsive animals. Revolted by the sight he eagerly pursues his way along the beaten road, hoping to find some human habitation. But, almost at once, he meets with one of the unpleasant creatures, full in his path:

> The ugly Monster, when he saw me, distorted several Ways every Feature of his Visage, and stared as at an Object he had never seen before; then approaching nearer, lifted up his fore Paw, whether out of Curiosity or Mischief, I could not tell: But I drew my Hanger, and gave him a good Blow with the flat Side of it; for I durst not strike him with the Edge, fearing the Inhabitants might be provoked against me, if they should come to know, that I had killed or maimed any of their Cattle.
>
> (*Gulliver's Travels*, Part IV, Chapter 1 (p. 244)[1]

This is how Swift begins his narrative of Gulliver's sojourn among the Houyhnhnms, or rational horses. The creatures he saw, first in the field and then in the road, are of course not Houyhnhnms but Yahoos. Only gradually does it become clear, to Gulliver and to the first-time reader, that the bestial Yahoos are in fact human beings (that the horses are rational is revealed much more rapidly). The writing, as usual, is spare and colourless. But this does not so much preclude as enhance a certain dream-like intensity. When I say 'dream-like' I mean just that: like a dream – *not* like most literary versions of dreams. The resemblance has something to do with a combination of distinctness and paucity of information and also with the way the horrible animals are first seen at a safe distance in an ordinary field and then, without transition or preparation, one suddenly appears in the human territory of the road. Childhood memories of some huge cow or bull, dung-encrusted, encountered unexpectedly in a lane, may play their part. But what Gulliver sees is, of course, much worse.

Such is the immediate impression made by the passage: an absolute, undoubted nastiness (not an evil; we need the more childish word) threatening the person with whom we are for the moment entirely identified, occurring in an almost blank environment. The elementary impression of something utterly and manifestly revolting is, and remains, the most important feature of the passage, but other things are happening. Even a first-time reader is caught for a moment in a faint-counter-identification with, of all things, the Yahoo. The dry prose finds space to make us aware that, just as Gulliver is seeing something he cannot name, so the creature before him is staring 'as at an Object he had never seen before'. Thus even within this narrative of primary, utterly objective, repulsion there is a moment of implied reciprocity, or relativism. The first-time reader may even wonder, 'When the other raised his fore-paw, was he perhaps making a gesture of friendship, as it were, offering to shake hands?' The complex distortion of the visage carries, moreover, an implicit suggestion of human facial expression, so much richer and more various than anything we see in brutes. Even if the thought is not there when we first read the passage, it can gradually enter our sense of what must have happened as we read on and become aware that the Yahoos are human.

But in that case Gulliver is wildly astray; he would, but for a ludicrously misconceived apprehenson, have killed without provocation an unarmed fellow human being who had done no more than extend his hand. The other may even have been smiling.

The passage, with its strong and its weak signals, is doubly disorienting. Gulliver is of course immediately surrounded by the Yahoos, who attack him by dropping excrement on him from the branches above his head. But Gulliver, the intruder in Utopia, is the aggressor. The Yahoos, themselves no party to the happiness of Houyhnhnms Land, attack (ineffectively) with excrement. Later the Houyhnhnms themselves will repel Gulliver's intrusion in an opposite manner; as they deal with diseases by 'a great *Evacuation*' (IV. 6 (p. 253)) so they will deal with this unwanted invasion of the body politic by a simple act of extrusion.

What I have called 'the weak signals' in the present passage are, as it turns out, immediately congenial to the prejudices of the twentieth century. If we try to write 'Gulliver' in the 'little language' of the *Journal to Stella* we get 'Gullible' and this, it might be said, is the key. There is, however, a snag. *Gullible* is not known to the *Oxford English Dictionary* before the nineteenth century, though the puzzling word *cullible* (having the same meaning) appears to have been in use in Swift's time (see, for example, Swift's letter to Pope of 16 July 1728).[2] Meanwhile the verb, *to gull*, was of course common currency. Certainly Gulliver is from the first entirely deceived by appearances. The reader quickly intuits that the horses Gulliver admires so fervently are cold, passionless, and, at the last, cruel. This impression, faint at first, is overwhelming by the end of the book, when Gulliver shrinks from the obviously virtuous Portuguese captain and prefers the society of his horses to that of his wife and children. No one, at the end of Gulliver's last voyage, can doubt, it is said, that the hero is mad.

Such is the critical orthodoxy of the twentieth century, though it is true that since the beginning of the 1960s various powerful voices have been raised in dissent.[3] There is moreover one forceful technical argument which supports this orthodoxy. Gulliver's fourth voyage is, quite clearly, a comic extravaganza. If there is one observation which applies as plainly to the first readers of *Gulliver's Travels* as it does to the most recent, it is that this book astonishes by reversing the ordinary disposition of characters; it turns human beings into dumb animals and it makes horses into grave sages. The logical implication of this is simple and unavoidable; in ordinary life it *must* be the other way round: horses must be dumb animals and such sagacity as is available must be gleaned from human beings. Were it otherwise the book would not be extravagant, would not be comic. Where did Swift find the characteristics, the thoughts, the behaviour of the Houyhnhnms, unless from human beings in their graver moments (especially, say, from certain Stoics of antiquity)?

The argument cuts cleanly but every good Swiftian will wish to resist it. The Dean would never have wasted time on the vacuous irony of mere reversal. He will always wish to fold into the most extravagant image, the most preposterous invention, an element of nagging likeness, or even of mere truth. The argument from comic extravagance needs to be put, however, because its failure is instructive. We begin to realise in consequence that all the great ironists, since Socrates said that he knew he knew nothing, have at some level always meant the thing they said in jest. Even tragic irony (a different but related thing) actually works most potently through an unlooked-for coincidence with truth rather than by any pleasure we may take in the manifest error; when Oedipus says he will track down the murderer of Laius he errs in supposing the culprit to be someone other than himself, but the force of the tragic irony lies in the fact that he will, in due course, carry out his promise to the letter. Swift, we know in our bones, will want us to think, if only at moments and against the odds, 'What are we but Yahoos?'

Certainly it is not enough to point to the coldness of the Houyhnhnms, as if the manifest repulsiveness of frigid rationality will settle the case outright. That Swift might have preferred coldness to warmth is not just conceivable, it is probable. Moreover, the implication of this preference, that intense love is ruled out, is precisely the kind of unwelcome corollary he would delight in adducing. He may even have seen himself at such moments less as the English Rabelais than as the successor of that Siger of Paris whom Dante describes: *leggendo nel vico delli strami, sillogizzo invidiosi veri* (*Paradiso*, x, 137; 'Lecturing in Straw street, he set forth in syllogisms truths his hearers hated').

That Gulliver's misanthropy is to some extent shared by Swift was the common presumption until the present century. William Warburton spoke for many when he accused Swift of *degrading his species* and carrying satire to the point of mere destruction: 'And now the Fig-leaf is so cleanly plucked off, what remains but bravely to strike away the rotten Staff, that yet keeps our doting Parents on their last legs.'[4] One half suspects the presence of a Freudian equivocation in 'the rotten staff' immediately following the removal of the fig leaf, as if Warburton with some part of his mind perceived that Swift's real motive was a hatred of sexuality, so that he sought not only to degrade but also to emasculate mankind. Moreover, Swift, notoriously, accepted the charge of misanthropy. 'I hate and detest that animal called man,' he told Pope, 'although I heartily love John, Peter, Thomas and so forth', and added, 'Upon this great foundation of Misanthropy (though not Timons manner) The whole building of my Travells is erected' (*Correspondence*, III, 103). Writing to Charles Ford on 19 January 1723/4 he affirms that he hates Yahoos of both sexes: even Stella and Madame de Villette are 'onely tolerable at best, for want of [the society of] Houyhnhnms' (*Correspondence*, III, 4). On 11 September 1725 he wrote to Thomas Sheridan: 'You will every day find my Description of Yahoes more resembling' (*Correspondence*, III, 94). To be sure, the tone is jesting, especially in the second of these. But (once more) few Swiftians will suppose that the irony is of the kind which simply cancels the apparent assertion. As the *Examiner* (7 June 1711), Swift wrote: 'Nothing can well be more mortifying, than to reflect, that I am of the same Species with Creatures capable of uttering so much Scurrility, Dulness, Falshood and Impertinence, to the Scandal and Disgrace of Human Nature' (*Works*, III, 171–2). The piece was anonymous but the voice is Swift's own.

Yet the peculiar *frisson* at one's biological kinship with the most odious of all creatures is precisely what is to charge the most powerful moment in *Gulliver's Travels*: Gulliver goes swimming on a hot day and a certain female Yahoo, seeing him, makes amorous advances. It is then that he knows, by a test used to this day by working scientists, that he is of the same species as the Yahoos, though of course the biologist requires, as Swift does not, that the union be fertile. Odysseus, the first traveller in European literature, wanted above all to go home. Gulliver's 'poor Wife' (IV. 1 (p. 221)) seems to have been quite as faithful as Penelope, but she and his home are alike odious to him after he has been permitted to kiss the hoof of the Houyhnhnm. The horror of wife, family, and home is, at its root, identical with the horror of biological kinship. Yet here, in the extremity of his madness, Gulliver can speak with what is recognisably the voice of Swift:

> My Reconcilement to the *Yahoo*-kind in general might not be so difficult, if they would be content with those Vices and Follies only which Nature hath entitled them to. . . . This is all according to the due Course of Things: But, when I behold a Lump of Deformity, and Diseases both in Body and Mind, smitten with *Pride*, it immediately breaks all the Measures of my Patience.
>
> (IV. 12 (p. 296))

Quite clearly the same savage indignation tore at Swift's heart: Patrick

Delany tells how Swift asked a friend whether 'the corruptions and villainies of men in power did not eat his flesh and exhaust his spirits?' When his friend answered that they did not, Swift cried out in a fury: 'Why, why, how can you help it, how can you avoid it?'[5] Of the two reactions Gulliver's is the more temperate.

W. B. Carnochan, reviewing these materials, concedes that at the end of the book Gulliver, like Timon or Molière's Alceste, is himself satirised. But, he adds, the joke is a painful one; he endorses the view of John F. Ross that it is 'at the expense of a very important part of himself'.[6] Claude Rawson, similarly, finds a certain doubleness in the final Timonian misanthropy of Gulliver. Plainly, he says, Gulliver is insane, but his reclusiveness and ranting stand for a position which is seriously asserted by Swift; meanwhile, however, the ranting, the *manner*, is Gulliver's, not Swift's. In this way Swift can distance himself from the charge of extremism while contriving to press his own central accusation against the human race.[7] This is criticism at its best, lucid, discriminating, and sensitive, but I am not quite persuaded that it is right. Carnochan suggests a simple clash of sympathies: Swift both despises and sympathises with the misanthropy of Gulliver. Rawson suggests a more organised tension: both Swift and Gulliver despise the human race but Swift implicitly dissociates himself from *extreme* misanthropy. I would prefer to say that Swift simultaneously asserts both the full, extreme misanthropy of Gulliver and its human absurdity, knowing that the two are, at root, not opposed but logically interlocked.

Everyone knows, in a primary, perhaps a biologically primary, fashion that to be repelled by one's wife and child merely on account of their humanity is a kind of madness. Swift, who, to put it mildly, was no fool, certainly knew this. At the same time, if humankind stinks, then Gulliver is absolutely right. Here also the thought burns in Swift's mind with a primal force, rooted in infantile responses, growing powerfully from an instinctive to a fully ethical revulsion. By their dung ye shall know them: the human variety is so much more offensive than the equine. The horse is a comelier, more fragrant thing than this beast which, alone among animals, maims and tortures its own kind.

It may be that the point at issue between myself and Rawson is a vanishing one, for in the essay I have cited he immediately qualifies the opposition I described by adding: 'But his [Gulliver's] are the final words which produce the taste Swift chose to leave behind: it is no great comfort or compliment to the reader to be assaulted with a mean hysteria that he cannot shrug off because, when all is said, it tells what the whole volume has insisted to be the truth' (p. 73). These words close the gap I would have closed. Indeed it was shut fast from the beginning by the latent logic of the narrative. The effect of this is to expose an anomaly in ethics; moral discourse is sometimes species-based in a radical manner, sometimes not. Species-based morality makes love of mankind primary; to desire the destruction of the human race is, in this scheme, *axiomatically* wicked and no moral defence of such a desire is even conceivable. Non-species-based morality, on the other hand, recognises no such practical axiom (it is, in G. E. Moore's terms, more clearly 'non-naturalistic').[8] It permits one to step back, even from one's own species, and to form an ethical judgement on it. Within this morality it is perfectly possible to argue, for example, that the human race taken as a whole is more bad than good, so that a collective suicide of the species is in truth our ultimate duty. Because the structure of species-based morality is simultaneously in force, this proposition immediately registers as both wicked and lunatic. But, because the non-species-based morality also figures powerfully in our conceptual scheme, the proposition 'man is vile' can be cogent. In *Gulliver's Travels* Swift, working simultaneously from a wicked humour and a black conviction of depravity, chose to cross the lines of nature and convention in a manner calculated to create the maximum disturbance.

The newly fashionable cultural relativism of the Enlightenment, which led even the staid Locke to write with a kind of glee about the Christian Mengrelians who bury their children alive, gave Swift the opportunity for the necessary initial disorientation: what is bad here may be good there.[9] But then he switches from relativism to an absolutism so stark as to be shocking. Lawrence Manley observes that Swift satirises the very relativism of the travel writers when he shows that the apparent differences between civilisations are in fact real differences, 'so that the Lilliputian disgust with Gulliver and Gulliver's disgust with the Brobdingnagians are a function of their real degree of magnitude and magnanimity'.[10] When we come to the rational horses this strategy undergoes a further, brilliant, transformation. For the unnaturally sagacious horses are themselves (in what anyone but the almost cultureless Gulliver will perceive to be a Stoic mode) followers of Nature: their own morality can be construed as thoroughly species-based, and at this level it simply mirrors the species-based presumptions of human beings. Thus far, Swift has shown us a novel figure in the dance of cultural relativism. If this were all, the Houyhnhnms would be subject to the same satiric scourge as mankind, in a precisely parallel manner. But in Houyhnhnm society we are gradually made to suspect that, after all, no fissure can ever be made to appear (as it can in our world) between the species-based and the absolute ethic. *Their* species really is superior. It follows that in their more or less Stoic philosophy reason will be in accord with this condition of nature and will in consequence exhibit no problems: 'Their grand maxim is, to cultivate *Reason*, and to be wholly governed by it. Neither is *Reason* among them a Point problematical as with us, where Men can argue with Plausibility on both Sides of a Question' (IV. 8 (p. 267)).

Thus, while human Stoics were constantly exercised by the transition from descript to prescript, no such difficulty arises for the Houyhnhnms. The Stoics affirmed that man was a rational animal and thereafter urged strenuously that he labour to become so. 'You are rational' was habitually

followed not by 'Therefore relax' but by the (in the circumstances wholly
irrational) 'Therefore subdue your passions'. We have moved, by implication, from 'You are rational' to 'You are, properly, rational', or 'You are
basically/originally/at your best rational'. But the Houyhnhnms, unlike the
ancient human Stoics, have no vast body of literature on the subjection of
passion because they actually are as they say they are (there is indeed a mild
inconsistency in Swift's having them continually dwelling in their poems on
instances of benevolence (IV. 9 (p. 274)), since there can be no reason to
praise that which is merely given by nature). The Stoic conception of man, it
might be said, is noble and therefore the opposite of misanthropic. But
because Stoics were in practice everywhere assailed by the rampant
irrationality of real human beings, misanthropy seems to have come easily to
them: 'One is sometimes seized', says Seneca, 'with hatred of the whole
human race.'[11] It is as if the old Pindaric tag, 'Become what you are' (*Pythian
Odes*, II. 72) came, with the rise of Stoicism, increasingly to express a state of
disquieting tension. Indeed this slippage to the Stoic perception of human
nature almost becomes a synchronic equivalent of the Christian conception
of the fall of man.

The definition 'Man is a rational animal' reminds one that the fourth book
of *Gulliver's Travels*, with its parade of inverse definitions ('The horse is a
rational animal', 'Man is beast'), is parodically linked with logic manuals of
the later seventeenth century. R. S. Crane was the first to point out that men
and horses provide the running example of rationality and its converse in the
treatises of Franco Burgersdijck, Narcissus Marsh (Swift's despised 'Primate
Marsh'), and others.[12] Indeed the connection with *Gulliver's Travels* may be
more intricate even than Crane saw. Narcissus Marsh, in his manual
designed 'for the use of the young academicians of Dublin', has a way of
generating (*per accidens*) distinctions and paradoxes which can appear
essentially Swiftian.[13] One of the simpler comic mechanisms in *Gulliver's
Travels* works through the ambiguity of 'animal' in English. Because we
commonly use this word to mean 'non-human' or 'beast' the phrase 'Man is
a rational animal' carries a whiff of paradox from the start. But the Latin
animal has the same ambiguity, and Marsh, in his plodding progress, makes
sure that we are aware of the fact. In the very Preface of his book he offers the
following syllogism:

> *Nullum animal est homo.*
> *Omne rationale est homo.* Ergo
> *Nullum rationale est animal.*
> No animal is a man. Every rational being is a man. Therefore,
> no rational being is an animal.
> (*Protheoria Syllogistica*, Q.6)

After which (still in the 'Preface') horses and apes come crowding in (it will
be said that there are no apes in the fourth book of *Gulliver's Travels*, but it is

hard to avoid the sense that the Yahoos are, in a way which Swift cannot acknowledge, partly based on a simian original).

> *Si Simia non sit irrationalis, est homo*
> *Sed Simia non est homo.* Ergo,
> *Est irrationalis.*
> *If an ape be not irrational, it is a man.*
> *But an ape is not a man.* Therefore
> *it is irrational.*
>
> (Q.8)

All of this of course is also sober sense, though when we come to the section on the Individual we may wonder a little at Marsh's obvious partiality for *horses*:

> [Individuum incertum] exprimitur per Nomen commune et Pronomen particulare: ut, *Aliquis homo. Quidam equus.*
> We express the indeterminate individual by means of the common noun and the particularising pronoun, *Some man.*
> *A certain horse.*
>
> (pp. 9–10)[14]

But it is when we come to the examples of bad syllogisms that we really strike pay-dirt. On page 144 he offers the wholly witless:

> *Nullus homo est brutum.*
> *Nullus equus est homo.* Ergo,
> *Nullus equus est brutum.*
> *No man is a brute. No horse is a man.*
> Therefore *no horse is a brute.*

On pages 149 and 153 we have the following standard Undistributed Middles:

> *Omne brutum est animal,*
> *Omne homo est animal.* Ergo,
> *Omnis brutum est homo.*
> *Every brute is an animal.*
> *Every man is an animal.* Therefore,
> *every brute is a man.*
> *Omnis homo est animal.*
> *Omnis equus est animal.* Ergo,
> *Omnis equus est homo.*
> *Every man is an animal. Every*
> *horse is an animal.* Therefore
> *every horse is a man.*

And so the rattling mechanism of Marsh's pedagogy goes on its way. On page 167 the eye is caught by *Homo est brutum*, 'Man is a brute', and a page later by *Homo est Bucephelus*, 'Bucephelus [Alexander's famous horse] is a man'. There can be no doubt that all this had its effect on Swift. When he wrote his parodic syllogism on the Aeolists in *A Tale of a Tub* he followed the typographic habit of Marsh, italicising the terms but leaving 'Ergo' in Roman: *'Words are but Wind; and Learning is nothing but words*; Ergo *Learning is nothing but wind.*[15] It is easy to see in what spirit the young Swift would have read the *Institutiones Logicae*, making it a point of honour to believe the syllogisms laboriously offered as errors by his master and to disbelieve the rest. All this, note, was long before Locke attacked Stillingfleet's views on the nature of man. On this side we have clever undergraduate humour; on that, springing from and then freezing the game, a queerly absolute judgement a priori, a judgement fenced with every sort of irony yet inescapably asserted.

So far I have argued in terms of commonplaces of the age: reason, temperance, benevolence, and nature provide the framework. But if the effect of this is, as it were, to flatten Swift, to merge him with his background, then once again one is probably going wrong. For Swift's brand of misanthropy (and I mean Swift's, not Gulliver's) has its own note of hysteria, its own special extremism. Setting aside the precise medical character of Swift's final illness, we may still be struck with the way contemporaries and near-contemporaries of Swift doubted his sanity while admiring his intellect. I will say nothing here of the obsession with excrement. Suppose instead that we add to the materials assembled by Carnochan and others the following passage from Swift's 'Letter to a Young Lady on her Marriage' (1723): 'Besides, yours was a Match of Prudence, and common Good-liking, without any Mixture of that ridiculous Passion which hath no Being, but in Play-Books and Romances' (*Works*, IX, 89). This corresponds with the dispassionately eugenic marriages of the Houyhnhnms so much admired by Gulliver (IV. 8 (p. 268)), and yet once more it is Swift, not Gulliver, who is speaking.

I have, however, another reason for singling out this passage. It is marked by a special tremor of the intellect which perhaps betrays much. For Swift. congratulates Deborah Staunton on the absence of something which (he says it himself) does not exist outside the pages of books. We may seek to expunge the absurdity by saying that Swift obviously means to congratulate the young lady on being free of the *delusion* of supposing herself in love, since love outside playbooks and romances is always a mere tissue of illusions. But this rescue operation is not altogether comfortable or convincing; a sufficiently vivid delusion of being in love might surely constitute *real* 'passion'; it is, after all, passion that Swift hates and it is surely wonderful if humankind is wholly free of it, so that it lingers only in works of fiction. The almost unbearable, icy, patronising blandness of this letter, with its deliberately unlovable combination of stylistic majesty with personal intimacy, is, at this point, disturbed by something which even Swift, perhaps, did not fully understand. It seems to be *fear* which, for the length of a sentence, here outruns the intelligence. The same fear shows in the 'Resolutions when I come to be Old' which Swift set down more than twenty years before he began to write *Gulliver's Travels*: 'Not to marry a young Woman. . . . Not to be fond of Children, or let them come near me hardly' (*Works*, I. xxxvii).

Johnson in his 'Life of Swift' makes his distaste for Swift's inhuman and obsessive rationality very clear. He is horrified by the way Swift lent to the poor, fixing a date for repayment and suing defaulters.[16] He describes Swift's private rule of giving one coin at a time when tipping and of always storing 'his pocket with coins of different value' (p. 58). Johnson's celebrated observation of Swift's 'inverted hypocrisy' is offered not in admiration but with some dismay (p. 54). Already one smells what the twentieth century has learned to call schizophrenia. The impression grows stronger when Johnson allows himself a freer rein with anecdotes of personal eccentricity, such as Pope's wonderful account of the occasion when he and Gay called on Swift: Swift asked if they had eaten and, on learning that they had, became very agitated by the thought that he would otherwise have had to give them lobsters, tarts, and a bottle of wine, at a cost of $2s. 6d.$ each; he was unable to rest until he had persuaded each of them to accept half a crown (pp. 58–9). I suspect that Johnson's obvious hostility springs in part from his recognition of obsessional tendencies within himself; certainly *he* dealt with them very differently. His pausing to tell us how Swift continually washed his face forms part of the same general picture (p. 55). It is as if Johnson can more easily forgive Kit Smart for not changing his shirt than he can forgive Swift for his cleanliness.[17] Meanwhile, however, one cannot feel that Johnson's anxieties are wholly misplaced.

The Portuguese sea captain is the strongest evidence in the fourth book for Swift's essential sanity, or so we are told. He is manifestly generous and Gulliver, conversely, is manifestly unbalanced in his response to that generosity. When I considered the behaviour of Gulliver on being reunited with his wife and family, I insisted on listening to the voice which said 'And the heart of the jest is that Gulliver is right, because human beings stink and horses are better than men.' Against all the odds (which is exactly how Swift loved to write) the same voice may even be heard here, if we care to listen. R. S. Crane got it right when he said that if Swift was to convey the full force of his indictment and shock the reader from his or her anthropocentric complacency it was necessary to include in the now-extended ranks of the Yahoos a person who would seem to most of us, in our innocent arrogance, virtuous and admirable. Or, as John Traugott put it more succinctly, 'Even good Yahoos are Yahoos.'[18] Your ordinary racist hates Jews because he believes that they poison wells or (in more recent times) destroy the economy. Your fundamental racist hates Jews because they are Jews and for no other reason. Among friends he will take pleasure in affirming that a good Jew is still a Jew, since in this way he can isolate the element of pure contempt. So with Swift. There is a part of his mind which has attained (so to speak) pure misanthropy, untainted by ordinary human reasons. This then obliges him to bring Gulliver face to face with the best of humankind – and then have his hero shrink in disgust. Of course he knows that the reader will laugh at the folly of Gulliver, but that is now an essential part of Swift's

increasingly private joke. For what is the reader but another Yahoo? In the
last resort Yahoos will stick together. Even now the joke is not quite over, for
what is Swift himself?

If this really is the inner logic of the Don Pedro episode then it must be said
that it carries a hint of insanity. If a Yahoo cannot be admired for his decent
benevolence, then neither can a Houyhnhnm. Non-species-based (absolute)
morality allowed Swift to accuse mankind as a whole of cruelty, mendacity,
and pride. In this way he could establish a misanthropic base. Then the
system gives a shake and, lo, we are presented with an inverse species-based
morality. Instead of 'even a bad man is still a fellow human being' we have
'even a good man is still, ugh!, a man'. It may be thought that in contriving
this mirror effect Swift's design was to satirise further the species-based
morality which he earlier threw off, but this is one subtlety which I believe
we must deny him. The writing is too dark and hot, the links with words
uttered *in propria persona* are of the wrong kind.

When Gulliver catches sight of his face in a pool (IV. 10 (p. 278)) his
reaction is the opposite of Narcissus' in the myth. Gulliver hates what he
sees. In Ovid (*Metamorphoses,* iii. 339–510) Narcissus is an innocent and lives
in the childhood of what is to become our own world. He has never seen his
face before and as soon as he sees it he loves it. Indeed, even the shaggy
Cyclops likes his face when he first sees it reflected (*Metamorphoses,* xii. 842–3).
Gulliver, who saw his face many times in the world of men, finds himself
translated to a counter-world in which innocence and truth are in a manner
recoverable. Once again his reaction can be seen comoedically as part of the
relativist game (what is fair here is foul there and vice versa). But at another
level (and that the more important) it is as if the effect of his sojourn among
the horses is to make the scales fall from his eyes. He can now see truly, but,
although he has somehow strayed into Arcadia, what he sees is corruption.

In emphasising an element of authentically Swiftian misanthropy I have
perhaps privileged the tormented ego of the author above his more liberal
and free-ranging imagination. Another way to express the antithesis is to say
that the book is an altogether richer thing than its proudly invidious thesis.
There is a sense in which simple imaginative postulates, such as 'Let us
imagine people six inches high', can generate an increasingly rich variety of
situations, almost of themselves. 'Let the horses be rational and the men
brutes' is such a postulate. Admit to the scheme a rational man and the
possibilities are richer still. Ancient structures of the imagination, ideal
Commonwealths, Utopias, transposed pastorals, Paradises penetrated and
overthrown begin to figure in the picture. It is as if a monomaniac central
impulse is made to work within a polymaniac field of reference.

I have resisted the notion that the coldness of the horses implicitly
condemns them. If, however, we substitute 'negative' or even 'stupid' for
'cold' the case is somewhat altered. The horses live by *reason* but they have no
skill or facility in *ratiocination.* They are sages who never philosophise. The

most frequent locution applied to them is that beginning 'They have no conception of . . .'; 'Power, Government, War, Law, Punishment, and a Thousand other Things had no Terms, wherein that Language could express them' (IV. 4 (p. 244)); 'The Inhabitants have not the least Idea of Books or Literature' (IV. 3 (p. 235)); 'they have no Word in their Language to express Lying or Falsehood' (IV. 3 (p. 235)); 'when I asserted that the *Yahoos* were the only governing Animals in my Country . . . my Master said [it] was altogether past his Conception' (IV. 4 (p. 240)). In addition they have no conception of the use of money (IV. 6 (p. 251)) or of what a ship is (IV. 3 (p. 235)), only an imperfect conception of illness (IV. 6 (p. 253)), and no conception, of course, of the various vices described by Gulliver (IV. 4 (p. 244)); *love* has 'no Place in their Thoughts' (IV. 8 (p. 269)), and the Sorrel Nag 'had no Conception of any Country beside his own' (IV. 10 (p. 281)).

This is in part an effect of genre. 'They have no word for "lie"' is a recurrent topos of travel literature and early anthropology. But in Swift the topos is immensely extended, and all the odder, it might seem, when we are dealing with paragons of rationality. More importantly we need to remember how rationality is treated by Stoic thinkers. The basic generative sentence of *Gulliver's Travels*, Part IV, 'Man is a rational animal', is not, as is commonly supposed, an Aristotelian commonplace, but is largely the property of the Stoics. 'Man is a political animal', on the other hand, is the key sentence of Shakespeare's *Timon of Athens* and is a genuinely Aristotelian tag.[19] Aristotle is certainly keenly interested in man as an animal capable of acquiring knowledge, but this, as I shall argue, is too dynamic a conception for either the Stoics or Swift.[20] Similarly, Aristotle is willing to describe man as the only animal capable of deliberation.[21] The nearest he comes to the stock phrase of the logic books is perhaps in the *Politics* when he says (at 1332 b 3) that the rational principle is not found in brute animals. The central phrase, 'rational animal' (*zōon logikon*) occurs as far as I can discover only once, and in a most dubious manner. In a fragment of Aristotle which we owe to the Pythagorean Platonist Iamblichus (fourth century AD) we are told that among the secret doctrines of the Pythagoreans was one which ran, 'There are three kinds of rational animal: gods, men and beings like Pythagoras.'[22] It is hard to be sure, but it looks very like a joke. With the Stoics the phrase comes into its own. Chrysippus leads the way, using it in a work revealingly entitled *On the Failure to Lead a Consistent Life*.[23]

It is clear that Aristotle is interested in activity, in the things human beings do with their intelligence. What the Stoics are interested in is, despite the rhetorical ordonnance of the Senecan style, rather less perspicuous. Important in the scheme is a notional fusion of 'follow nature' with 'follow reason'. It is commonly said that in the technical philosophy of the seventeenth and eighteenth centuries reason is increasingly restricted to the deductive faculty, with a corresponding shift away from the traditional cognitive conception (reason as a just perception and moral appraisal of what is really the case). 'The traditional conception' appears to owe far more to Stoicism than to Aristotle. A powerful moral stress on cognitive reason can lead to the terminal notion of an inert conformity with nature (where 'nature' means not 'the green world' but That Which Is, considered as a divinely ordered whole). Seneca, in his *Moral Epistle* 'On the God within Us', explains the matter with an almost Chadbandian vacuousness:

> Praise in him that which can neither be torn from him nor given to him, that which is the Property of Man. You ask, what may that be? It is soul, and reason perfected in the Soul. For man is a rational animal. And so the highest good is accomplished if he has filled the role for which he was born. And what is it that is demanded from him by this 'reason' of which I speak? The easiest thing of all, to live in accord with his own nature.[24]

There, to be sure, he ends, trapped in a subjective circle: 'Your nature is rational, what is reason? This life in accordance with your own nature; what is your own nature? Why, to be rational.' Elsewhere the circle is broken and he says, simply, 'Follow nature', the practice being firmly associated with the possession of a sane unclouded mind.[25]

The Stoic assimilation of reason to both internal and external nature is accomplished through a covert act of prescription. Man's *real* nature is rational (the 'honorific' use of *real*). The prescriptive identification was followed by the usual long rebellion of the *de facto* against the *de jure*. When the Stoics affirmed the rationality of following nature they intended 'nature' in the sense opposed to 'convention' (*physis/nomos*): 'Scorn luxury and wild opinion, attend to what is truly noble.' But even in antiquity *nature* was also opposed by *art*, and it is this second opposition which lies behind all pastoral writing and will ultimately yield the 'green' nature of Romanticism. Meanwhile, what is the opposite of reason? In Stoicism it is passion. But by the pastoral opposition it is the passions which seem most obviously natural, while reason belongs with art (we may remember at this point that *nomos*, which is the Greek for 'convention', also means 'law').

We may now be in a better position to understand the Houyhnhnms. Their minds and values, being perfectly adjusted to nature, need never stir from the consequent sleep: until, that is, they are visited by one whose rationality is of the dangerous, dynamic, *ratiocinative* kind. Until Gulliver occasioned the first debate in Houyhnhnms Land, these were sages who never once disputed any question. Is it not possible that Gulliver's sessions with his Master Horse are really (though Gulliver would be profoundly shocked at the description) strange tutorials in which Gulliver (not the Horse) is the teacher? The Yahoos are described as unteachable (IV. 8 (p. 266), 9 (p 271)) but if we look for the opposite character we shall find it, not in the incurious Houyhnhnms but in *homo sapiens* as described by Gulliver. The Master Horse is obviously quite unable to account for the malignity implicit in Gulliver's very cleverness; reason ought to be a point in his favour yet it seems to be working the other way. A little desperately he suggests that it is because man has been given only a 'pittance' of reason, which is somehow susceptible of misuse, that he goes wrong (IV. 7 (p. 259)), as if a larger ration of the same would somehow have been all right.

Gulliver's description of the ship is a nice specimen of Enlightenment 'defamiliarisation': 'I came over the Sea, from a far Place, with many others of my own Kind, in a great hollow Vessel made of the Bodies of Trees' (IV. 3 (p. 235)). He has learned to speak as if to a child. The Master Horse's response is touched with inadvertent pathos: 'He was sure no *Houyhnhnm* alive could make such a Vessel, or would trust *Yahoos* to manage it.'

The truth is that the Houyhnhnms are just not very clever. Not only do they abstain from disputes, but they have no technology. When Gulliver makes two chairs, using his knife, the Sorrel Nag, for all his undoubted membership of the Master Race is, comfortably and without comment, assigned the simpler and more laborious tasks (IV. 10 (p. 276)). When, later, Gulliver goes Crusoe-like to work in his ingenious 'Canoo' the Sorrel Nag once more plays the part of Man Friday, performing 'the Parts that required most Labour' (IV. 10 (p. 281)).

The Stoics were driven to philosophise, to engage in pursuasive discourse, only because man was not in practice invariably rational in the way he was expected to be: the active rationality of Seneca, such as it is, can live and breathe only in the space afforded by the failure of that primal definition. But the horses really are thus and, as the gap is closed, we realise that we are indeed confronted by a species of rationality which has no tincture of the ratiocinative. Such rationality is indeed not so much the correct appraisal of nature as a mere identity with nature, a surrender of thought. We are very close to saying that Swift might, with greater consistency, have used perfectly ordinary well-adjusted horses, without entangling himself in the treacherous business of anthropomorphism; how could he think that he could dignify a noble horse by making him resemble the Yahoo Seneca?

The presentiment that Part IV might be, in some remote fashion, a transposed pastoral is not so wide of the mark. The pre-Argonautical Houyhnhnms, like the men of Virgil's Golden Age, know not the use of iron (*Georgics*, i. 143; *Gulliver's Travels*, IV. 9 (p. 274)).[26] Their use of sledges (IV. 2 (p. 231), IV. 9 (p. 275)) suggests that they may not even have invented the wheel, though 'carriages' are mentioned at IV. 9 (p. 274). Their world is indeed a green one. I have asked, in effect, when Gulliver converses with the Master Horse, which is the teacher, which the taught? There is an obvious sense in which Gulliver's pride in mechanical contrivance is exposed by the horse, but this also conforms to the pastoral pattern. Gulliver encounters not the authority of intellect but the authority of innocence. Spenser's Sir Calidore, who with all his civil courtesy brings change and death to a pastoral society, is similarly wrong-footed by innocent wisdom: he makes the mistake of offering money to the aged shepherd Melibee (*Faerie*

Queene, IV. ix. 32–3). One lesson, we find, the Master Horse is capable of learning; when Gulliver first explains how horses were castrated in his own country the Master is shocked, chiefly no doubt because the operation is performed on horses (IV. 4 (pp. 241–2)). Later the Master proudly announces how it is possible to learn from the lower animals, and that rebellious Yahoos might be rendered more tractable by castration (IV. 9 (pp. 272–3)). This time it is we who are shocked, chiefly no doubt because the operation is to be performed on men.

Like Milton's Satan, Gulliver brings with him dynamism and change, transforming the world of unfallen Stoics. He shows how any world in which the intelligence will function as a live thing will contain evil as well as good. Unlike Satan, however, he is no rebel but, had they only known it, their first and only perfect pupil. For Gulliver's abject submission was wholly unfeigned. He swallowed everything, the Spartan (Hitler Youth) exercises, the pride of caste (like Nietzsche's archaic Greeks in *The Genealogy of Morals*, who draw their terms of disapproval from synonyms of 'slave', the horses derive theirs variously from the word *Yahoo*), the moral platitudes, the equine Pindaric odes on athletic victories – the lot.[27] But they decided he was a potential revolutionary and therefore expelled him (IV. 10 (p. 279)). It may be said that they were wise, since Gulliver, whatever his intentions, carried the corrupting taint of the civilised Yahoo which would in due course have had its effect. At that level, however, it is likely that the subtle damage was already done. What the Houyhnhnms actually suggest is that Gulliver would have led the local Yahoos in revolt, and it is difficult to resist the conclusion that the Assembly, with its habitual stupidity, simply got it wrong. Gulliver himself, whose attitude to the Assembly is a little like that of George Herbert towards God, makes no complaint.

There was one Houyhnhnm, however, who got it right. Near the end of the story Gulliver tells how he put out to sea in his makeshift boat, watched by the Master Horse and some friends. When he was almost out of sight, he says, 'I often heard the Sorrel Nag (who always loved me) crying out, *Hnuy illa nyha maiah Yahoo*, Take Care of thy self, gentle *Yahoo*' (IV. 11 (p. 283)). Not 'seditious', notice, but 'gentle'. The parenthesis '(who always loved me)', after so many pages of rational benevolence and the perfunctory 'better feelings' of the Master (IV. 10 (p. 279), has a sudden power. It is here rather than in the Don Pedro eposide that the Swiftian fear of love is shaken. In the first ideal Commonwealth they expelled the poet. Swift himself with his breathtaking, ever-moving intelligence would have been expelled from Houyhnhnms Land more rapidly, one surmises, than Gulliver. But to tell Swift this would be to tell him what he already knows, that he must include himself in his misanthropy.

It is always unwise to patronise good writers, but it is especially unwise in the case of Swift. We must allow him to say what he must say, however it offends us. Like the tree with which Stoic Aeneas is compared by Virgil, his roots are in hell (iv. 446). Even so, however, pious Aeneas is too high-minded a hero for our purpose. If Boswell is allowed to compare the mind of Dr Johnson to the Colosseum, perhaps we can say that the mind of Swift resembled the Augean Stable, remembering only that he was also his own Hercules, labouring within it.[28] But, if we remember the word *lacerare* from Swift's epitaph in St Patrick's cathedral, we may think of him as not a Luciferan but an ascetic Prometheus, tormented on his rock, yet able still to torment posterity.

Notes

1. *Gulliver's Travels* is quoted from *The Prose Writings of Jonathan Swift*, ed. Herbert Davis and others, 16 vols (Oxford, 1939–74), XI (revised 1959). Other references to this edition of the prose writings (*Works*) are indicated by volume and page numbers in parentheses.
2. *The Correspondence of Jonathan Swift*, ed. Harold Williams, 5 vols (Oxford, 1963–5), III (1963), 294.
3. The satirist satirised view is most ably argued, perhaps, by Roger C. Elliott in his *The Power of Satire: Magic, Ritual, Art* (Princeton, New Jersey, 1960), especially pp. 211–21. W. B. Carnochan, 'The complexity of Swift: Gulliver's fourth voyage', *Studies in Philology*, 60 (1963), pp. 23–44 (p. 23), provides a useful summary of criticisms pursuing the view that in the fourth book it is Gulliver and the horses who are satirised, rather than the human race. R. S. Crane, 'The Houyhnhnms, the Yahoos and the history of ideas', in *Reason and Imagination: Studies in the History of Ideas, 1600–1800*, ed. J. A. Mazzeo (New York, 1962), pp. 231–53, gives a similar but shorter list (pp. 231–2). Carnochan and Crane are themselves both 'dissenting voices' as are (to varying degrees) J. Traugott, 'A voyage to nowhere with Thomas More and Jonathan Swift: *Utopia* and the voyage to the Houyhnhnms', *Sewanee Review*, 69 (1961), pp. 534–65; I. Ehrenpreis, 'The meaning of Gulliver's last voyage', *Review of English Literature*, 3 (1962), pp. 18–38; James L. Clifford, 'Gulliver's fourth voyage: hard and soft schools of interpretation', in *Quick Springs of Sense: Studies in the Eighteenth Century*, ed. L. S. Champion (Athens, Georgia, 1974), pp. 133–51; Donald Keesey, 'The distorted image; Swift's Yahoos and the critics', *Papers on Language and Literature*, 15 (1979), pp. 320–32; and C. J. Rawson, 'Gulliver and the gentle reader', in *Imagined Worlds: Essays on Some English Novels and Novelists in Honour of John Butt*, ed. Maynard Mack and Ian Gregor (London, 1968), pp. 51–90. This last is reprinted, with some changes, in C. J. Rawson's book, *Gulliver and the Gentle Reader* (London and Boston, Massachusetts, 1973), pp. 1–32.
4. *A Critical and Philosophic Enquiry into the Causes of Prodigies and Miracles* (London, 1727), in *Swift: The Critical Heritage*, ed. Kathleen Williams (London, 1970), pp. 71–2.
5. Cited by W. B. Carnochan ('The complexity of Swift', pp. 37–8) from Delany's *Observations upon Lord Orrery's Remarks on the Life and Writings of Jonathan Swift* (London, 1754), pp. 148–9.
6. Carnochan, 'The complexity of Swift', p. 32; John F. Ross, 'The final comedy of Lemuel Gulliver', *Studies in the Comic*, University of California Publications in English, 8 (1941), pp. 175–96 (p. 196).
7. 'Gulliver and the gentle reader', *Imagined Worlds*, p. 79.

8. Naturalistic morality permits sentences containing the term 'ought' to be translated, without logical remainder, into ordinary indicative sentences or else to be derived from such sentences. For G. E. Moore on naturalism, see his *Principia Ethica* (Cambridge, the 1962 reprint of the first edition of 1903), especially pp. 39–41, 58, 59. See also John Hospers, *An Introduction to Philosophical Analysis* (London, 1956), pp. 568–74.

9. *An Essay Concerning Human Understanding* (1689), 1. 3. 8; ed. Peter Nidditch (London, 1975), p. 71.

10. *Convention, 1500–1750* (Cambridge, Massachusetts, 1980), p. 330.

11. *De Tranquillitate Animi, Moral Essays*, edited with an English translation by J. W. Basore, 3 vols (Cambridge, Massachusetts, 1935), III, 273.

12. Crane, 'The Houyhnhnms, the Yahoos and the history of ideas'. See also C. T. Probyn, 'Swift and the human predicament', in *The Art of Jonathan Swift*, ed. C. T. Probyn (London, 1978), pp. 57–80.

13. *Institutiones Logicae in usum Juventatis Academicae Dublinensis* (Dublin, 1681).

14. *Aliquis* and *quidam* in Latin, unlike 'a certain' in English, can figure as pronouns.

15. Ed. A. C. Guthkelch and D. Nichol Smith (Oxford, 1958), p. 153.

16. *Lives of the English Poets*, ed. George Birkbeck Hill, 3 vols (Oxford, 1905), III, 57.

17. See Boswell, *Life of Johnson*, ed. George Birkbeck Hill, 6 vols (Oxford, 1887), I, 397 (24 May 1793).

18. Crane, 'The Houyhnhnms, The Yahoos and the history of ideas', p. 35; Traugott, 'A voyage to nowhere', p. 562.

19. In referring to Aristotle I use the standard Bekker numbers. These are given in all good editions including English versions, for example, Sir David Ross, *The Works of Aristotle translated into English*, 12 vols (Oxford, 1926–52). See *Nicomachean Ethics*, 1097 b 11, 1162 a 17, 1169 b 18; *Eudemian Ethics*, 1242 a 22–7, 1245 a 11–27; *Politics*, 1253 a 2, 30, 1278 b 20.

20. *Topics*, 130 b 8, 132 a 20, 133 a 21, 134 a 15, 140 a 36.

21. *De Anima*, 433 a 12; *Historia Animalium*, 488 b 24; *De Partibus Animalium*, 641 b 8; *Politics*, 1332 b 5; *Rhetorica ad Alexandrum*, 1421 a 11.

22. Fragment 187 (Rose's numbering), in Ross, XII, 137.

23. Quoted by Plutarch, *On Moral Virtue*, 450 D, in Plutarch's *Moralia*, with an English translation by W. C. Helmbold, Loeb Classical Library, 15 vols (London, 1927–69), VI, 72.

24. *Epistulae Morales*, 41. 8–9, in *Ad Lucilium Epistulae Morales*, with an English translation by R. M. Gummere, Loeb Classical Library, 3 vols (London, 1917–25), I, 276–8. The translation is mine.

25. *On the Happy Life*, 3. 3, in *Moral Essays*, with an English translation by J. W. Basore, Loeb Classical Library, 3 vols (London, 1927–35), II, 106.

26. See Margaret Anne Doody, '*Gulliver's Travels* and Virgil's *Georgics*', in *Augustan Studies and Essays in Honour of Irvin Ehrenpreis*, ed. Douglas Lane Patey and Timothy Keegan (Newark, Delaware, London, and Toronto, 1985), pp. 145–74, especially p. 171.

27. *The Genealogy of Morals*, 1. 4 and 10, in *The Birth of Tragedy and the Genealogy of Morals*, trans. F. Golfing (New York, 1956), pp. 162, 171–2.

28. Boswell, *Life of Johnson*, II, 106 (26 October 1769).

MOVING CITIES

Pope as translator and transposer[1]

The criticism of Pope has never been the same – or ought never to have been the same – since Empson declared that he would enter 'the very sanctuary of rationality' and applaud the poets of the eighteenth century 'for qualities in their writings which they would have been horrified to discover'.[2] Empson had critical designs on Popean zeugma which, he saw clearly, worked through a tension between apparent, or formal symmetry and a latent asymmetry. The result is wit (not rationality), a contained wildness of the mind. My own design in this essay is to follow Empson's lead, to pursue further the idea of instability in stability, the dynamic imagination within the static.

It might be thought that the very last place in which we should look for such tensions is eighteenth-century translations of classical authors: to look, as Empson looked, for the fluid within the fixed is surely to seek the anti-Augustan within the Augustan; what is hinted at in such an enterprise is the possible presence of proto-Romantic elements in an otherwise firmly classical body of work; that part of the work which is actually derived by direct translation from classical antiquity will scarcely exhibit the required character. 'Classic' and 'Romantic' are terms which criticism can neither define nor do without. I will content myself here with a single observation and make no further use of them in this essay. It is impossible absolutely to confine either term to a given historical period. Broad areas of literature may seem to fall under one flag or the other but then a narrower scrutiny of a single area will cause us to make the same distinction again, and then again. Thus it might be argued that the eighteenth century is Classic while the nineteenth is Romantic, but then, that within the eighteenth century the Graeco-Roman materials are alone truly classic. Or, to cast one's net differently, one might urge that the whole of European literature from the Middle Ages constitutes a Romantic antithesis to the authentic classicism of Homer and Virgil; but move back into the ancient period and Virgil, with his celebrated 'subjective style', his dream-like fluidity, his sense of landscape, becomes Romantic to Homer's Classic; move back once more and the magical *Odyssey* is Romantic when set not with but against the austere *Iliad*. We shall do better if we drop these terms altogether and confine ourselves to the contrast between stability and flux, and in particular the literary extension of flux to that which is itself properly stable, as a means of expressing movement in the subject.

Let us begin, not with a Greek but a Roman. A strange poem called the *Dirae* (either 'Curses' or 'Furies') has been handed down to us as one of the works of Virgil. It appears in many good early manuscripts of Virgil and is listed as Virgil's by both Servius and Donatus. The Renaissance scholar Scaliger (who thought this poem was the work of Virgil's friend Varius) classed it separately, with certain other minor poems, as part of what he called the *Appendix Vergiliana*. Most modern scholars regard much of the *Appendix* as non-Virgilian. Although the *Dirae* is almost certainly not by Virgil himself, it is concerned with the special Virgilian experience of dispossession. Virgil, unlike Shakespeare, say, but like Dante, perceived a significant shape in his own life and projected it on the whole of human history in his major work.[3] Like Aeneas he was first expelled from his own land and then brought home. Virgil never forgot the traumatic loss of his farm, requisitioned for veterans returning after the Battle of Philippi. 'Traumatic' is not too strong a word. The picture of Virgil which has come down to us is of one gauche in all things but poetry, at once rustic and over-educated, almost neurotically attached to a certain landscape. In Virgil's *Aeneid* the hero is unparadised from Troy and finds his way, through varying images of ruined pastoral and spectral cities, to a home more anciently his than Troy had ever been. In the *Dirae* (as in certain of the *Eclogues*) we have the personal story. Grief and imprecation are strangely mixed. The poet does not curse those who threw him off his land. Instead in a sort of hysteria he curses the land itself, as certain suicides seek to involve their own loved ones in their self-destruction. The rough usurping soldiers are barely glimpsed, in a single, Marvellian line (I accept the conjecture *succidet* in place of the impossible *succedet*):

> Militis impia cum succidet dextera ferro . . .
> (31)
> When with his iron axe the soldier's impious hand shall fell . . .

The lines which follow accelerate the impending destruction of the sweet especial rural scene and then, abruptly, seek to retard the process of change:

> Tardius a miserae descendite monte capellae.
> (91)
> Ah, slowly, slowly now, my goats, come down from the hill.

The most remarkable lines of all (and the more Latin poetry one reads the more startling they become) are those in which the poet describes his own departure from the place:

Hinc ego de tumulo mea rura movissima visam,
hinc ibo in silvas: obstabunt iam mihi colles,
obstabunt montes, campos audire licebit:
'dulcia rura valete, et Lydia dulcior illis,
et casti fontes et, felix nomen, agelli'.

(86–90)

From this mound I shall look for the last time at my lands and then go into the woods; now hills will block, now mountains, but the levels will still be able to hear, 'Goodbye, sweet country places and Lydia sweeter still, goodbye, chaste springs and you little fields of happy name.'

These lines stand out from the relatively coarse, sub-Virgilian versification of the *Dirae*. Eduard Fraenkel went so far as to say that whoever wrote these lines, it could not be the poet of the *Dirae*, and to stress a connection, indirect but nevertheless intimate, with the authentically Virgilian fifth Eclogue.[4] The passage is remarkable for its subtle hypallage from subject to object, not all of which can be conveyed straightforwardly in an English version. For example, the Latin does not actually say, 'I shall look for the last time at my lands', it says, 'I shall look at my newest (latest) lands'; the character of the looking (looking for the last time) is ascribed to the thing looked at. This is not a mere trick or metrical convenience. It is *used* poetically.

Partly, the effect is of an extreme subjectivism: where the *pathos* of the viewer is as strong as this it can, so to speak, appropriate the object in act of wilful perceptual tyranny, but at the same time this is a poem about expropriation and we are aware that this small, defiant movement of the imagination is futile. The notion of a last embrace, hackneyed in English, but poetically powerful in the *Aeneid*, may lie behind the thought here. Thus, together with the rhetorical appropriation we sense the opposite of appropriation: that the subject is drained, that a richness of identity properly his has passed into the landscape. There is even a faint paradox within the single word *novissima*, where, because this is a time poem, we hear for an instant the basic sense, 'newest', before it is contested and defeated by the dominant sense 'last'. But then we have a firmly personal assertion: *ibo in silvas*, 'I shall go into the woods', followed at once by *obstabunt iam mihi colles*. I translated these words, with all the inelegance of a studied neutrality, as 'now hills will block'. In ordinary Latin *obstabunt* following *ibo* must mean 'will bar my path'. But the context of intense subjective perception, of looking and listening (or being heard) ensures that we do not take it so. It is as if the poet is walking with head turned, so that *obstabunt* can mean (as the Loeb translator takes it) 'will block *my view*'. The agency is mysteriously transferred, once more, from the subject moving through the landscape, to the landscape itself. We cannot quite say that the poet makes the hills move (these hills are not like the striding mountain in the first book of Wordsworth's *The Prelude*[5]). Yet the repetition of the verb and the changing scale of its subject (first hills then mountains) suggest as it were a covert action on the part of the landscape, as if the ground moves to interpose its masses when the poet is not looking. In these lines we have, then, a certain linguistic and logical oddity, deployed to a subtle literary effect. These hints are then allowed to flower in the full-blown poetical figure of the levels still hearing the poet's melancholy valediction, a version of the quintessentially Virgilian trope of the pathetic fallacy, since we infer sympathy in the listening fields.

If these lines are not by Virgil they are by someone who, as they used to say in the sixteenth century, was deeply inward with his work. Though the *Dirae* never lost its place in the Virgilian *corpus* it seems to have been little taught in the Roman schools and to have escaped the kind of learned commentary which accreted round Virgil's *Eclogues, Georgics* and *Aeneid*. These lines especially are thoroughly Virgilian in their subtle manipulation of subject and object and in their heart-tearing sense of place. Virgil is rightly famous as the poet of *idem in alio*, who reworked the war and the wanderings of Homeric epic until they became instinct with futurity, with the divine history of a single city. Rome. At the same time, as I have suggested, Virgil was aware of a correlative personal history, of his own eviction, wandering and home-coming. This is picked up and accented in the *Dirae*, together (it must be confessed) with a quantity of sub-standard writing of quite another order.

I have explored this passage in some detail because it is a peculiarly rich example of something rare in Latin literature: a kind of poetry in which the moving subject implicitly imputes his own movement to the landscape, producing a strange effect of exacerbated, disorienting subjectivity. It is an effect which without further apology we may agree to call Virgilian, not least because it is given audacious expression in the *Aeneid*, where Italy *flies* before a pursuing Aeneas through a world of evanescent visions and ghost cities which rise and fall before our eyes. I chose the *Dirae* as my main specimen in preference to the more opulent tropes of the *Aeneid* because of the very smallness of the scale and the sharpness of the visual/spatial effects which go with such intimacy. I chose it because it is more Popean. Yet we cannot be quite certain that Pope ever read it. The *Dirae* is excluded from the Daniel Heinsius edition of the *Works of Virgil* (Leyden, 1636) which Pope is known to have possessed.[6] It is included in Michael Maittaire's *Opera et Opuscula Veterum Poetarum Latinorum*, a book Pope is again known to have owned.[7] But the *Opera et Opuscula* did not appear until 1713, it ascribes the *Dirae* not to Virgil but to the more readily negligible Valerius Cato and, most infuriatingly of all, prints *nec adire* in place of *audire* at line 88.[8] This changes the sense from 'the levels will be able to hear' to 'it will not be possible to reach the levels', which in its turn reduces *obstabunt*, 'will block/My vision)', to the commonplace 'will bar my path'. It would really be more to the point to ask whether the *Dirae* was known to Sir William Trumbull, the friend and mentor (especially in matters classical) of Pope's youth. Pope refers on a number of occasions to the *Appendix Vergiliana* but always to the *Culex* (never the *Dirae*).[9] One particular early reference, in a letter of 11 November 1710, suggests (though we may remind ourselves that Pope liked to wear his learning heavily) a serious engagement with Virgilian *dubia*; he points out that a borrowing from the conclusion of the *Culex* occurs in the *Prolusiones Academicae* (1622) of Famianus of Strada.[10] The question remains uncertain. I therefore offer the lines from the *Dirae* not as a source for Pope but as a remote, early parallel – another example of the fertilising effect of Virgil's poetry. Of Pope's awareness of the grander, epic versions there can be no doubt, for these had been imperiously transposed and integrated in English literary culture through Dryden's translation:

> . . . arva . . . Ausoniae semper cedentia retro
> (*Aeneid*, iii. 496)

appears in Dryden as

> Fields of flying *Italy* to chase
> (*Virgil's Aeneis*, iii. 643)[11]

and

> Italiam sequimur fugientem et volvimur undis
> (*Aeneid*, v. 629)

appears as

> Through stormy sea
> We search in vain for flying *Italy*
> (*Virgil's Aeneis*, v. 819)[12]

The ancient poet who is *not* like this at all is, of course, Homer.

When Pope was about nineteen he worked up a free translation of a number of neighbouring passages in the thirteenth book of Homer's *Odyssey*. This we now know as 'The Arrival of Ulysses in Ithaca'. By the second couplet we can see Pope Virgilianising his author:

> At once they bend, and strike their equal oars,
> And leave the sinking Hills, and lessening Shores.
> (4–5)

The first line is Homerically objective, the second is like a Virgilian antiphony, at once mirroring and modifying the first, with its insinuation of a projected subjectivity. There is nothing in the Greek about sinking hills or lessening shores, nor is there in the English versions of Hobbes, Ogilby or Chapman.[13] In a similar manner at lines 21–4 one couplet conveys the objective splendour of Homer (weakened only marginally by the faint personification of 'promis'd') while the next counters with a Virgilian moving landscape – not a diminuendo this time, but a crescendo:

> But when the morning Star with early Ray
> Flam'd in the Front of Heav'n, and promis'd Day,
> Like distant Clouds the Mariner descries
> Fair Ithaca's emerging Hills arise.

There is, again, no warrant in Homer for the second of these couplets but, as Audra and Williams observe,[14] Pope may actually have had Dryden's Virgil in mind at this moment:

> When we from far, like bluish Mists, descry
> The Hills, and then the Plains, of *Italy*.
> (*Virgil's Aeneis*, iii. 684–5)

Because feelings are freer than facts, a certain easy extremism of language enters with the subjective style; hyperbole, in a manner, becomes merely natural. One result of this is that, while it is clear in the Greek that the vessel which conveys Odysseus is a *magic* ship, moving with preternatural speed, we are unsurprised when Pope tells us that the ship flew faster than an eagle (13–14); any ship may *seem* to do that. Here what is perhaps the finest image of the *Odyssey*, the sleeping hero whirled across the sea, is unforgivably reduced.

In Pope's version the Phaeacians set Odysseus/Ulysses ashore, as they do in Homer, and he hides his treasure so that no one can steal it. Here Pope does not elaborate but instead curtails his author. Homer is much more interested than Pope in the practical business of concealing the treasure, telling us, as Pope does not, that it was in a place aside from the road, where no wayfaring man would come upon it (*Odyssey*, xiii. 123).

At line 55 we have the minor but still significantly un-Homeric hypallage 'solitary shore', for strictly speaking it is the hero who is alone, not the shore, and then, with almost no warrant from the original, five lines of studied art, in which grief is expertly mingled with visual perception:

> Pensive and slow, with sudden Grief opprest,
> The King arose, and beat his careful Breast,
> Cast a long look o'er all the Coast and Main,
> And sought around his Native Realm in vain;
> Then with erected Eyes, stood fix'd in woe.
> (68–72)

Homer says simply that Odysseus 'looked upon his native land' (xiii. 197). Otherwise, of these lines only the second can be said to occur in Homer, at xiii. 198 (though there the hero smites not his breast but his thigh). At 224 Pope again adds a note of Virgilian visual pathos with the words, 'Now lift thy longing Eyes.' The intruded line 133,

> Where Troy's Majestic Ruins strow the Ground

is, once more, Virgilian in tone, though here it is a different strand in Virgil which is being drawn upon.

But not all Pope's departures from Homer are Virgilian. The adjectives at 106–7 –

> Her decent Hand a shining Javelin bore,
> and painted Sandals on her Feet she wore

– are not in Homer but are, so to speak, Augustan-Homeric: 'painted' is influenced by Homer's ποικίλος, which happens not to be used here but easily could have been. 'Decent' is indeed a Latinism, but the influence here is Horace rather than Virgil (say, *decentes malas*, Horace, *Odes*, III. xxvii. 53–4, transmitted through Milton, *Il Penseroso*, 36, 'decent shoulders'). Elsewhere Pope's changes are in the direction of gentility, as when he introduces the 'Peasant' at 124. Here the result is that the interest in farming on Ithaca, which for Homer is immediate, is distanced as the proper province of subordinate persons. Or else he is sententious, as at 86–7, where he offers the reader an elevated reflection on the rarity of virtue in the Great. He omits entirely the conversation of Zeus and Poseidon together with the turning to stone of the Phaeacian ship (xiii. 125–87). The full list of omissions and additions is a long one but it is the Virgilian changes which most crucially affect the atmosphere of the whole and colour the poetry. Homer's ancient, magic world is humanised, refined, imbued with sensibility.

All the while Pope, the craftsman, is learning from this crossing of cultures. Every translator knows occasions when he is tempted to convey not only the sense but the linguistic character of the original, to drop the game of equivalences and instead to transpose, by a kind of bodily violence, vocabulary, idiom or syntax from the source language to the receiving language.[16] Where a language is relatively poor, as was Middle English, say, when the Latin for 'remorse of conscience' had to be rendered by 'again-bite of in-wit', the receiving language is actually enriched and extended by such forcible incursions from the major culture. Later phases of transposition have subtler effects. The aureate diction of Sir Thomas Browne played the transposed polysyllables of Latin and Greek against Saxon simplicities to suggest a running ambivalence or balancing of equivalents in the world and in the mind. Milton's despotic transpositions of alien syntax and idiom created for all the poets who followed a strange secondary music in the given medium of literary English.

English-Augustan classicism is an altogether less radical, more urbane affair than Milton's. Its typical effect is a certain finesse, a precision which may look for a moment, but a moment only, like imprecision. Thus in calling his poem 'The Rape of the Lock' Pope knew that the grosser, ordinary meaning of *rape* (which, by the way, the reader is never allowed quite to forget), inappropriate as it is to a lock of hair, must be swiftly replaced by the Latin sense, 'seizure' (now perfectly appropriate and free, after all, from any offence).

If all translators from the Latin and Greek had followed the implicit code of, say, the Penguin Classics, in which those quirks of linguistic and conceptual organisation which may be deemed to be embedded in the ancient language as such are suppressed, the varying streams of more or less classicised diction would never have entered the language, to be poetically exploited in due course by such as Pope. Of course, as long as there were

people about who knew the ancient languages, abrupt translinguistic
allusions like Milton's 'happy-making sight' at line 18 of *On time* were always
possible (here the seemingly artless phrase is ponderously *faux-naif*; a
Saxonised version of *beatifica visio* and so a small prize for the learned reader).
But Pope, whose learning in ancient tongues was not profound, had
nevertheless an ear sharply attuned to the literary effects of transposition,
whether from Greek, Latin or from contemporary high-polish Romance
cultures such as French. The writer of a radically classical style gives the
reader a sense of an utterly hard infrastructure of meanings which are both
alien to us and clear. Milton does so systematically and Pope does not. Jane
Austen inherited certain verbal habits of precision from the classicising
eighteenth century but employed them without any sense of the original
infrastructure. She is therefore classical in the comic form of her novels but
not in their intimate verbal texture. In our own century Evelyn Waugh is
found repellent by some not only because of his politics but also because of
the hard, alienating gloss of a radically, but not ostentatiously, classical style.
Something must have gone into his head at Lancing College.

The distinction between translation and transposition is, it will be noticed,
a rough and ready one, with further sub-distinctions lurking within it. The
translator, unlike the transposer, selects from the receiving language
equivalents *which shall be wholly natural to the receiving language*. Where the Latin
poet says (indeed with no religious intention) that bulls 'breathe Vulcan
from their nostrils' (Ovid, *Metamorphoses*, vii. 104) the modern translator will
say they 'breathe fire' (since that is what *we* would say). But at this point a
certain sort of reader, curious as to how ancient poetry was actually pieced
together, will resent the modification while another sort of reader will be
gratefully acquiescent. It may be that this example artificially biases the
argument in favour of the literalist transposer, for it is certainly true that an
exaggerated fidelity to form and idiom can result in an utterly faithless and
distorted rendering of meaning (now the notion of *equivalence*, the watchword
of the translator, begins to look strong again). Yet – the argument oscillates
more and more rapidly – this too can beget difficulties which arise from the
fact that even fictional ancient literature is engaged at certain points with
historical actuality. There will be times when *praetor* may be rendered
'magistrate' and times when the translator must write, even in English,
'praetor'. In eighteenth-century England there was a perfectly clear cultural
equivalent for Rome, namely London, yet to *translate* Juvenal's *Roma*
'London' is to stretch translation so far as to turn it into what Dryden called
'imitation' (as opposed to 'paraphrase' or the still tighter 'metaphrase').[17]

The eighteenth century knew how to enjoy such ultra-translation just as it
appreciated the opposite pleasure of linguistic transposition. If Johnson's
London (a version of Juvenal's third Satire) may stand at one end of our
continuum, the calque may stand as its polar opposite. A calque is a
transference of a special, subordinate use of a given word in language 'A' to

the corresponding word in language 'B', where that special use had not existed previously. 'Foot' in the sense 'metrical foot' is a calque from Latin *pes*, which carried just such a subordinate technical sense. A calque is quite distinct from what is called *borrowing*, where the *form* of a word in language 'A' is simply replicated, with the minimum necessary adjustments, in language 'B'. 'Admonition' is a borrowing from Latin *admonitio* and preserves the form of the original almost exactly. Calques became less and less common as the English language developed and borrowings were felt to be more cultivated. They are commonest in the Anglo-Saxon period.[18] A learned freedom at the 'imitation' end of the spectrum (where the receiving culture is lavishly enfranchised) is answered at the other end by a tiny localised usurpation of the natural rights of the receiving language – not by the mere importation of the polysyllabic alien *form* of the word but by a more fundamental invasion of the *seme*, or meaning-structure. To refer to 'the third foot' of a line of verse is, even today, not quite natural English. Dickens makes a free and very coarse use of calques to convey the Frenchness of France in *A Tale of Two Cities* and at the beginning of *Little Dorrit*. Charlotte Brontë does the same thing, though less exuberantly, in *Villette*. Pope's touch is far too light for such gross effects.

Let us take, from nowhere, a Latin sentence: *Et blaesa voce numeris locutus sum*. This can be translated, 'I lisped in verse-time.' A bad case of form-transposition might give 'I balbutiated metrically' (where the borrowings are from other Latin words). Transposition of the subordinate sense gives, 'I lisped in numbers', and this, of course, is Pope. As soon as we read, 'in numbers' we sense Augustanism and, if we enjoy it, what we are enjoying is a subtle counterpointing of semic systems. 'Numbers' is a calque, for here the English word is used in a way which is, still perceptibly, unnatural. It is used as *numerus* is used in Latin. For some learned readers the intuition of Latinity in 'numbers' would be strengthened by the fact that at this point in the *Epistle to Dr Arbuthnot* Pope happens to be echoing a particular passage of Ovid (*Tristia*, IV. x. 21–6). Of course calques may be gradually naturalised by frequent use in the receiving language until they are no longer felt as calques – for example certain uses of *chair*, influenced by Latin *cathedra*, or *left* in the political sense, influenced by French *gauche*. It is characteristic of Pope that he should use a partly naturalised calque with a surviving stylistic sense of its linguistic nature. It is not for him but for hardier spirits to introduce wholly new calques.

When the young Pope essayed the translation of Homer he brought to the task not the self-abnegating, objectivist zeal of the scholar but a civil art of interwoven tones and nuances. Was he not soon to be the foremost social poet of the age? He knew perfectly well that his job was to temper style with style, to gain point and dynamism by modulating from austerity to urbanity. But as soon as he began to write he found that such modulation did not work through a simple encounter of the (severe) ancient and the (polished) modern; ancient literature itself prescribed a startlingly rich variety of tone. The matter is further complicated – almost beyond analysis – by the varying mediations of existing translations, but for all that we continue to find an intelligible music of styles rather than a mere chaos. Certainly the *Odyssey*, as we hinted earlier, is deeply different from the *Iliad*. The later poem is spatially indistinct, magical, humorous, and to bring this out Pope found himself drawing on Virgil, who is different again. The result is not a faithful rendering of Homer (a thing worth chasing but impossible to hit) but a shimmering of styles and languages. To the eighteenth century (and still, to some extent, to us) the ancient world was marble: Vitruvian, regular, arched, pillared, founded in reason and nature. Where the modern world presents an obscure flux, the ancient presents a sunlit stability. Such is the 'mental set', the elementary binary codification of material from which we must begin. Pope's way with English poetry was always subtly to thwart or undermine seemingly stable structures, restoring harmony only at the last (and not always then). But when he engaged directly with ancient literature he found his way to what is perhaps the most imaginatively original element in Virgil: the rendering fluid of that which is normally the very paradigm of the stable, the earth under our feet, the buildings through which we move.

To be sure, in the England of Pope's day the baroque was very much a living force. In the great *sotto in su* paintings of the period heroes, saints and demi-gods fly up on clouds above our heads and the architecture from which they rise, columns and pediments seen in an aggressively perspectival manner from below, seems to be on the point of following the figures up, wildly, into the firmament. Giovanni Battista Gaulli had painted his *Adoration of the Name of Jesus* on the ceiling of the Gesù in Rome before Pope was born, but Sir James Thornhill's Painted Hall at Greenwich was not finished until 1727. Borromini, the great architect of the baroque, took the rectilinear classical façade and caused it to undulate in serpentine curves. Strictly speaking, a curving wall is as stable and unmoving as a straight one but imaginatively, perhaps because in general we expect straightness, undulation immediately suggests movement. But the architects and architectural painters were not placed quite as Pope was placed. There was no real analogue within ancient literature for the spectacular subversions of stability they sought to introduce. Nevertheless Pope found, primarily in Virgil, a non-baroque precedent for his own less grandiose, more intimate subversions. I began with the *Dirae* as something separate and unique, neglected in the commentaries and yet exhibiting in a curiously poignant manner the imaginative trope of *movement imputed to the landscape*. Latin is, after all, capable of such things. Pope, from his side, infuses his translation of Homer with an imaginative fluidity which is recognisably akin to what we find first in the *Dirae* and then, more largely, in the *Aeneid*.

As early as the Pastorals, written in 1704, the verbs, always revealing in Pope, show this distinctive quality. Often they are inchoative, either in form or in sense:

Here where the Mountains, less'ning as they rise
Lose the low Vales, and steal into the Skies.
(*Autumn*, 59–60)

The first part of *Windsor Forest*, that 'which relates to the country', was written at about the same time as the Pastorals. Here too we find the same note struck. The phrasing of line 24, 'blueish hills ascend', may seem unremarkable, but the sense that even here the Virgilian influence may be at work is strengthened by the odd and beautiful word 'bluish' used, as we have already seen, of hills in Dryden's Virgil. A couple of lines earlier we have an intuition of a landscape which seems to shift and redispose itself as we move through it in the words 'interspersed in Lawns and opening Glades', where the important word is 'opening'. At line 213 we have the marvellously judged classicism of 'pendant' in:

The watry Landskip of the pendant Woods.

First there is the latent *linguistic* precision of 'pendant', a precision not quite natural in English. Then, behind that, we have the *imaginative* precision-within-a-seeming-inappositeness of woods seen as hanging. In Virgil's first Eclogue the shepherd apostrophises his goats:

Non ego vos posthac viridi proiectus in antro
dumosa pendere procul de rupe videbo.
(75–6)

No more, stretched out in some green cave, shall I watch
you in the distance, hanging from a bushy crag.

Wordsworth's comment on *pendere* is famous. He observes doggedly that goats do not in fact hang as parrots hang, that rather the word presents 'to the mind something of such an appearance, the mind in its activity, for its own gratification, contemplates them as hanging.'[19] Wordsworth is right on the essential point: that the character proper to the act of seeing is imputed to the thing seen, so that the passage contrives to be both about goats and about seeing at the same time. But of course there is more to it than that. Things threatened can seem more precious than things secure: that which hangs can fall. At the same time there is a contrary sense of a diminished reality, of a back-cloth *suspended* before the eye (for a visual presentation of a goat, however intense, is somehow less than the goat itself). Virgil more than any other poet taught this art to the ages which followed and Pope was not the least apt of his pupils. Thus Pope's pendant woods may owe something to the landscape description at *Aeneid*, i. 164. The famous phrase *silvis scaena coruscis*, translated by R. G. Austin as 'a backdrop of quivering woods',[20] where the sense of a painted curtain becomes explicit, is followed by *horrentique atrum nemus imminet umbra* (165), 'The grove hangs dark over it with its bristling shade' (*imminet* is parallel in Latin to *impendet* and *pendentibus* itself appears in the very next line, applied to the hanging rocks of the cave).

There is a lesson in all this for us. The twentieth-century reader of Pope

needs in a manner to have his ear educated by Virgil if he is to read the
English poet with full understanding. *Sapho to Phaon* belongs to the same year
(1707) as *The Arrival of Ulysses in Ithaca*. Here the dominant influence is Ovid,
but Virgil is not wholly absent. The *silvis scaena coruscis* passage is perhaps the
most influential piece of natural description in all ancient literature and its
fainter echoes persist even where direct influence is unprovable. Let us try to
catch the more fleeting Virgilian affinities in the following lines:

> As if once more forsaken, I complain
> And close my Eyes, to dream of you again.
> Then frantick rise, and like some Fury rove
> Thro' lonely Plains, and thro' the silent Grove,
> As if the silent Grove and lonely Plains
> That knew my Pleasures, cou'd relieve my Pains.
> I view the *Grotto*, once the Scene of Love,
> The Rocks around, the hanging Roofs above . . .
>
> (157–164)

Here we do not have the trope of imputed movement, but the subject's
progress through plains and conscious (in the old sense) woods is reminiscent
of the *Dirae*, while the word 'Fury' evokes the stricken and sleepless Dido,
roving maddened through the night at the beginning of *Aeneid*, iv (*uritur infelix
Dido totaque vagatur/urbe furens*, 'Unhappy Dido burns and wanders fury-like
through the whole city'). Meanwhile the 'Grotto', the 'Scene' of love and the
'hanging' roofs take us back to *silvis scaena coruscis*, felt through Ovid, *Heroides*,
xv. 135f. We must concede, I think, that Pope's 'scene' is a degree or two less
assertive of the theatrical metaphor than Virgil's *scaena*; one can watch the
word weakening in successive English imitations of Virgil before Pope.
Milton at *Paradise Lost*, iv. 137 writes 'sylvan scene' and then goes out of his
way to make sure that the image is kept alive by 'woody theatre' immediately
afterwards. Dryden, translating *Aeneid*, i. 164, writes 'a Sylvan Scene/
Appears above'[21] and we sense that the word is paler than it was. But in both
Dryden and Pope the word *scene* certainly retains the theatrical image more
strongly than it does today. Virgil's poetry was then still feeding the word.

The case is similar with the (for us) unremarkable '*Alps* on *Alps* arise'
which occurs in the *Essay on Criticism* (232) in a sharply visual context ('tire
our wandring Eyes' ends the preceding line). The line about the Alps can be
linked with *Eloisa to Abelard*, 290: 'Rise *Alps* between us! and whole oceans
roll', where we are discernibly in the world of the *Dirae* (*obstabunt montes*, the
mountains which interpose themselves between the subject and the loved
object).

Sometimes indeed the effect is more full-blown and closer to the baroque.
Take the ascending, swelling, bending architectural splendours of *Windsor
Forest*, 375–80:

> Behold! th'ascending Villa's on my Side
> Project long Shadows o'er the Chrystal Tyde.

> Behold! Augusta's glitt'ring Spires increase,
> And Temples rise, the beauteous Works of Peace.
> I see, I see where two fair Cities bend
> Their ample Bow, a new *White-Hall* ascend!

It may be said that this is at best an impure specimen of the trope since the buildings to which Pope referred were actually rising. The point is less important than it appears. Even when a building is being raised the eye does not *see* it rising in the accelerated manner of these lines. When we come to the two fair bending cities the reader is not sure whether the sense is that building works are joining them (as in fact they were) or whether they simply appear thus. It is characteristic of such poetry that questions of this sort do not trouble us but are instead merely suspended. Some may have been reminded of Aeneas at the site where Rome is later to rise, *Aeneid*, viii. 355–6, especially as in the Latin the word *oppida*, 'towns', is mildly surprising, occurring when, metre apart, we might rather have expected some such word as *arces*, 'citadels':

> Haec duo praeterea disiectis oppida muris
> reliquias veterumque vides monumenta virorum.

In Dryden:

> Then saw two heaps of Ruins; once they stood
> Two stately Towns, on either side the Flood.
> (*Virgil's Aeneis*, viii. 467–8)[22]

The same, more grandiose manner appears (but this time with a downward motion) in

> . . . Tow'rs and Temples sink in Floods of Fire.
> (*The Temple of Fame*, 478)

Years later Pope could not resist a Virgilian expansion when he translated the lament of Andromache for Hector (*Iliad*, xxiv. 725–45). Homer makes her say that, before her child will grow up, πόλις ἥδε κατ᾽ ἄκρης/πέρσεται (728–9), literally 'This city will be destroyed from the top down'. The phrase which I have rendered 'from the top down' is however less vivid in the Greek than in the English and Lang, Leaf and Myers have some justification in translating it simply as 'utterly'.[23] But Virgil, contrariwise, blew on the spark and made it blaze, not once but twice:

> Ruit alto a culmine Troia.
> (*Aeneid*, ii. 290)
> Down from her high pinnacle Troy is falling.

> . . . divum inclementia, divum
> . . . sternitque a culmine Troiam.
> (ii. 603)
> The gods, the merciless gods scatter and
> lay low Troy from her pinnacle down.

Pope, translating the original Greek phrase, writes, surely with a sense of the Latin *ruit* in his 'Ruin':

> For *Ilium* now (her great Defender slain)
> Shall sink, a smoaking Ruin on the plain.
> (Pope's *Iliad*, xxiv. 916–17)[24]

Compare with this Pope's *Odyssey*, iii. 614–18 (the third book of the *Odyssey* is one of the books which Pope undertook to translate himself, without waiting for a prior version by Fenton or Broome):

> Beneath the bounding yoke alike they held
> Their equal pace, and smoak'd along the field.
> The tow'rs of *Pylos* sink, its views decay,
> Fields after fields fly back, till close of day:
> Then sunk the Sun, and darken'd all the way.[25]

The Greek here is rendered, almost word for word, by Butcher and Lang as follows:

> Nothing loth the pair flew toward the plain and left
> the steep citadel of Pylos. So all day long they swayed
> the yoke they bore upon their necks.
> Now the sun sank and all the ways were darkened.[26]

In Pope's version the bounding yoke and the darkened way are both reasonably Homeric. The words 'alike' and 'equal' may look like a sheer importation of Augustan order and balance into the headlong motion of the original, but in fact Pope may here be responding to the dual form of the verb and to ἀμφίς ('both', or 'the pair'). The rest is a compound of Virgil and Pope's own, unsubduable gift. This passage is linked to the one previously cited by 'smoak'd', but its chief interest is that it returns us to the trope of imputed motion. The towers sink as Telemachus and Pisistratus leave them behind. Virgil's fields of flying Italy are somewhere in the penumbra of the poetry, but meanwhile the startling phrase 'views decay' is very much Pope's own. Thomas Hobbes in his *Leviathan*, with no lyric intent, called imagination itself 'decaying sense'.[27] Pope's use of the word is full of lyric sensitivity but is at the same time in a manner neutral (there is no sinister suggestion). He may be writing in a classicising mode, with an awareness of the word's remoter derivation from Latin *decidere*, 'to fall'. What he writes is certainly poetry. Later the word is to appear again in the terrific conclusion of *The Dunciad*, in which creation itself runs backwards to a hell of unbeing:

> *Fancy's* gilded clouds decay,
> And all its varying Rain-bows die away.
> (1742, iv. 631–2)

This time the implication of corruption and malaise is admitted by the poetry. Within five lines we have the finest, and the most disquieting, line Pope ever wrote:

The sick'ning stars fade off th'ethereal plain.
(636)

In *The Dunciad* Pope is no longer teaching himself by cross-breeding his predecessors but is writing at the height of his powers. The auditory relativity of Virgil is thoroughly transformed, appearing now in the fully Popean evocation of London, the sounding city, flooded and overwhelmed by a rising tumult:

> But far o'er all, sonorous Blackmore's strain;
> Walls, steeples, skies, bray back to him again.
> In Tot'nam fields, the brethren, with amaze,
> Prick all their ears up, and forget to graze;
> Long Chanc'ry Lane retentive rolls the sound
> And courts to courts return it round and round,
> Thame wafts it thence to Rufus' roaring hall,
> And Hungerford re-echoes bawl for bawl.
> (1742, ii. 259–66)

Pope can be seen in training for this passage in his early version of Statius (1703), with its echoing cities and remurmuring river-banks (164, 166), followed by the baroque exhilaration of the 'guilty Dome' and the bright pavilions invaded by obscuring clouds (172–3). That Statius should himself sound like Virgil is, of course, scarcely surprising. Now, however, the language is thoroughly naturalised, not least as a result of the London place-names. It will be said that they are there for bathetic effect and are intended to contrast, according to the ordinary rule of mock heroic, with an implied array of Roman names. Yet the sheerly heroic energy of the lines is too strong. If ever Pope were, against all the odds, to be comparable with Blake, it would be here.

In *The Dunciad* the verbs are as important as ever:

> Thro' Lud's fam'd gates, along the well-known Fleet
> Rolls the black troop, and overshades the street,
> 'Till show'rs of Sermons, Characters, Essays,
> In circling fleeces whiten all the ways:
> So clouds replenish'd from some bog below,
> Mount in dark volumes, and descend in snow.
> (1742, ii. 359–64)

The simple forward motion of 'Rolls' is overtaken by the inchoative 'whiten'. 'Whiten' is used many times in the translation of Homer, mostly in descriptions of the sea, and 'blacken' is commoner still (twenty-four instances), usually with reference to storm and clouds. In the early (1707) translation of 'the Episode of Sarpedon' from the *Iliad*, an army of warriors, likened to a storm, is seen as 'black'ning in the field' (58). In the *Dunciad* passage, the recurrent Homeric formula 'All the ways were darkened' is working somewhere in the back of Pope's mind. 'Blacken' is used most powerfully in *The Elegy to the Memory of an Unfortunate Lady* (1717):

>   While the long fun'rals blacken all the way.
>   (40)

In *The Dunciad* blackening and whitening are combined and the combination
is at once brilliantly mirrored in the ascending darkness of the clouds
followed by the falling pallor of the snow.

Both the passages I have cited from *The Dunciad* will stand as spectacular
examples of dynamic townscape, but in neither of them do we find the radical
figure of imputed movement. There is perhaps a kind of vertigo in the image
(from the second passage) of flying manuscripts filling the streets, which
links it to certain baroque conjurings of flying buildings, but in both passages
London itself remains rooted, while the human chaos swirls through it. In
the vision of the Fall of Rome in Book iii the movement of the buildings is not
imaginatively imputed but is actual, a real fall brought about by barbarian
hands:

>   See, the Cirque falls, th' unpillar'd Temple nods,
>   Streets pav'd with Heroes, Tyber choak'd with Gods.
>   (1742, iii. 107–8)

Yet, even though all this actually happened, it is given a dream-like quality,
an air of licentious imagination, by the surrealism of the second line.

Some thirty lines further on the poetry gathers to a head in the ancient
figure, known as the *adynata* or *Impossibilia*[28] (fishes in the trees, suns in the
sea), in which nature herself runs lunatic. This special, cosmic version of
imputed movement has its own literary history and I have done my best to
keep it out of this essay. But six lines must be quoted:

>   Thence a new world to Nature's laws unknown,
>   Breaks out refulgent, with a heav'n its own.
>   Another Cynthia her new journey runs,
>   And other planets circle other suns.
>   The forests dance, the rivers upward rise,
>   Whales sport in woods and dolphins in the skies.
>   (1742, iii. 241–6)

Here the landscape moves mightily, as it does in the *Epistle to Burlington*,
where the golden corn flows over and buries Timon's vanity (173–6). The
splendour of the lines quoted is quite untouched by the distinctive colouring
of subjective visual perception we found earlier. They are as much Greek as
Roman (look at Herodotus, v. 92a); they are as Horatian (look at *Odes*, I. ii.
5–10) or as Ovidian (*Metamorphoses*, i. 293–303) as they are Virgilian.

To rediscover the subjective inflection we must leave the major sonorities
of *The Dunciad* and go back in time. In *Eloisa to Abelard*, the shrines tremble
(112) with Eloisa's trembling consciousness and when Abelard's image rises
in her mind,

>   Priests, Tapers, Temples, swim before my sight.
>   (274)

Otherwise, we may turn to that almost perfect minor poem, the *Epistle to Miss Blount, on her leaving the Town, after the Coronation*, written in 1714. The poet, in a reverie, standing in a London street, imagines Miss Blount in her tedious country exile, imagining (in her turn) the metropolitan splendours of the court. The poem is thus an intricate Chinese box of imaginings within imaginings. Then, to represent the evanescence of an image as it is replaced by common perception, Pope uses the image of a suddenly moved fan, imputing the visual occlusion and revelation occasioned thereby, as movement, to the objects imagined or perceived. So much for the hard, marble clarity of Augustan verse.

> In some fair evening, on your elbow laid,
> You dream of triumphs in the rural shade,
> In pensive thought recall the fancy'd scene,
> See coronations rise on ev'ry green;
> Before you pass th' imaginary sights
> Of Lords, and Earls, and Dukes, and garter'd Knights;
> While the spread fan o'ershades your closing eyes,
> Then give one flirt, and all the vision flies.
> Thus vanish sceptres, coronets, and balls,
> And leave you in lone woods, or empty walls.
>
> (31–40)

I have argued that 'scene' in Pope carries a stronger theatrical connotation than is always perceived by modern readers. In these lines (perhaps because of their historical relation to the Coronation) Pope seems to be thinking partly of a pageant or masque and masques were of course remarkable for their transformation scenes. Stage scenery, unlike mental imagery, is part of the physical fabric of the public world, but that does not mean that the whole tenor of this passage is merely objectified, as when the falling towers really fall, toppled by the barbarian hordes. Because scenery consists of picturings, more or less flimsy and impermanent, it is naturally analogous to mental imagery. Several scholars have sensed an allusion to masque in the most famous of all the moving-architecture passages of English poetry, the rising to music of Pandemonium in *Paradise Lost* (i. 710–17).[29] In Miss Blount's reverie it is not 'Doric pillars overlaid / With golden architrave' that whirl from her but 'sceptres, coronets, and balls', things which are in any case mobile in themselves. When, however, we are returned to the consciousness of Pope himself, the very streets assail him and clamorously usurp his dream:

> *Gay* pats my shoulder, and you vanish quite;
> Streets, chairs and coxcombs rush upon my sight.
>
> (47–8)

I have at times in this essay written of these effects as if they were heroic or sublime. But where they are unequivocally placed as free-floating imaginings they are of course immediately diminished. Pope, jealous to preserve, especially in a potentially sexual context, his own lightness of manner, is often anxious to secure this very diminution. Gay's hand on Pope's shoulder enables him to show Miss Blount that he is not, after all, her abject slave but an urbane man with friends and interests of his own. Pope skilfully curtails the flirtation (remember that this word has to do, as the poem itself shows us, with the use of the *fan*) and contains his own, briefly vagrant imagination. But the rushing streets are not a dream or an illusion: they are reality itself, importunate and loud. Thus Pope resists the easy baroque sublimity which by his day was virtually inherent in the trope of imputed movement. It is common, everyday London, not heroes and palaces, which is here behaving so uncommonly. One searches in vain for a just analogue in painting, something like Thornhill's ceiling if it had been painted instead by Hogarth. Gillray was later to draw mock-baroque tableaux with caricatured political personages, and I am sure that Pope would have been delighted by Cruickshank's picture of London spreading into the surrounding country-side, squirting smoke and bricks in fountains. But both these examples (quite apart from the fact that they post-date Pope) are far too coarse in their technique.

I have tried to show how, when Pope entered the altered landscape of another culture, he chose not only to translate classical meanings into English meanings but also to transpose certain alien habits of speech and thought. He did this because, like all great poets, he cared about language and form, and knew that the language of English poetry itself would be strengthened and enriched by the minor violations to which he was willing to subject it. He also found that the ancient world itself was far from being a uniform field. I have written about Pope's Virgilianising of Homer as if it were a matter of strenuously artificial interference. In fact it would have required a most artificial vigilance on Pope's part to keep Virgil *out*. Pope, who never published a set translation of Virgil, had Virgil in his bones and accepted the consequence. This was a dynamic, ever moving modulation of tone. The whole can be seen, thus far, as a marvellously managed interplay of cultural perspectives. But then we notice that the Virgilian passages are all actually *about* individual, perspectival seeing and perceptual relativities. Pope found, in the ordinary practice of translation, that a Virgilian subjectivity could quicken his page. He had to make the landscape of the past live and move and, lo, there within that very landscape was a poet who made the natural landscape live and move. Meanwhile there is a certain analogy with the situation in English poetry. Johnson said that Dryden found English literature brick and left it marble.[30] Not, of course, that Dryden is uniformly marmoreal. Johnson himself observes, earlier in the same life, 'Sometimes the marble relents, and trickles in a joke.'[31] Elsewhere, one might add (a little more warmly), Dryden is full of life and energy. Nevertheless, Pope following Dryden may well have sensed that, stylistically, English poetry had been fixed in a classic mould. He knew that he must both defer to this and oppose it with his own more delicate genius, and the Virgilian infiltration of the objective epic showed him one way in which this might be done. There is, all the same, a certain irony in the fact that Virgil reached Pope partly through Dryden's version.

Pope was not the only poet to employ the trope of imputed movement any more than Virgil was the only Latin poet to do so. But there is a sense in which the fluid, subjective mode remains Virgil's property. If it is found in the *Appendix Vergiliana* it is because whoever wrote those passages loved and wished to be like Virgil. If it is in Ovid it is because he learned not only from the Hellenistic poets but also from Virgil. As for Statius, his debt to Virgil is immense. When Pope writes,

> Then Marble soften'd into life grew warm
> And yielding metal flow'd to human form.
> (*The First Epistle of the Second Book of Horace, Imitated*,
> i.e. 'The Epistle to Augustus', 147–8)

he owes nothing to Horace, a little to Virgil (*Aeneid*, vi. 847–8) but most of all to Ovid (e.g. *Metamorphoses*, x. 283f.). Pope utterly lacks Virgil's love of his own soil, his religious intensity, his special pathos. Yet, in an age of mannered aggression and social vigilance Pope found a way to keep poetry alive, and Virgil helped.

Notes

1. I am indebted for criticisms and suggestions to C. A. Martindale. All references, unless otherwise specified, are to *The Poems of Alexander Pope*, a one-volume edition of the text of the Twickenham Edition, ed. John Butt (London: Methuen, 1968). References to Homer are to *Homeri Opera*, ed. D. B. Monro and J. W. Allen (Oxford: Clarendon Press, 1917–19), those to Virgil are to *P. Vergili Maronis Opera*, ed. R. A. B. Majors (Oxford: Clarendon Press, the corrected 1972 reprint of the 1969 edn). References to the *Dirae* are, except for one specified case, to the edition by E. J. Kenney in the *Appendix Vergilia*, ed. W. F. Clausen, F. R. D. Goodyear, E. J. Kenney and J. A. Richmond (Oxford: Clarendon Press, 1966).
2. *Seven Types of Ambiguity* (London: Chatto and Windus, 3rd edn, 1963), pp. 68f.
3. Many scholars now doubt the biographical reference of the first Eclogue. See the copiously documented discussion by I. M. le M. Du Quesnay, 'Virgil's first *Eclogue*', *Papers of the Liverpool Latin Seminar*, ed. Francis Cairns III (1981), pp. 29–182, esp. pp. 30–5.
4. 'The Dirae', *Journal of Roman Studies*, LVI (1966), pp. 142–55, p. 152.
5. 1850, i. 412.
6. See Maynard Mack, *Collected in Himself: Essays Critical, Biographical and Bibliographical* (London and Toronto: Associated University Presses, 1982), p. 424.
7. Ibid., p. 459.
8. Michael Maittaire (ed.), *Opera et Fragmenta Veterum Poetarum Latinorum* 2 vols (London: J. Nicholas, B. Tooke and J. Tonson, 1713), vol. II [pp. 1588–9]. The sequence of pages 1525–1612 occurs twice in this volume, the earlier run being distinguished by square brackets.

9. See for example Pope's *Essay on Homer*, Twickenham Edition, vol. VII, p. 52 and his letter to Jervas of 29 November 1716, in *The Correspondence of Alexander Pope*, ed. George Sherburn, 5 vols (Oxford: Clarendon Press, 1956), vol. I. p. 376.
10. *Correspondence*, vol. I, p. 103.
11. In *The poems of John Dryden*, ed. James Kinsley, 4 vols (Oxford: Clarendon Press, 1958), vol. III, p. 1136.
12. Ibid., vol. III, p. 1193.
13. Thomas Hobbes, *The Iliads and Odysses of Homer*, 2 vols in one (London: Will. Crook, 1677), John Ogilby, *Homer his Odysses* (London: Thomas Roycroft, 1665); George Chapman's translation (complete version 1616 but preceded by earlier versions) is best consulted in *Chapman's Homer, the Iliad, the Odyssey and the lesser Homerica*, ed. A. Nicoll, 2 vols (London: Routledge & Kegan Paul, 1957).
14. Twickenham Edition, vol. I, p. 466.
15. In *The Poems of John Dryden*, ed. Kinsley, vol. III, p. 1137.
16. See C. A. Martindale's admirable discussion in his 'Unlocking the word-hoard. In praise of metaphrase', *Comparative Criticism*, VI (1984), pp. 47–72.
17. See his Preface to *Ovid's Epistles, Translated by Several Hands* (1680), in John Dryden, *Of Dramatic Poesy and Other Critical Essays*, ed. George Watson, 2 vols (London: Everyman, 1962), vol. I, pp. 262–73.
18. See Barbara M. J. Strang, *A History of English* (London: Methuen, 1970), esp. p. 316.
19. Preface to *Poems* (1815) in *William Wordsworth*, ed. Stephen Gill, the Oxford Authors (Oxford: Oxford University Press, 1984), p. 631.
20. *P. Vergili Maronis Aeneidos, Liber Primus*, with a commentary by R. G. Austin (Oxford: Clarendon Press, 1971), p. 73.
21. *Virgil's Aeneis*, i. 233–4, in *Poems*, ed. Kinsley, vol. III, p. 1070.
22. Ibid., vol. III, p. 1274.
23. *The Iliad of Homer*, trans. A. Lang, W. Leaf and E. Myers (London: Macmillan, 1914), p. 500.
24. Twickenham Edition, vol. VIII, p. 574.
25. Ibid., vol. IX, p. 117.
26. *The Odyssey of Homer*, Trans. S. H. Butcher and A. Lang (London: Macmillan, 1903), p. 46.
27. *Leviathan*, Part I, ch. ii, ed. A. R. Waller (Cambridge: Cambridge University Press, 1904), p. 3. Pope is known to have owned a copy of the Leviathan; see Maynard Mack, *Collected in Himself*, p. 414.
28. See Ernst Robert Curtius, *European Literature and the Latin Middle Ages*, trans. William R. Trask (London: Routledge & Kegan Paul, 1979), pp. 95f. and pp. 68–81 above (Fishes in the Trees).
29. See Fowler's note *ad hoc.* in *The Poems of John Milton*, ed. John Carey and Alastair Fowler (London: Longmans, 1968), p. 502.
30. *Lives of the English Poets*, ed. G. Birkbeck Hill, 3 vols (Oxford: Clarendon Press, 1905), vol. I, p. 469.
31. Ibid., vol. I, p. 438.

ADAM'S DREAM AND MADELINE'S

On 22 November 1817, Keats wrote[1] to his stiff, clerical friend Benjamin Bailey. Bailey, it seems, was upset. The painter Haydon had offended him in some way and Keats, in a turbulent overflow of good feeling and excited speculation, sought, so to speak, to set his friend on his legs again. Haydon is one of the few private citizens in relatively recent history to consider putting up a plaque to his own glory.[2] His thoughts ran naturally and easily on his own genius and Keats was content to run alongside. Accordingly Keats's reassurance of Bailey turns without warning from ordinary comfort to a disquisition on genius. There is a kind of argument in this part of the letter: one cannot be offended by defects of character in a genius since it is the essence of artistic genius to have no character at all, to be open to all influences, all colours. Although Keats may well have taken his cue from the grandiose self-description of Haydon, this brief, anticipatory sketch of what is to become in other letters[3] the theory of Negative Capability really has little to do with Haydon and much with Shakespeare. It has still more to do, perhaps, with Keats's sense of his own amoral latitude of imaginative sympathy. But here Bailey, it seems, had Doubts (like Prendergast): is not the imagination, so far from being inaccessible to moral censure, an inauthentic thing, indeed a source of lies and self-deception? In response to these doubts Keats, generously anxious to share his joy with Bailey, redoubles his pace:

> O I wish I was certain of the end of all your troubles as that of your momentary start about the authenticity of the Imagination. I am certain of nothing but of the holiness of the Heart's affections and the Truth of Imagination – What Imagination seizes as Beauty must be truth – whether it existed before or not – for I have the same Idea of all our Passions as of Love they are all in their sublime, creative of essential Beauty – In a Word, you may know my favourite Speculation by my first Book and the little song I sent in my last – which is a representation from the fancy of the probable mode of operating in these Matters – The Imagination may be compared to Adam's dream – he awoke and found it truth. I am the more zealous in this affair because I have never yet

been able to perceive how anything can be known for truth by consequitive reasoning – and yet it must be – Can it be that even the greatest philosopher ever [when] arrived at his goal without putting aside numerous objections – However it may be, O for a Life of Sensations rather than Thoughts.[4]

Here Keats philosophises. The movement of his mind is hyperbolical, elliptical, hesistant, incoherent, but it is real philosophy. The philosophising of Keats (unlike that of Coleridge, say) is all home-made, cobbled together in the back yard of his mind. Where Coleridge cocooned his thought in self-protective tissues of learning, ancient and modish, Keats had neither time nor natural aptitude for such stratagems.

His first – thoroughly endearing – indiscretion is to protest too much. Just as the phrase, 'As a matter of fact', is commonly used to introduce a lie, so people say 'I am certain of nothing but . . .' when they are not, in fact, quite certain or when, as here, they are by an act of will substituting the certainty of faith for the ordinary certainty of rational conviction. But Keats's level of self-awareness is high. He is conscious of the apparent wildness of his thought and seeks to strengthen his position by getting behind the usual structures of rationality. And what he produces is in fact highly challenging: a sort of 'innocent eye' empiricism, utterly unlike the artificially reduced empiricism of the scientific revolution. His thought runs like this: what the imagination seizes as beauty must be truth even if the thing it seizes never existed before the act of seizure; for the passions create actual beauty; one awakes with a start and realises that the imagination is not a mere web of illusions but on the contrary provides the primary material of knowledge; meanwhile mere chains of deductive reasoning of themselves tell us nothing – they are as strong or as weak as their premises, and those premises are not themselves rational sequences.

The story of empiricism – the philosophy which says that all our knowledge must arise from experience – is a curious one. Empiricism is associated in England with the rise of science. But the scientists found that they could not work without certain pre-empirical restrictions on the matter of their enquiry. Controlled experiments are more informative than uncontrolled experiments. Bacon, early in the seventeenth century, had urged scientists to let the rain come in, to let the wind blow through the laboratory, since to do otherwise was to 'rig' the experiment, to point it towards a pre-selected result. But the scientists wanted specific answers to specific questions and therefore sought to exclude irrelevant variables. As their methods sharpened it became increasingly clear that science was not the child of experience alone, but of experience and mathematics (the English tradition of Locke infiltrated by the French tradition of Descartes). The mathematical imperative was to exclude all that is not exactly quantifiable or measurable and the impact of this imperative is nowhere so evident as in the strange doctrine of Primary and Secondary Qualities. According to this doctrine length, breadth and weight are real qualities of objects as they actually exist, whereas sounds, tastes, smells and colours are not. These were termed secondary qualities and were commonly understood to exist only in the mind of the perceiver (who, notice, becomes forthwith the inventor rather than the perceiver of such qualities). If no other living thing existed a rose would be as broad, as long and as heavy as it is, but, until someone or something with a nose comes along, it has no fragrance.

The doctrine is prominent (with certain curious hesitations) in Locke's great work,[5] but before the *Essay concerning Human Understanding* it had already crept into the consciousness of the age. Look, for example, at Galileo's *Il Saggiatore* of 1623.[6] Taken strictly, the doctrine scarcely licenses the inference that colours and smells are entirely subjective to the perceiver: the rose must be *such* that it affects the nose as fragrant rather than foul, *such* that it strikes the eye as red not blue, which is as much as to say that the Secondary Qualities may, at a microscopic level, prove to be *bene fundatae* in the Primary and hence, after all, a characteristic of the objective world. But most people were not so careful in their inferences. The measurable world alone was real and the world of colours, sounds and smells was abruptly crowded into tiny cells of illusion, within the human skull. Experiment and Experience, though etymologically cognate, shudder and move austerely apart. But meanwhile the flag of empiricism still flies over the fortress of science. Here we reach the heart of the paradox. For experience is made of Secondary Qualities. Poets had always been the experts on experience in this simple, fundamental sense of the word: on the way the world looks, feels, tastes, smells, sounds. And all this stood condemned – in the name of empiricism!

The story of English Romanticism is largely the story of the artists' reaction – in part hysterical, in part cogently destructive – to this intolerable reduction of experience. The reaction was indeed violent, but it scarcely occurred to any of the Romantics to recapture the flag. Instead of offering real Experience to counter the artificially gutted Experience of the natural philosophers, they marshalled under the flag of Imagination, a word whose central reference is to the fiction of images, implying, therefore, a submission, before the battle has ever begun, to the arrogantly dismissive truth-claims of the opposition. Blake wrote,

> The atoms of Democritus
> And Newton's particles of light
> Are sands upon the Red Sea shore
> Where Israel's tents do shine so bright[7]

The scientist who felt himself momentarily threatened by these lines could recover as soon as he remembered the word 'imagination'; 'Ah,' he might say with an indulgent smile, 'you are *imagining* this?', and he would turn again to his experiment.

Keats in the face of this challenge is a degree more radical than most Romantics. Note that, if colour and sound are Secondary, beauty must be *a fortiori* still more Secondary, or perhaps we need to say Tertiary. There are similar 'tough-minded' implications for ethics. But beauty certainly figures in real experience, fused with colour and fragrance. If one is a genuine empiricist that first experience has absolute authority. It is what we are given before we think, that without which we cannot think and therefore it is mere idiocy to attempt to encroach upon this primary gift with posterior distinctions of reason.

But like the other Romantics Keats speaks not only of sensation but also (and more prominently) of imagination. The ordinary distinction between the two, as long as it survives, is potentially embarrassing to his theory, but it may be that this commonplace contrast ('Sensation is of real objects, imagination of unreal') can be blurred or removed altogether if one's empiricism is radical enough. Unjudging, with a wise passiveness, the mind simply welcomes whatever is presented to it. Here Keats can almost touch hands with Hume; in the first part of the *Treatise* Hume refused to ground the difference between mental images and perceptions in the fact that the objects of perception are real while the objects of imagination are unreal. To make external reality a criterion in this way is to step outside experience, and that the good empiricist can never do. Accordingly Hume distinguished perceptions as having a greater *vivacity*. The mind of the reader can respond to this in two ways: either it will be acknowledged that reality has been simply surrendered, 'reduced out', and an implicitly solipsistic scheme substituted, or else it may be inferred that in some way mere vivacity can now guarantee reality in the old full-blooded sense of the term. But if more or less vivacity is the mark of a greater or lesser degree of reality it is now open to the Romantic to argue, on Hume's own ground, 'Since *my* images are more vivacious than my percepts, their title to reality is, in a manner, incontestable.' Keats's word for 'vivacity' is 'intensity'.

We are now in a position to see why it is that commentators on Keats often hesitate over the question whether his observations about beauty, imagination and sensation are to be referred to the world of subjective images or to the perceived world. To the radical, psychologising empiricist this distinction simply ceases to be important; the barriers between the two are dismantled, the passport office stands unmanned. The presentations are of varying intensity and that is all. In the most radical versions of the theory there is finally no implication even of subjectivism or solipsism, since the ego is as much a secondary construction as is the causally governed 'external world' of the scientist.

But Keats, as we have seen, stays with the *term* 'imagination', and as long as the term is used the implication of subjective fiction is not quite dead. 'Imaginary' and 'real' are natural opposites. The Romantics, most notably Coleridge, strove to abolish this opposition by making the imagination an organ of perception (think what it would be like explaining that to Dr Johnson). The fact, increasingly evident to nineteenth-century thinkers, that all perception involves an element of interpretation, that we bring to the act of perception certain expectant schemata which can be satisfied or disconfirmed by the real, seems, in part at least, to have been picked up by Coleridge. Here indeed is a place where, perhaps, the imagination may be enlisted as an organ of truth. Bacon's dream that we can 'put our notions by' and proceed directly, without expectation or hypothesis, to 'the things themselves' is a philosophical nonsense. We operate through certain schemata of expectation which are corroborated or disconfirmed in specific experience. Some great figures in the history of mimetic realism work by re-activating schemata of expectation in the viewer. As we begin to look at a face painted by Rembrandt, certain mechanisms of perception are set in motion with an added energy and the result is that Rembrandt makes the ordinary world (other-real-faces in the gallery) look different for a time. The picture gives, not an extension of our factual knowledge but rather a deepening of our hypothetical awareness of what a face can be like, together with a temporary sharpening of associated perceptions. The knowledge which is deepened is *connaissance* rather than *savoir*, *Erleben* rather than *Wissen*. Literary art meanwhile, with its larger command of the temporal dimension, can focus hard on probable *sequences*, and in this way the intent imaginings of a great realistic novelist can even come to resemble the 'Thought Experiment' of the scientist. At this point, Aristotle's classic theory of hypothetical mimesis (the poet tells us 'what kind of things would happen', *Poetics*, 1451a) can be joined to Coleridge's defence of the imagination as the living agent of all perception. We know via a prior sense, which may be more or less intense, of possibilities and likelihoods.

Yet certain discomforts remain. The art I have just described is that generally known as realistic. The Romantics placed little emphasis on such skills and were concerned rather to redeem ideal or wildly improbable art. Moreover, 'imagination' is perhaps a misleading term to apply to the formation of probable schemata of the kind that work in close harness with the specificities of experience. Hume indeed invoked imagination to shore up his disintegrating epistemology but that was entirely deliberate on his part. For him, the stable shapes composed by the mind are not tested against the real but rather complete and fill out the ragged and discontinuous data of the senses. Thus he invokes the imagination, precisely, as a *fictive* power and not as an organ of veridical knowledge. In the last resort, says Hume, we *feign* the existence of ordinary public objects.[8] He is certainly providing an account of what is normally called 'knowledge' but his account is violently reductive. He offers only a way of arguing that what we took to be knowledge is not really knowledge at all. The reader may be forgiven for suspecting that the only difference, at bottom, between the petrifically reductive Hume on the one hand and the sanguine, inflationary Coleridge on the other lies in the fact that Hume knew what he had done. Certainly Coleridge seems to have had no precise notion of the way a Gestalt is put to work in Gestalt psychology.

The sense of strain persists. Of course, if we change the *meaning* of the word 'imagination' so that it is the same as the meaning of 'perception', the novel proposition 'Imagination is an organ of perception' will soon collapse into the inert tautology, 'Perception is perception'. If, on the other hand, a genuine synthetic proposition is being offered – either 'Perception is partly imagination' or 'Imagination is involved with our perceptions' – the fictive character of imagination is allowed to remain and the ghost remains unexorcised. Indeed for most people statements of the second type have the flavour of scepticism, suggest that the truth-claims of perception are less absolute than we thought. This inference is drawn (once more) because the primary meaning of the term perception (which is of the real) has been infiltrated by imagination (which is of the unreal).

In Keats's letter to Bailey, the sentence starting with the words 'What the imagination seizes . . .' begins in heady confidence, but before it is over this confidence is flawed. The root meaning of 'imagination' has begun to assert itself. The word 'seizes' implies a thoroughly cognitive imagination, grasping that which is other than itself. The verb 'must' is the first signal of an area of acknowledged ignorance or doubt (think of the way a mathematician will say, 'This proof has got to be right'). The words 'whether it existed before or not' make the doubt manifest. That which is grasped or seized is there before it is grasped or seized. That which is imagined begins and ends with the act of imagining. But, to be sure, we are in the world of the radical empiricist and so is Keats, at least as long as he holds to the highest pitch of excitement. Bishop Berkeley wrote *Esse est percipi*,[9] 'To be is to be perceived', which effectively eliminates any *separate* object of perception transcending the act of perception itself. The tree in the quad lapses into unbeing as we turn our heads away, just as images fade within our minds. The notion is notoriously counter-intuitive. It affronts the usual sense of what is required or implied in our notion of reality. That it could nevertheless fascinate the Romantic intelligence is clear from the axiom declared in Shelley's *Defence of Poetry*: 'All things exist as they are perceived.'[10] Keats, less stridently confident than Shelley, half-acknowledges the element of Berkeleian paradox in his thought, but then drives on. By implication, however, he has shifted the meaning of 'imagination'. We move from the cognitive to the fictive imagination with the words 'creative of' (already quite different from 'seizes').

Of course things made are no less real than natural things. Artefacts exist as securely as cows. For that matter, mental images *qua* images certainly exist (though some philosophers have tried to deny the fact). But the parenthesis, '*qua* images', is all-important. No one in Keats's time doubted – not even the hardest of the scientists – that dreams exist, as dreams. What was denied by common sense was the substantial rality of their contents. Last night, perhaps, I really did dream that there was a rhinoceros in the library but no rhinoceros was in the library. The dream itself, as is the way of dreams, was an illusion. Here Keats may be resorting to philosophical sleight of hand, trusting that we will not notice the fluid transition from tenor to vehicle (or indeed perhaps not noticing it himself). Clearly the imagination may form images of beauty and these creations, *qua* creations, are to be added to the fabric of reality. It may also be that the regular forming of such images may alert our perceptive powers to the presence of beauty in the real surrounding world. But none of this makes the imagination itself an organ of truth. All we have gained is the real existence in the world of imagined beauty (as well as real beauty), which is exactly the account the hardest reductionist would give.

The story I have told so far is, however, much too confident and misses entirely the glancing, vital movement of Keats's mind. The word 'creative' may carry a larger burden than I have so far allowed. Keats is indeed beset by doubt but at the same time he senses that he has almost within his grasp an overwhelmingly simple answer. Let us try, then, to give a stronger sense to 'creative'. When the mind intuits beauty it does not merely grasp that which is coldly external to itself, nor does it pretend that something is the case; it gives full being, by a miracle, to the category of beauty which forthwith leaps up in the world. If we ask how this is to be distinguished from mere feigning, the answer may lie with the irreducible substance and character of beauty. It cannot be stitched together from strands of consecutive reasoning. Sensation, indeed, is more conceivable as supplying the material, but only as long as sensation is allowed to be informed by aesthetic passion, by the full diapason of *feeling* (another favourite word of Keats). The excitement of this passage is like the excitement which some have found in Anselm's celebrated Ontological Proof of the Existence of God – the excitement of watching something which appeared to be merely conceptual turning real before one's very eyes.

Anselm in the eleventh century argued that, if we allow that God must be greater than we can conceive, it follows that he exists.[11] An island which actually exists is better (richer, stronger) than an imagined island. But if God did not exist we could immediately suppose him made better by mentally attributing existence to him. But *ex hypothesi* he is better than we can imagine and so must already possess all the virtues which we might attribute to him. So he must already have existence; that is, he exists.

Anselm says that any denial of this consequence generates a contradiction:

> Even a fool, then, must be convinced that a being than which none greater can be thought exists at least in his understanding, since when he hears this he understands it, and whatever is understood is in the understanding. But clearly that than which a greater cannot be thought cannot exist in the understanding alone. For if it is actually in the understanding alone, it can be thought of as existing also in reality, and this is greater. Therefore if that than which a greater cannot be thought is in the understanding alone, this same thing than which a greater cannot be thought is that than which a greater can be thought. But obviously this is impossible. Without doubt, therefore, there exists, both in the understanding and in reality, something than which a greater cannot be thought.

To most people in the twentieth century Anselm's argument carries no
conviction at all. It continues, however, to fascinate philosophers although
refutations of it abound. Anselm urges us to see that in this one case a logical
necessity must also be an ontological or practical necessity: 'God would not
be thus great if he lacked existence: the definition of God requires the real,
not notional existence of God.' Someone who refuses to accept the shift from
one sort of necessity to the other might well reply, 'You have shown that if
God did exist, in order to conform to the definition he would have to exist;
meanwhile the definition need refer to no existent.'

In so far as Anselm's notion of greatness seems to be associated with
'richness of being', it may seem to approximate to the 'vivacity' of Hume and
the 'intensity' of Keats. But Anselm does not psychologise his conception; the
greatness to which he refers is a power of objective existence rather than a
measure of the impact on the perceiver. He is, however, entirely willing to
turn existence into a predicate, and this is sufficiently odd. It is as if one were
to say that although Hamlet is on the whole a better person than Hitler,
Hitler beats Hamlet hollow with his score on existence, since poor Hamlet
has only a shadowy, fictional degree of being. Indeed, it can almost be said
that Anselm fetishised existence and so became master of exactly the right
potent magic to heal the solipsistic wound of the Romantics. On the one hand
we have a generation which has been authoritatively instructed that its most
valued experiences are merely subjective and on the other we have a new
version of the philosopher's stone: a device for turning mere concepts into
reality. Keats, in his proper darkness, stretches out his hand towards the
Anselmian solution.

The difference meanwhile for the psychologising Hume is crucial.
Anselm's fetish is credited with miraculous redemptive powers. Hume could
have nothing to do with this. With Keats, however, it is otherwise. For all his
radical empiricism, he continues to hope for a miracle by which the old
transconceptual, truly independent reality might be restored, which is as
much as to say, he retains the old, unreduced conception of reality. Hume
could not permit himself to be excited by the miracle of the image
brightening into reality, since there is no longer a chasm to be crossed: he has
revised the very notion of reality so that it is itself no more than an image
presentation. The transformation envisaged by Keats would appear in
Hume's redaction as merely a further increase in the vivacity of the image.
Thus Keats makes use of radical empiricism just long enough to establish
that intensity alone may constitute a primary claim to reality but the fervour
with which he then pursues his thought is eloquent of his refusal to go all the
way with the empiricist reduction of reality. He employs the hard-won
primary equivalence of presentation to an inflationary rather than a
reductive end. Instead of saying, 'So called percepts are no more real than
images: all you *have* is a flux of ideas', he says 'images, no less than percepts,
may be images of truth'. Instead of saying 'reality comes down to vivacity',

he says 'It is sensation, not argument, which gives us substances; therefore the stronger the sensation the stronger the substantial reality; it must be so because that is what reality *is*'. In the last clause the analogy with Anselm's thought is striking: 'That is what the word "God" means.' In radical empiricism the notion of existence seems to be knitted into the notion of experience at a pre-philosophical level; for Anselm the notion of existence, not notional existence but real existence, is built into the idea of God. Each glimpses the chance of showing that his highest value (God for Anselm, the world of beauty for Keats) might after all be self-authenticating. For Hume all this would be futile mumbo-jumbo.

But Keats's air of triumph in securing an equivalence which for Hume would have been merely analytic shows, as I have suggested, that he regards full existence as entailing more than mere presence-to-the-mind. If we ask 'What more?' we shall find the old requirements of independence and stability (in contrast with the flickering character of 'merely mental' images). I suspect that Keats begins to think in this way and then finds himself in difficulties. Intuitions of beauty, though intense, are notoriously evanescent. We find the thought about stability and independence peremptorily crushed in the words 'whether it existed before or not'. This leaves us with beauty as a matter of recurrent creation, its claim to independence still strong because of its transcendent, irreducible nature. Remember that the artist is himself colourless, without identity, and could therefore never have spun such a thing as beauty from his own substance. Once again there is a theological parallel: Descartes in his *Discourse on Method* found in the idea of God a richness which proved that the idea itself could not have been produced by the human mind and in his *Meditations* he advanced an ontological proof of God's existence which is substantially identical to that advanced by Anselm.[12] For Keats this combination of evanescence and transcendence naturally pushes his thought in the direction of religion. The effect of this can be seen in the words 'holiness', 'creative', and of course in the allusion to Adam's dream.

To be sure Keats had no learning in philosophy. The names of Anselm and Hume would have meant little or nothing to him. The line which runs from Hume to Coleridge, in which the imagination is invoked, in the face of the unmeaning flux of presentations, to feign (Hume's word) or else to compose the continuous identity of public objects cannot be traced in Keats, though it is likely that he listened to others talking about such things. But the profound Romantic imperative to blot out the hierarchical opposition of knowledge and imagination is obeyed by Keats, which is enough to show that we are dealing here with a need which is both simpler and more fundamental than the technical shifts of Coleridge's philosophy. But at the same time Keats is thinking very hard and it is of the nature of real philosophic thought that it connects with other philosophic thought, even where there is no contact by way of reading or direct influence. Keats, after an astonishing feat of honest intelligence, seemed to have won through to a marvellous conclusion: the reductionists are wrong; poetry and aesthetic experience are not an idle delusion; they are parts of reality.

But if Adam's dream proved to be truth, what are we to make of Madeline's dream in *The Eve of St Agnes*? It is a fallacy to suppose that the highest energies of thought will always appear in an author's prose writings. *The Eve of St Agnes* is one of the most feeling-saturated, purely Romantic poems ever written, but at the same time the thought of the poem is more alive, more exquisitely tormented and divided than anything we found in the letters. The story told in the poem mirrors the story of Adam's dream in Milton, but the sexes are transposed. Adam dreamed of Eve, awoke and found that she was really there. Madeline dreamed of Porphyro, awoke and found that he was really there. The dominant effect of the poetry is to enforce the likeness of the two stories, the sense of miracle and joy. But there are other effects, of a less docile character. Keats warned us of the anarchic latitude of the poetic imagination. As soon as we begin to read *The Eve of St Agnes* we become strongly aware of a feature largely suppressed in the debate so far (that is, in the letter to Bailey), namely sexual love, though the letter does speak of 'the heart's affections' and Keats also wrote 'as of love'. Adam's dream in Milton, we should remember, was a love dream. When Milton writes in *Paradise Lost*, viii. 463 how Adam 'saw the shape' of Eve, the great Latinising poet shows that he knows exactly when to use the native, Saxon word; had he used the Latinate equivalent, 'form', all the tenderness would have been lost. He then permits himself a Donne-like moment of near-surrealism when he describes how Eve was made from Adam's rib, drawn from a wound, 'with cordial spirits warm/And life blood streaming fast' (466–7). In the objective primal myth God simply does this while Adam sleeps. In Milton's version an eerie effect is obtained by having Adam dream of something which is actually happening, just as Madeline in Keats's poem dreams of consummation at the moment when it occurs. The idea of flesh transmuted has here the faintly licentious force of dream imagery. Some twenty lines later it is raised to the Miltonic sublime: 'Bone of my bone, flesh of my flesh', echoing the marriage service, pre-echoing the terrible moment of the Fall (ix. 914–15). Eve's looks breathe 'the spirit of love and amorous delight' (iv. 477), 'she would be wooed, and not unsought be won' (503) and Adam leads her to the nuptial bower 'blushing like the morn' (511). The whole passage in Milton is an essay in the New Protestant idiom of sanctified sexuality. God conducts Adam to Eve and oversees the marriage rite. Sex and religion are harmonised (though Eve's blushes worried C. S. Lewis).[13]

Keats followed Milton in many things but he did not reproduce the Miltonic harmonisation of sexuality. He knew as an artist that he must turn instead to an older tradition, in which sexuality and religion co-exist in a tense and uneasy relationship, the tradition of medieval Courtly Love, blurred by its transmission through the Elizabethans and the Gothic Novelists. The central empiricism of Keats's thought (remember 'proved upon our pulses'[14]) is in fact subjected to restrictive pressure from two directions, from religion and from sexuality. This was something which Keats could not handle philosophically, but the organisation of poetry is not the organisation of a philosophical treatise and in *The Eve of St Agnes* he found a way to dramatise these polarities.

Courtly Love is laced with schizophrenia. When the lover in Chrétien's poem genuflects outside his lady's room[15] the action represents both an element of spiritual devotion in the love and, at the same time, hell-brink blasphemy. Aquinas had condemned passionate sexual love as a *ligamentum rationis*, a binding up of reason.[16] Profound love is worse, perhaps, than casual sexuality, since it carries with it the danger of idolatry. The cynical amorist, oddly enough, is in less danger of forgetting that God is the most valuable, most lovable thing. That this feeling could survive into the Romantic period is shown by Coleridge's note on *Romeo and Juliet*, 'All deep passions [are] a sort of atheists, that believe no future.'[17] As love is exalted through the language of religion the danger of blasphemous parody or even idolatry is increased. That is why the medieval writers again and again conclude their poems and treatises with pious recantations. Nor, by and large, do they pretend that love can be merged with the major system – say, by marriage. Sexual love remains the dangerous, beautiful obverse of true religion.

When Shakespeare's Romeo and Juliet speak of shrines, palmers, pilgrims and saints, profanity and gentle sin (I. v. 92–108) the starkness of the old conflict has gone but a certain tension remains. Similarly when Donne writes 'us Canonized for love' ('The Canonization', 36) the conceit is almost a joke, made from the security of love, but still with a consciousness of that latent unease which nourishes all jokes. With the rise of Gothic Romance this *frisson*, this illicit echoing of the sacred in the erotic, is made the vehicle of a mild pornography. Virginity at risk among murky Gothic buildings became the order of the day. Pope set the tone with the brilliant avant-garde bad taste of *Eloisa to Abelard* (castration and frustration in a Gothic setting). This, rather than the high moral tone of *Paradise Lost*, supplied Keats with the tradition he needed. The result is that, even while the lyric power of the poem enforces the intuition of miracle, it simultaneously offers an erotic parody of the myth, which in itself implies the presence of an unsubdued scepticism towards the new, high-minded Romantic harmonisation of knowledge and imagination.

For Porphyro stage-manages the awakening of Madeline. The miraculous brightening of the dream to reality is a trick. Like all seducers Porphyro promises not to 'displace one of her soft ringlets' (148) and proceeds in due course to do rather more than that. Most important of all, when Madeline first wakes, her first reaction is horror:

> Her eyes were open, but she still beheld,
> Now wide awake, the vision of her sleep –
> There was a painful change, that nigh expelled
> The blisses of her dream, so pure and deep . . .
> How changed thou art! How pallid, chill and drear . . .
>
> (298–301, 311)

The high-minded love-myth of Romanticism is accompanied in this poem by a low-minded love-myth, and this low-minded strand is essential to the Gothic character of the whole. The low sexual sequence has been brilliantly analysed and documented by Jack Stillinger in his article, 'The Hoodwinking of Madeline'.[18] Stillinger points out that what Porphyro proposes is a 'stratagem' (139) variously characterised by Angela as 'cruel', 'impious' and 'wicked' (140, 143). Porphyro wishes, voyeur-like, to 'see [Madeline's] beauty unespied' (166). Critics since Swinburne have noted, with varying degrees of reluctance, the similarity between Porphyro and the vile Iachimo in *Cymbeline*, II. ii. At 340 we have the image of robbing a nest (denied, but also in a way, asserted). Stillinger notes that the 'tongueless nightingale' at 206 is an illusion to the ugly–elegant Ovidian story of the rape of Philomel. In *Cymbeline* Imogen had been reading this story before Iachimo found her sleeping. At 257 Porphyro wishes he had a 'Morphean amulet', that is a means of drugging Madeline. This, Stillinger observes, links him with Lovelace in *Clarissa* (and also one might add, with Humbert Humbert in *Lolita*). Most tellingly of all, he finds such allusions as there are to *Paradise Lost* tend to associate Porphyro with Satan. At 224 Porphyro grows faint before the beauty of Madeline. Keats wrote in his copy of Burton's *Anatomy of Melancholy*, beside a passage describing how the Barbarians stood silent before a fair woman, 'Abash't the devil stood.' Here the reference is to *Paradise Lost*, iv. 846 (Satan before Zephon). There is a similar moment at ix. 463 where Satan is momentarily arrested in his evil design by the beauty of Eve. At one point in the revision of 314–22 which Keats made in September 1819 (Woodhouse and Taylor, Keats's publisher, found the revised version too sexually explicit and induced him to change it almost completely) the phrasing recalls Satan at the ear of the sleeping Eve (*Paradise Lost*, iv. 800). Keats wrote that Porphyro's 'close rejoinder flows/Into her burning ear'.

I have said that the story of *The Eve of St Agnes* mirrors the story of Adam's dream but that the sexes are transposed. Now we begin to see what can flow from that transposition. There are two important dreams in *Paradise Lost*, Adam's and Eve's. In Keats's poem the second dream, that planted in the mind of Eve by Satan, is allowed to infiltrate the first. Indeed the dream which Eve relates (v. 31–92) has an oddly Keatsian flavour. She tells how she was drawn into the moonlit garden and there urged to eat the apple of the tree 'with fruit surcharg'd', to ease its load and taste its sweet (v. 58–9). Perhaps all *Romantic* poets really are of the Devil's party without knowing it?

When Adam's dream ends in *Paradise Lost* there is a moment of chill dereliction: 'she disappeared, and left me dark' (viii. 478). Just as *The Eve of St Agnes* may be related to the 'happy understanding' Keats reached with Fanny Brawne on Christmas Day, 1818,[19] so, in a darker manner, Adam's dream may be related to the death of Milton's beloved second wife, Katherine Woodcock, in February 1658, Milton having already embarked upon the composition of *Paradise Lost*. The terrible sonnet[20] on the dream which followed that death ends with the words, 'I woke, she fled, and day brought back my night'. Keats's knight at arms in 'La Belle Dame Sans Merci' awoke to find himself 'on the cold hillside' (44). In Milton the natural trauma of waking from a wish-fulfilment dream is healed by God's gift of Eve. In *The Eve of St Agnes* it is healed by the amorous prowess of Porphyro himself, lover, redeemer of fallen reality, ravisher.

At the lowest level of Gothic Romance Madeline's horrified reaction is needed for the sheer base excitement it can provide. At a slightly higher level some suspense is needed if the miracle is to be felt as truly miraculous. But the very efficacy of these literary mechanisms betrays the original philo-sophical insight of the letter to Bailey. Even there, indeed, all was not well. What I have called the radical empiricist argument insists that the reality-claim of any experience should be measured, quite simply, by the presentational intensity of that experience. Dreams, mental images and the feigned worlds of romance can be exceedingly vivid and may therefore be as real as anything else. But if we then use the language of change – 'The image *brightens* into reality' – we implicitly concede that the image (dream, poem) was itself less than real; otherwise there would be nothing to applaud in its unlooked-for transformation. Of course the brief period of suspense necessary to our sense of miracle could be supplied from a mere failure of comprehension: it is not that Adam's dream gradually became real but that *we* find – gradually – that the dream was real all the time. To adjust the sentence in this way is to save the philosophy at the expense of the myth (for myth naturally deals in objective events disposed in time). But poetry operates at the mythic end of the spectrum and myth has a way of remaining obstinately linked to commonsense notions: Adam dreamed and when Eve came along in person reality replaced delusion. The whole effect is dependent on our not confusing the categories.

So too in *The Eve of St Agnes* the common sanity of the inherited story-pattern impedes the blurring of the distinction between dream and ordinary reality, although philosophically Keats urgently requires that this line should be blurred. One must grant indeed that there are certain moments of exciting confusion in the poem. For example, we are given contradictory indications of the nature of Madeline's dream. In the brutal jargon of the 1980s we may ask our question directly: is it a sex dream? At 301 we are told of 'the blisses of her dream' but, in the same breath, that they were 'pure'. In the cancelled revision of 314–22, though Madeline's repose is 'serene', her dream is 'wild'.

Moreover the revision stresses the slightly perverse idea that when Porphyro consummates the union Madeline is still dreaming her (presumably congruent?) dream.

Intensity alone is not enough to guarantee reality. The other requirement we make, that a thing should be stable, should be there still when we go back to look again, is met neither by dreams nor by the visionary heights of passion: the very drama of the poem implicitly acknowledges this common-place truth. When the Romantics sought to beat back the 'hard reality' of the scientists, their shrillness in debate again and again betrayed their cause. The imagination is invoked as an organ of truth but, as we saw, the very word 'imagination' implies something other than ordinary perception, some creative activity of the mind. It is at this point that Romantic Platonism can come in, with what may seem to be a saving effect. Using the Neo-platonic shift whereby the artist, instead of being doubly removed from reality as he is in Plato's *Republic* (597), is allowed direct access to the Forms,[21] all the base empirical requirements of stability and the like can be referred to the transcendent realm (where, indeed, they assume the exaggerated form of eternity). What this world calls imagination may in fact be perception of transcendent ideal forms, which are conceived as having an independent existence. Blake wrote in his *Jerusalem*, 'Imagination is the Real and Eternal World of which the Vegetable Universe is but a faint shadow, and in which we shall live in our Eternal or Imaginative Bodies when these Vegetable Mortal Bodies are no more.'[22] Such Platonism is really a postponed empiricism, guarded from falsification by the terms of the postponement. If it is pressed hard, this idea can come to oust ordinary experience (think of Blake's remark that 'Natural Objects always did and now do deaden, weaken and obliterate Imagination' in him[23]). What is inescapable is that the primary opposition between imagination and common perception has reasserted itself. The gap Coleridge sought to close has opened once more. Thus one finds an other-worldly reference in Romantic poetry which is tantamount to a confession that common reality is, after all, not to be sought from poets.

And yet – irony of ironies – *The Eve of St Agnes*, with a strange candour, dramatises all these tensions and is therefore startlingly *true* – true, that is, to the divided mind and heart of the age. Many critics have sensed a transcendent or even a religious direction in the poem. E. R. Wasserman says it teaches us that it is only in heaven that empyreal imaginings are true.[24] W. W. Beyer suggests that the poem is rooted not in the senses but in our dream of God.[25] R. A. Foakes sees in the union of Madeline and Porphyro a 'Sacramental image of all that is good, as through their love they are made immortal'.[26] Newell F. Ford, in his excellent study, *The Prefigurative Imagination of John Keats*,[27] finds clear evidence that Keats sometimes construed the deliverances of imagination as a foretaste of some eternal joy to come.

All these things figure in the writing. But the *poem* is sure of none of them. In his 'Ode on a Grecian Urn' Keats makes lyric use of the idea that the requirement of stability is met by the marble stillness of a work of art; only the notoriously affirmative words 'Beauty is truth, truth beauty' fall with desperate crassness in a poem which is elsewhere marvellously alive to all the real ironies involved. To find an unequivocal immortality at the end of *The Eve of St Agnes* is surely very strained. Prospero in *The Tempest* says that we are such stuff as dreams are made on and that at the last we leave not a rack behind. The commentators laboriously interpret this as meaning the exact reverse, that we are eternal. So at the end of *The Eve of St Agnes* Porphyro and Madeline dislimn before our eyes. 'Like phantoms' (361) they pass through the hall and then, with that marvellous modulation of tense, 'they are gone' (370). In all this story it was the higher intelligence which fell victim to enchantments, never the lower modes of understanding. The rich, amoral interplay of sex and ideality, stratagem and magic, dream and waking is mistaken for the desired fusion of these things, for the long-withheld healing of the Romantic wound. Even the Grecian Urn, once one had entered the world of its fictive forms, proved live and mobile in its stillness. A poem may achieve a kind of palpable reality by the very force of its impact – that is implied in the letter to Bailey. But poems may also, by stressing poignancy or irony, confess the frailty of those same moments of vision. The narrow Romantic theory which sees poetry as concerned only with glory is affronted by this. Coleridge's 'Dejection', a successful imaginative expression of the failure of the glory-giving imagination, shows how the practice of the Romantic poets could on occasion transcend their theories. In like manner Keats's poem is not only a larger thing than the critics allow, but also a larger thing than Keats himself, who wrote the best of all literary letters, could ever have explained. I am pleading, notice, for the presence of a kind of realism in both 'Dejection' and *The Eve of St Agnes*. The term 'realism' is now out of favour, but if the imagination really is to convey truth, what else should we expect but realism?

I have a sense that this essay has probably failed signally to produce the result which many of its readers will have desired and expected from it. The anxieties of Romanticism are still with us and we look eagerly for authoritative voices (from Coleridge to Barfield, from Barfield to Mary Warnock) telling us that the imagination gives truth. Keats in his letter to Bailey enforced the doctrine with as much authority as anyone could well produce, but the poem in which the idea is acted out is both ravishingly enchanting and mercilessly sceptical. No critic in his right mind could claim that *The Eve of St Agnes* is a cynical poem. To find beauty and wonder poignant because fugitive and involved with illusion is not cynical but only profoundly humane. But, in Keats's case at least, one has to say that the philosophic credo of the letter to Bailey does not survive when tested in the fire of a real poem.

Notes

1. Letter No. 43 in H. E. Rollins (ed.), *The Letters of Keats, 1814–1821.* (Cambridge, Mass.: Harvard University Press, 1958), vol. I, pp. 183–7.
2. See Ian Jack, *Keats and the Mirror of Art* (Oxford: Clarendon Press, 1967), p. 23. The plaque was to read, 'Here Haydon painted his Solomon, 1813.'
3. See, 'To George and Thomas Keats', 21, 27 (?) December 1817 and 'To Richard Woodhouse', 27 October 1818, in Rollins's edn, Nos 45 and 118, vol. I, pp. 191–4 and pp. 386–8.
4. In Rollins's edn, vol. I, p. 184–5.
5. *Essay Concerning Human Understanding*, II. viii. 7–10, in the edn by A. C. Fraser (New York: Dover Publications, 1959), vol. I, pp. 168–71.
6. See *Discoveries and Opinions of Galileo*, trans. Stillman Drake (New York: Doubleday, 1957), pp. 273–5.
7. 'Mock on, mock on, Voltaire, Rousseau', in *Poetry and Prose of William Blake*, ed. Geoffrey Keynes (London: the Nonesuch Press, 1956), p. 107.
8. *A Treatise of Human Nature*, I. iv. 6, in the edn by L. A. Selby-Bigge (Oxford: Clarendon Press, the 1964 reprint of the edn of 1888), p. 254.
9. *Of the Principles of Human Knowledge*, i. 3, in *The Works of George Berkeley, Bishop of Cloyne*, ed. A. A. Luce and T. E. Jessup (London: Thomas Nelson and Sons, 1948–57), vol. II, p. 42.
10. *A Defence of Poetry*, in *The Prose Works of Percy Bysshe Shelley*, ed. R. H. Shepherd (London: Chatto and Windus, 1906), vol. II. p. 34.
11. *Proslogion*, ch. ii, in *Anselm to Ockham*, ed. and trans. E. R. Fairweather, vol. X (1956) of the *Library of Christian Classics*, pp. 73–4.
12. *Discours de la Méthode*, iv and *Méditation Cinquième* in *Œuvres et lettres de Descartes*, ed. A. Bridoux (Paris: Gallimard, 1953), pp. 149 and 312–13.
13. See his *A Preface to Paradise Lost* (London: Oxford University Press, 1960), p. 123.
14. 'To Reynolds', 3 May 1818, in Rollins's edn, vol. I, p. 279.
15. Chrétien de Troyes, *Lancelot*, 4716–17, in the edn with an English translation by W. W. Kibles (New York and London: Garland Publishing, 1981), p. 196.
16. *Summa Theologiae, Prima Secundae*, Quaest. 34, Art. I.
17. *Coleridge's Shakespearean Criticism*, ed. T. M. Raysor (London: Constable, 1930), vol. I. p. 10.
18. *Studies in Philology*, LVIII (1961), pp. 533–55.
19. See Aileen Ward, 'Christian Day, 1818', *Keats and Shelley Journal*, X (1961), pp. 15–27.
20. 'Methought I saw my late-espoused saint.'
21. See for example, Plotinus, *Enneads*, V. viii, I (32–6) in *Plotini Opera*, ed. P. Henry and H-R. Schwyzer (Oxford: Clarendon Press, 1964), vol. II, p. 269.
22. *Poetry and Prose of William Blake*, ed. Keynes, p. 535.
23. *Ibid.*, p. 821.
24. See his *The Finer Tone* (Baltimore: Johns Hopkins Press, 1953), p. 107.
25. See his *Keats and the Daemon King* (New York: Oxford University Press, 1947), pp. 124–5.
26. See his *The Romantic Assertion* (London: Methuen, 1958), p. 94.
27. Stanford: Stanford University Press; London: Oxford University Press, 1951.

JACK THE GIANT-KILLER

I

In his inaugural lecture at Cambridge C. S. Lewis introduced himself as a cultural dinosaur, a sort of doomed, stranded anachronism and therefore the proper object, at the very least, of curiosity. This antic pedagogical posture was not wholly disingenuous. Lewis subscribed, with a sort of secondary, achieved simplicity, to objectivist ethics, an objectivist aesthetic and an objectivist religion and knew that, although he had many like-minded friends, almost all of them had been dead for centuries. It might be thought that at least he was at home with fellow Christians, but there were some discomforts even there. As the years passed, he became conscious of a certain political obligation to preserve Christian unity in his apologetic writings and therefore avoided criticism of his co-religionists, but it is nevertheless clear that not all Christians were Lewis's kind of Christian. For example, despite his long association with Owen Barfield, he was never truly[1] part of that English tradition descending from Coleridge which stresses the role of imagination in the formation of knowledge. Newman, whom Stephen Prickett has shown[2] to be deeply indebted to Coleridge in his conception of the organic development of doctrine, was never as important to Lewis as Aristotle or Hooker. To be sure, he revered Plato, and this may seem to blur the contrast I have just drawn. But Lewis's Plato is not the psychologised Plato of the Romantics, but is rather the philosopher who affirmed that ideas are not 'thoughts'[3] and held that the supernatural realm was more, not less, definitely objective than the world displayed to our senses. This shifting 'middle term' in Lewis's intellectual journey was not 'Imagination' but 'Myth'.[4]

Since Lewis so described himself the drift towards subjectivism has if anything become more marked. Philosophy has swung back to idealism from positivism (a philosophy which, despite its damnable elimination of ethics, nevertheless contained much that Lewis could almost love, as may be seen from the character MacPhee in the Romances and the account of 'the great Knock' in *Surprised by Joy*). At the same time we have seen a second efflorescence of structuralism which, in its more radical moments, implies that our most fundamental beliefs are subjective not indeed to the individual but to our culture, thereby resolving substance into formal relationship. In these circumstances it might be thought that 'Lewis the dinosaur' is no longer in any sense a joke but is rather a plain description: he was losing touch even then and is now thoroughly exploded.

This view is certainly wrong. Lewis would have been surprised by nothing that has happened since. He was prescient of all these things. His objectivism was always dialectically set forth, in a manner which anticipates both current and subsequent opposition. To say this is not to imply that his 'plain man' stance was *faux naif*. His central beliefs were indeed simple, but his intelligence and his consciousness of his context were acute.

Even within his professional discipline of English literature, Lewis is discernibly anomalous, a prescient reactionary. He appears at first as the docile heir of W. P. Ker and Gilbert Murray, virtually untouched by the rise of New Criticism. Yet, if we consider the more recent history of literary criticism and the various artillery which has been brought to bear, it is Lewis, rather than any particular New Critic, who will be found to have constructed the better defences (he may even prove in the end to be the sole survivor). It is generally agreed that there was a tendency in New Criticism to treat the history of literature as a series of discrete events, to fasten immediately on the text as given and almost to repress prior questions to do with the context, literary, social or intellectual, of the work. Of course the better New Critics could not avoid knowing some history and other literary works, and this knowledge mercifully mitigated the austerity of much of the criticism. But in so far as they admit such prior knowledge they tend to lose their distinctness as New Critics and, conversely, in so far as New Criticism has an identifiable theory, the playing down of history and context must be seen as part of that theory (the other principal element being the denial that an author's intention can be relevant to a critical assessment of his work). In his long epistolary dispute with E. M. W. Tillyard, *The Personal Heresy* (1939), Lewis in fact chose a position which was 'modern' in so far as he denied that the author's mind was the proper object of literary criticism, but at the same time he steadfastly insisted on the importance of literary history and context (a proviso which makes him either old-fashioned or ahead of his time, according to your taste). His British Academy Shakespeare Lecture for 1942, 'Hamlet: the Prince or the Poem?', shows him to have been receptive to the contemporary fashion, led by L. C. Knights, of emphasising themes and images at the expense of characterisation. His later book *An Experiment in Criticism* (1961), long before most people in England had heard of the new attention being paid in France to the reading-process, suggested that poems might be better assessed by the modes of reading they elicit than by the supposed processes of composition. In broad terms, structuralist literary theory has embraced the second proposition but has powerfully opposed the first. The fundamental impulse of structuralism is the contention that meaning is conferred by context: a syllable heard in isolation means nothing, but a syllable heard within a word begins to have meaning; a word alone means little, but a word within a sentence means much more (I speak of *operative* meaning: there is of course a sense in which the range of potential meaning is progressively narrowed by each fresh specification of context). This principle is then extended to the intelligible import (rather than 'meaning' in the restricted linguistic sense) of poems, social conventions and ideologies. The underlying philosophical theorem is the contention that substance is resolvable into a nexus of relationships: whenever we try to say something about an object in itself we in fact implicitly describe its relation to other objects. Thus the structuralist can attack effectively at various levels: he can ask, 'Don't you want to know what these words mean?' or he can ask, 'Don't you realise what kind of literary trope is being used here?' and in either case the moral of his question is, 'You cannot hope to know a thing before you know its context.'

Lewis's *A Preface to Paradise Lost* (1942) begins thus:

> The first qualification for judging any piece of workmanship from a corkscrew to a cathedral is to know *what* it is – what it was intended to do and how it is meant to be used. After that has been discovered the temperance reformer may decide that the corkscrew was made for a bad purpose, and the communist may think the same about the cathedral. But such questions come later. The first thing is to understand the object before you: as long as you think the corkscrew was meant for opening tins or the cathedral for entertaining tourists you can say nothing about them. The first thing the reader needs to know about *Paradise Lost* is what Milton meant it to be.
>
> This need is especially urgent in the present age because the kind of poem Milton meant to write is unfamiliar to many readers. He is writing epic poetry which is a species of narrative poetry, and neither the species nor the genus is very well understood at present.[5]

It is at once apparent that the writing is dialectical, is tensely argumentative. The main thrust of the structuralist attack on New Criticism is clearly anticipated and indeed employed by Lewis, but in a characteristic style. A blunt opening 'What is it?' rapidly leads him, with the help of the notion of purpose, to genre and precedent. He does not suggest that substance must be resolved into formal relationship; instead he employs a language at once simple (almost 'hearty') and learned. His credentials are not Saussure or Lévi-Strauss but Aristotle. We sense a willingness to engage, if necessary, in fundamental philosophy but that the philosophy Lewis would give us would be one remote from fashion and yet close to the conceptual practice of the ordinary person.

Thus, in one page of literary criticism the singular character of Lewis's mind begins to emerge: 'prescient-reactionary', currently paradoxical yet anciently orthodox. But the argument refuses to remain merely literary.

Lewis's greatest contemporary in philosophy was Ludwig Wittgenstein. Some may resent any comparison of the 'first order', highly original philosophising of Wittgenstein and the writings of Lewis, who delighted to own the scale of his debts to older thinkers (indeed, made a special point of the confession). A teacher of English may nevertheless be allowed to observe that this difference, though real in itself, is exaggerated by the style of either writer. Wittgenstein's style, especially in the *Philosophical Investigations*, seems expressly designed to suggest that every thought, whatever its real antiquity, is here struck out for the first time. Lewis's style, conversely, seems to minimise what is often a very real originality. Yet a more fundamental comparison is in any case possible. Let us take Wittgenstein's use of the concept 'game'. By way of this concept Wittgenstein sought not so much to solve as to resolve or 'shake free' certain puzzles; he suggested that, if one found out what 'game' was being played and identified the working rules, many apparent contradictions would turn out to arise from the confusion of one game with another. Allied to this is Wittgenstein's conception of 'family resemblance'; the existence of a single term need not imply a single property, common to all the things designated by the term; instead the term may have arisen from a phylogenetic pattern of characteristics. That Lewis was interested in this approach is apparent from his highly Wittgensteinian review[6] of George Steiner's *The Death of Tragedy*. He there suggests that our concept of tragedy may be founded, not upon a single unifying character somehow hidden in all the works called 'tragic', but rather on the mere fact of literary genealogy whereby Greek tragedy may, so to speak, be great-aunt to Elizabethan tragedy. He further suggests that the difference between tragedy and comedy was apprehensible in ancient times by such 'coarse' criteria as enable us to distinguish rugger from soccer. In this review Lewis responds momentarily to the attraction of a method which so coolly dispels 'deep' questions. But, although he shares Wittgenstein's interest in the *use* we make of terms, Lewis usually resisted the suggestion of formalism implicit in Wittgenstein's notion of language games.

One finds a similar impulse to reduce philosophical problems to the structure of their formal expression in Wittgenstein's extension of the term 'grammar' to cover what would formerly have been regarded as the logic of discourse. This stretching of terms has proved rhetorically deeply congenial to the age which followed. Once again, Lewis's consciously robust style is the signal of his refusal to follow the fashion. While Wittgenstein sought to defuse problems by making people aware of the varying forms of their discourse, Lewis sought instead to reawaken the sense of moral substance by showing what we actually do when we admire, approve, love. The exploration of context, therefore, means something different for either writer. Wittgenstein searches continually for the rules of the game, for the relevant criterion of use (there is sometimes a presumption that a concept is vacuous if no criterion of use can be specified). Ultimately, Wittgenstein's notion of a criterion is notoriously strained: the 'criterion of pain', for example, can scarcely mean anything but 'the symptoms of pain' or, perhaps, 'the defining character of pain'. It is as if Things are beginning to kick back against Language: the spectral model of linguistic propriety seems merely inapposite. With Lewis, on the other hand, exploration of context is seldom content with the merely Linnaean level of grammatical analysis but involves the ancient vocabulary of logic, so that *his* question is, 'What, here, is *presupposed?*'

But first he asks (herein differing from the structuralist) 'What do we actually do?' This is the method of Lewis's great rearguard defence of objective value, the three Riddell Memorial Lectures published with the title, *The Abolition of Man.*

Lewis begins by explaining that he has been sent, free of charge, a textbook intended for the upper forms of schools on literature and literary criticism: the book is pernicious but was probably not intended to be so. The authors, whose views must be attacked because they are dangerous, shall nevertheless be spared the humiliation of a public pillory. Instead of using their real names, Lewis announces that he will call them Gaius and Titius. Already a certain atmosphere is established. Lewis leaps into the ring like a boxer and his opening benevolence to his opponents seems almost designed to drain away any confidence they might have had. It seems not to occur to him that they might ever rebut his criticism; instead he assumes that they have no chance of doing so and regally offers them the protection of anonymity. Were I Alexander King (Gaius) or Martin Ketley (Titius) I fancy I would have considered it more truly courteous in Lewis to have attacked me under my own name.

Lewis takes as his text the comment by King and Ketley on the story of Coleridge overhearing one person describe a waterfall as pretty, and another call it 'sublime'.

> When the man said *'That is sublime'*, he appeared to be making a remark about the waterfall. . . . Actually . . . he was not making a remark about the waterfall, but a remark about his own feelings. . . . What he was saying was, really . . . 'I have sublime feelings'.[7]

Lewis's initial response to this must be quoted in full:

> Even on their own view – on any conceivable view – the man who says *This is sublime* cannot mean *I have sublime feelings*. Even if it were granted that such qualities as sublimity were simply and solely projected into things from our own emotions, yet the emotions which prompt the projection are the correlatives, and therefore almost the opposites of the qualities projected. The feelings which make a man call an object sublime are not sublime feelings but feelings of veneration. If *This is sublime* is to be reduced at all to a statement about the speaker's feelings, the proper translation would be *I have humble feelings*. If the view held by Gaius and Titius were consistently applied it would lead to obvious absurdities. It would force them to maintain that *You are contemptible* means *I have contemptible feelings*: in fact that *Your feelings are*

contemptible means *My feelings are contemptible*. But we need not delay over this which is the very *pons asinorum* of our subject.[8]

Lewis's first move is a plain denial of the fact. The man was not talking about his feelings, he was talking about the waterfall. The second move brings in the notion of presupposition: if one were to take the line that 'This is sublime' is a purely subjective observation, one would be instantly committed to explaining that the feelings involved were reverent. Thus the reader is forcibly reminded that ordinary language reserves one term for the object and another for the subject, as if each somehow has rights in the matter.

Here we see how it is that Lewis can show scholarly attentiveness to lexical difference and yet avoid formalism. He is, so to speak, more interested in the logical implications of grammar or linguistic usage than in the 'grammar' or quasi-linguistic rules of logical discourse. Thus his method was really closer to that of G. E. Moore than that of Wittgenstein. Indeed, Moore's practical demonstration in *Principia Ethica* that, whatever philosophers may say, ordinary people are quite clear that evaluation is one thing and the registration of pleasure another is so like Lewis's method as to suggest itself as a direct influence: 'Whoever will attentively consider with himself what is actually before his mind when he asks the question "Is pleasure (or whatever it may be) after all good?" can easily satisfy himself that he is not merely wondering whether pleasure is pleasant.'[9] Still closer is the following sentence, from Moore's *Ethics*: 'One point should be carefully noticed to begin with; namely, that we have no need to show that when we call a thing "good" we *never* mean simply that somebody has some mental attitude towards it.'[10]

The devastating confidence of Lewis's initial onslaught makes one wonder what kind of defence could be constructed for King and Ketley. One might argue as follows:

Lewis prides himself on his sense of history and yet he begins with a sheer howler. Moreover his blunder is not superficial but is essential to his argument. He cites, of all people, Coleridge, a Kantian Romantic, to show how, before 'quite modern times', everyone thought that aesthetic qualities were objective. But in fact the suggestion that the adjective 'sublime' is properly transferable to the subject is not a grotesque modern error but on the contrary is found in Kant himself, whom Coleridge revered.

In his *Critique of Judgement*, Kant wrote:

> We express ourselves incorrectly if we call any *object of nature* sublime . . . no sensible form can contain the sublime, properly so-called. This concerns only Ideas of the Reason, which, although no adequate presentation is possible for them, by this inadequacy that admits of sensible presentation, are aroused and summoned into the mind. Thus the wide ocean, agitated by the storm, cannot be called sublime. Its aspect is horrible; and the mind must be already filled with manifold Ideas if it is to be determined by such an intuition to a feeling itself sublime, as it is incited to abandon sensibility and to busy itself with Ideas that involve higher purposiveness.[11]

Again, a little later in the same work, Kant wrote:

> True sublimity must be sought only in the mind of the [Subject] judging, not in the natural Object, the judgement upon which occasions this state. Who would call sublime, e.g. shapeless mountain masses piled in wild disorder upon each other with their pyramids of ice, or the gloomy raging sea.[12]

It takes a philosopher to ask a rhetorical question which so infallibly provokes the undesired response, 'Almost everyone'. Nevertheless, it seems clear enough that, if we enlist the aid of historical scholarship, its tendency is precisely to vindicate King and Ketley and to discredit Lewis. Before he arrogantly corrected 'two modest practising schoolmasters who were doing the best they knew'[13] he would have been well advised to pause and consider whether they might conceivably have known rather better than he did.[14]

I offer the foregoing as a possible rejoinder, set forth in the sort of combative style that Lewis (who had a Johnsonian hunger for 'rational opposition') would have enjoyed. How far does it really destroy Lewis's main argument? It blows a small hole in his superstructure, but he remains sound below the water-line.

To begin with, it is always possible to argue about what Kant meant. Even if he really is saying that the sublime is a subjective sentiment, it would appear that this conception is, so to speak, an exception which proves Lewis's rule; for Kant makes it clear that a sharp distinction is to be drawn between the notion of sublime and ordinary aesthetic judgements, which are properly applied to natural objects. But there is in any case doubt as to whether even the concept of the sublime is, in Kant's philosophy, purely subjective in character. In the first passage quoted from *The Critique of Judgement*, just before he observes that no sensible form can contain the sublime, Kant writes, 'All that we can say is that the object is fit for the presentation of a sublimity which can be found in the mind.' With this concession of a certain *fitness* in the object, implying presumably that some objects are fitter than others, Kant might be said to have granted everything Lewis needs, namely that there is something about certain objects which renders the use in connection with them of the word 'sublime' appropriate. The term is, then, not merely free-floating, governed exclusively by subjective caprice. There appears after all to be some basis for that feature of ordinary language whereby the adjective is applied to natural objects.

One is reminded of the argument about 'primary' and 'secondary' qualities. A hundred years before Kant philosophers and natural scientists had been eager to point out that no object was really red; colours inhere in the subjective apparatus of the perceiver. But it gradually became clear that certain objects are *such* that they are seen as 'red' and a little later it emerged that this provided, after all, a sufficient basis for saying that these objects *are* red (this is what being red turns out to entail).

But there seems to be little doubt that Kant would have required some persuading that such an argument applies in the present case. It follows that

Lewis has chosen to hang his thesis on a dangerously ambiguous example. This, I think, is the full extent of his error. The thesis itself is virtually unscathed. At worst, the only adjustment necessary is for him to add, 'Perhaps Coleridge indeed thought thus, but if he did he was wrong, and must accordingly be placed as part of the historical emergence of the later philosophy to which I am opposed.' That said, the brisk analysis offered by Lewis is effective against Coleridge precisely as it is effective against Ketley and King (and Kant). On the other hand, if Coleridge did not follow Kant in this view, Lewis's original words may stand without supplement.

Lewis demonstrates that, whatever our more recent educators may say, in ordinary life people quite clearly ascribe value and beauty to objects and consider variations in ascription as substantial disagreements rather than 'empty' oscillations of subjective sentiment. It follows that any philosophy which denies the objective reference of ethical and aesthetic terms will be, in P. F. Strawson's words,[15] prescriptive rather than descriptive metaphysics. That is, it will not be the kind of philosophy which seeks to understand the rational structure of what we ordinarily do, but will rather be the kind which seeks to convert or at least to censure ordinary practice on the ground that it is confused or irrational. It is clear that an extra burden of proof falls on the prescriptive metaphysician since it is he that is proposing change.

But in the case immediately before us the proponent of change is, according to Lewis, uniquely disabled. His difficulty arises from the fact that each attempt to criticise the moral system presupposes that same system. If you say, 'It is unscientific to bother about honour or truth-telling; the only end to which the species is biologically committed is its own preservation', Lewis will answer, 'But it is more than doubtful whether there is such a thing as an instinct to preserve the *species* (as opposed to the instinct to preserve one's offspring). More importantly, however, the bare thesis "Organisms strive to preserve their kind" can have no force in either an ethical or an anti-ethical discussion. It is only when you say, "The species *ought* to be preserved" that you begin to be relevant, but this proposition turns out, lamely enough, to be derived from the very body of traditional ethical wisdom you seek to subvert.' As Lewis wrote in another essay, closely connected in spirit and date of composition with *The Abolition of Man*, 'The trunk to whose root the reformer would lay the axe is the only support of the particular branch he wishes to retain.'[16]

Meanwhile there remain those who, with greater apparent consistency, disclaim any thought of ethical reform but rather affirm that, since all ethical views are the result of conditioning, the time has come for man to assume control of those conditioning mechanisms which have hitherto controlled him. For these Lewis has an answer no less destructive than the previous one. The proposed triumph over nature can be neither more nor less than a subjection to nature far more complete than any which existed before. The old obedience to the moral law had been clear-eyed, rational and easily distinguishable from merely instinctive behaviour. But the conditioning of their fellows undertaken by ethical sceptics can be regulated by no principle other than instinct or mere fashion. Thus the new overlords who subjugate the minds of their own kind (for the power of Man over Himself always turns out in practice to be the power of some people over others) are themselves subject to blind nature. No one dethrones Good. They merely dethrone themselves.

Lewis traps the Common sceptic, then, by pointing out that as long as he uses words like 'better' he presupposes the system he hoped to destroy, and deals with the radical sceptic by modestly observing that he is standing on his own oxygen pipe. He outplays the moderns by bringing to bear a sense of context which is logically sharper than theirs. Meanwhile, he uses his sense of lexical meaning to show how certain conceptions are more deeply embedded in the fabric of our lives than many suppose. This sense of contextual or implied significance is very modern and it is this which equips him most effectively in his resistance to contemporary trends. The case of C. S. Lewis is not after all a simple instance of past culture refuting present culture. It is true that the sense of logical context which I have so far associated with Wittgenstein and Moore is most likely to have been found by Lewis in the works of G. K. Chesterton. Take, for example, this sentence from *Orthodoxy*: 'An optimist cannot mean a man who thought everything right and nothing wrong. For that is meaningless; it is like calling everything right and nothing left.[17] Nevertheless, there are major episodes in twentieth-century philosophy which are highly relevant to Lewis's position and really ought to have been cited by him. It is as if the mere fact of their belonging to the twentieth century, the degenerate age, led to an automatic suppression. He allows, indeed, the importance of I. A. Richards, Croce and Alexander, but of these the first two were respected opponents and the last was the source of a distinction (that between 'enjoyment' and 'contemplation') which led Lewis to avoid introspection. Indeed, the last thing Lewis was likely to notice would be something contemporary, working in his own intelligence. Always scrupulous in the distinctions he applied to others, in his own case he proved gullible to what must be seen at last as a misleading caricature, the dinosaur.

For the ethical theorem which lies at the heart of *The Abolition of Man* is what all the world knows as G. E. Moore's concept of the Naturalistic Fallacy, the error of supposing that one can draw an ethical conclusion from non-ethical premises.[18] Moreover Moore's argument was anticipated by, of all people, David Hume, the greatest of the sceptics, when he noted the illicit manner in which 'ought' is smuggled into seemingly consecutive reasoning and how the deductive chain always snaps at this point because of the fundamental discontinuity between the natural and the ethical.[19] It is therefore very curious and symptomatic of something more than mere chronological snobbery in Lewis that, in all the plethora of reference to Aristotle and Aquinas and the rest, there is no reference to the principal modern source of his governing idea.

Nevertheless, the argument as it unfolds is dazzling. It is in a way odd that a work which so thoroughly routs whole volumes of Nietzsche and Sartre is not more widely admired, especially as the style in which it is presented is brilliantly lucid. One suspects, indeed, that the very lucidity may in a curious fashion have impeded the cultural success of the work. Many people suppose that if a thing appears to be done with ease the thing itself must have been easy and therefore trivial. Others are repelled by the 'plain man' manner (although this stance is rationally integral to the argument). It is hard to avoid the inference that Lewis might have pleased the intelligentsia more if only he had taken the trouble to obfuscate his style. But doubtless the mere opposition of the *Zeitgeist* is the principal factor. At present people do not *want* to be told that value is objective. In a fallen world those who rationally resist fashion can hardly expect universal acclaim.

I have suggested that Lewis successfully outflanked the armies of those who hold that values are merely epiphenomenal upon biological process. This is high praise and indeed will remain so at the end of this essay. But though I applaud his victory I am not sure that I fully agree with him in every particular. I have so far in this essay (apart from a minor skirmish over Kant) held back my own criticisms, wishing to establish first the strong sympathy I feel for Lewis's general position. But Lewis would indignantly resent it if I did not say what I thought was wrong. I wish he was alive to answer.

II

Lewis refers to the great body of moral injunctions by which civilised man had lived for the last four thousand years as the Tao. He believes that the Tao is axiomatic, the premise of all rational discourse rather than the conclusion of any particular argument. There can, he says,[20] be no ethical reason for adopting any of the great systems of the Tao in preference to, say, instinctual hedonism. And yet, in a manner, it is clear that *The Abolition of Man* commends and argues for the Tao.

Lewis wants to say that the Tao imperiously claims our allegiance and hardly needs the assistance of C. S. Lewis in making good its claim. It is redundant to say, in any particular case, that one *ought* to perform the action which is good rather than the action which is bad, since a practical obligation is already contained in the word 'good'; this is what 'good' *means*. We must accept the obligation implicitly, because, if we demand a separate moral injunction which says, 'obey moral injunctions' we must then, by parity of reasoning, require authority for obeying *this* overriding injunction and so on *ad infinitum*. The situation is parallel to that which obtains in legal systems.

Some have argued that particular laws can have no force unless there is an overriding law which says 'Law must be obeyed'; little thought is needed to show that this generates an infinite regress. The choice is therefore between *implicit* obedience and total immoralism and there is no way in which implicit obedience can be 'commended' to one outside the Tao. Lewis is therefore in the curious position of so defining the issue that, on his own terms, he can only preach to the converted. He is mounting a crusade, with trumpets, weaponry and commissariat, to remind people that they are already in Jerusalem. Moreover, it appears that almost everyone *is* converted. To the person who says, 'We should follow instinct, not the Tao', he answers, 'As soon as you say "should" you are involved in the Tao'. But if the Tao is so inexpugnably present in the discourse of the moderns, why is Lewis so worried about them? Why the missionary zeal to reclaim those who are already within the Law?

It will be said that this misrepresents Lewis's position, since he is really reminding those who acept part of the Tao that they ought in consistency to accept it all. This sounds like common sense but we shall see that in fact this is not a position which Lewis can adopt. The 'all-or-nothing' character of his fundamental philosophy is in fact fatal to the strategy of the lectures themselves.

This becomes clear if we examine the manner in which Lewis argues against those who opt for Instinct. Since he can offer no ethical argument in favour of accepting the ethical, Lewis attempts an argument in the 'neutral' terms of logical consistency. Instinct, he observes, issues varying instructions and provides no clue to the manner in which they should be ranked. As soon as you exalt one instinct above another you are dependent on the Tao for your criterion. Already one senses that the thought is weaker. The fact that the Tao can 'rank' instincts is not of itself especially persuasive. Lewis says that if any portion of the Tao is retained, the entire Tao must be retained.[21] It would seem to follow that there is no ground within the Tao for 'ranking' its contents. Only an 'outsider' could perceive, say, that Buddhism was superior to Stoicism. But the instincts can, in their turn, 'rank' the various injunctions of the Tao. (I imagine that instinct places 'Love your children' above 'Render to every man his due'.) Meanwhile what Lewis calls the Tao is what Gilbert Murray called the 'Inherited Conglomerate',[22] that vast accumulation of injunctions, taboos and explanations which has, as Murray put it, very little chance of being true or even sensible. The relatively simple jarring instincts is as nothing beside the buzzing confusion of the Tao.

For this half of the argument Lewis was fully prepared. He denies that the confusion is anything but superficial and mounts a formidable case for the substantial unity of the Tao. This case is set out at length in the Appendix to *The Abolition of Man* and is put shortly in 'The Poison of Subjectivism':

> From the Babylonian *Hymn to Samos*, from the Laws of Manu, the *Book of the Dead*, the Analects, the Stoics, the Platonists, from Australian aborigines and

Redskins, he will collect the same triumphantly monotonous denunciations of oppression, murder, treachery and falsehood, the same injunctions of kindness to the aged, the young and the weak, of almsgiving and impartiality and honesty.[23]

Lewis is of course forced to concede that there are some differences between the different 'parties' of the Tao. His account of these differences is that they are mere shifts of emphasis and variations in what is omitted. Whatever is positively included or commended will be a part of the Tao, itself a rationally consistent body of doctrine.

This account is somewhat strained. The Tao says, 'Give to every man his due.' The Tao also says (at another time and in another place) 'Forgive those who wrong you.' It is quite possible to see the Christian injunction, not as a deepening and emphasising of something already present, but as ethical lunacy, a direct violation of the existing Tao. By the same token it might be seen as a radical innovation, of the kind which Lewis feels obliged to deny. Indeed Lewis is so strong on the impossibility of ethical innovation[24] that the question of the origin of the Tao begins to be somewhat pressing. I suspect that Lewis was not displeased to have a mystery at this point in his scheme (it suggests a religious solution). In his *English Literature in the Sixteenth Century, excluding Drama*, he writes with ill-concealed relish of Aristotle's insistence that the supreme power should administer a pre-existing law and should itself hardly be expected to legislate. 'I do not know', writes Lewis, 'that Aristotle ever tells us where this original and immutable law came from.'[25]

Sometimes a party within the Tao will raise 'a question of emphasis' to the status of a positive, independent injunction: 'Mercy transcends justice.' Deny that and you deny the Tao. Yet, in another country, the Tao may present a directly opposite injunction. After all, much blood has been spilled over these 'questions of emphasis'.

Similarly, some societies present injunctions which appear to outsiders to be merely accidental to morality. I believe Lewis was willing to eat pork and unwilling to drink the blood of his enemies. We are untroubled by the example, because we are confident that such injunctions are less than ethical, but the Tao, as a mere accumulation, can never tell us that. Lewis, in his essay 'Ethics',[26] argues somewhat desperately that such injunctions are typical of savage societies and that these are undeveloped exceptions to the rule of rational civility. This, coming from Lewis, is at least odd. He loved to tell others that what they took for a stable truth was really a mere *préjudice de siècle*. In such matters he made of chronology a favourite weapon. But in the history of *Homo Sapiens* the civilised state is the recent exception. Of the millenia passed by our species in forests and caves we can say little, but there is at least a presumption that our existence was like that of modern 'savages'. And what about the triumphantly monotonous moral orthodoxy of the aborigine and the Redskin? 'Lo, the poor Indian' indeed![27]

At this point we find a striking discrepancy between Lewis the literary critic and Lewis the philosopher. In *A Preface to Paradise Lost* Lewis affronted his traditionally-minded colleagues by rejecting what he called the doctrine of the Unchanging Human Heart:

> How are these gulfs between the ages to be dealt with by the student of poetry? A method often recommended may be called the method of the Unchanging Human Heart. According to this method the things which separate one age from another are superficial. Just as, if we stripped the armour off a mediaeval knight or the lace off a Caroline courtier, we should find beneath them an anatomy identical with our own, so, it is held, if we strip off from Virgil the Roman imperialism, from Sidney his code of honour, from Lucretius his Epicurean philosophy, and from all who have it their religion, we shall find the Unchanging Human Heart, and on this we are to concentrate. I held this theory myself for many years, but I have now abandoned it. I continue, of course, to admit that if you remove from people the things that make them different, what is left must be the same, and that the Human Heart will certainly appear as Unchanging if you ignore its changes. But I have come to doubt whether the study of this mere L.C.M. is the best end the student of old poetry can set before himself.[28]

Incidentally, Lewis, never strong on mathematics, really ought to have written 'H.C.F.' instead of 'L.C.M.', though to be sure, the words 'Highest Common Factor' do not of themselves carry the required suggestion of baseness. Given the jubilant contempt in this passage (note the ironically honorific capitals – a sure sign that Lewis is Having a Good Time) for those who cannot see the difference between what is anatomically essential and what is humanly essential, the standard response which tells us that in terms of the Tao Sidney's honour is a mere aberrant emphasis seems – once more – strained.

Again, when in a footnote Lewis's self-control slips a little and he lashes Gaius and Titius for their pusillanimous materialism,[29] it is hard to construe his words as no more than a courteous suggestion that their views, valuable as they are, might nevertheless be supplemented by further ethical reflections. It is rather as if (to borrow Lewis's own language from another, more forthright occasion) he hates what they love.[30]

But these are minor criticisms. The force of the argument from Lewis's doctrine of the Changing Human Heart, especially, can easily be overrated. In fact Lewis's historical scholarship is refreshingly distinct from that of his colleagues in one particular, his excited willingness to believe that the words of his author, however ancient, however picturesque, might have some chance of being true. Thus Hooker for him is not simply an interesting historical phenomenon, but someone who saw something important about the Church. In plotting all those subtle differences of mentality, Lewis never ceased to apply, in addition to the tests of *coherence*, the tests of *correspondence* with reality. Oddly enough, since reality is itself rich and multiform, authors may differ deeply from one another and yet touch severally upon truth. One senses Lewis's sympathy[31] with the syncretic eclecticism of Renaissance thinkers, with their habit of supposing that Plato and Aristotle were talking about the same thing, so that points of agreement might also be points of truth. In order to see the major contradiction we must recall the general form of Lewis's argument. He alleges that, if man is in any degree involved with the Tao, he must accept it all. There are no half measures. There is no way of ethically discriminating one element of the Tao from another. By this one argument he seeks to persuade the modern 'instinctualist', say, that since he is involved with Tao to the extent of valuing anything at all, he is committed to the rest. But the compulsion to value the rest is not logical. The fact that the sceptic values instinct in no way *entails* his valuing charity. All that Lewis can offer is the proposition 'Everyone else accepts the rest'. Having austerely rejected ethical commendation in favour of a neutral approach in terms of logical consistency, Lewis ends by relying on a sub-logical sense of consistency – mere conformity: that is, on an ethical exhortation of the weakest sort. Indeed his argument is doubly weak. First, if the thesis that everyone accepts the whole Tao were true, it would exert no compulsive force, because, as Lewis himself is anxious to point out on other occasions, in ethics the *de facto* can provide no ground for the *de jure* – you cannot base an Ought on an Is; Lewis's argument therefore terminates in the grossest ethical naturalism. Secondly, the thesis, 'Everyone else accepts the whole Tao' is simply false. Even if Lewis were able to hold the line that there are no actual logical inconsistencies in the Tao, he clearly concedes that some people leave bits out. Indeed, the very fact that the Sceptic prefers instinct shows that applications of the Tao are not uniform. The very existence of the malaise discredits the proffered cure. If Lewis's reply were true, there would have been no problem in the first place. The fact that the Sceptic needs to be reclaimed shows that the Tao can slip. Of course Lewis can preserve the majestic unity of the Tao by hastily shepherding strays back into the fold but, as he said himself, 'no man of high intellectual honour can base his thought on an exposed *petitio*'.[32] The realm of the *de facto* is a bleak democracy of facts. A preference for wholeness, for the 'developed' as against the 'merely savage', for the rich and complex as against the primitive and local, will always involve the illicit intrusion of the *de jure*.

Thus, although one easy way to deal with cultural variation might have been to observe that, although different societies may ascribe value to different things, they all have the practice of ascribing value (so that valuing is universal even if values are not), this is a stratagem Lewis could not use, since it exposes the discontinuity fatal to his argument, the discontinuity between the form and content of ethics, the concept 'good' and its variable paradigms. This would have been clearer if Lewis had attended to Moore's contribution. Lewis implicitly assents to Moore's contention that 'good' is non-natural, but part of that conception rests on the fact that it is logically and practically possible for a person to stand back from any object whatsoever and ask, 'Is this really good?' With this freedom, any compulsive force Lewis's appeal to the Sceptic might have had is lost.

Lewis would doubtless be quick to respond that this freedom is not regarded in ordinary discourse as unconditional. In so far as goodness is not deducible from empirical data (this is part of the impossibility of deriving Ought from Is on which Lewis is elsewhere anxious to insist), thus far it is indeed logically open to the subject to query the goodness of anything at all, but at the same time this freedom to withhold the ascription is not wholly unconstrained. When Smith says 'I think cruelty is a virtue' and Jones says 'No, cruelty is obviously a vice,' this is not like Smith's saying that he feels ill and Jones replying that he on the contrary feels fine. Yet the fact remains that there are no *defining* paradigms of 'good'; rather, every candidate for the title must be measured against *it*. Lewis himself said that the Tao was a premise rather than a conclusion.[33] So here 'good' is a prior criterion rather than a derivate of experience. In these circumstances, although there may be considerable cultural agreement on the more likely candidates for the title 'good' there can clearly be no final adjudication of the matter and, in particular, there can be no question of telling a proponent of a new ascription of 'good' that he is committed by his very use of the term to accept the ascriptions of others and repress his own. Lewis outlaws deviation and then congratulates the Tao on its unity.

In fact the tension that I find in Lewis between the idea of good as a non-natural conception and good as a rationally ordered perception permeates the philosophy of Moore. When Moore's attention is caught by the objective constraints on 'good' he uses unduly simple cognitive analogies[34] like colours, as if for him, as for Donne,

Good is as visible as green.[35]

Lewis, in a similar mood, likens moral defectiveness to colour blindness.[36] On other occasions, Moore stressed the independence of 'good' from any empirical determinant. Likewise Lewis. The truth lies somewhere between the two conceptions. I am not sure that the ethical philosopher has yet appeared who has correctly analysed the part played by empirical factors in the use of ethical terms. It is plainly not enough to say, as I have, that empirical objects are 'candidates'. It is necessary to specify in what a successful candidature would consist. In so far as *The Abolition of Man* is a hortatory tract to reform our educators, it implicitly acknowledges that the Tao is not as plain as the nose on your face or the redness of that pillar box, but is something to be carefully inculcated by disciplined and generous teaching, something now imperilled. It is merely false to tell the bad educator that his only error was his failure to perceive that he was already within the fold. This central uncertainty in the thought shows in Lewis's strange oscillation over the concept of nature. When he introduces the concept of the Tao on page 16 he tells us in one breath that it is 'beyond existence' and that it is 'Nature'. As long as he is pressing the idea of the Tao as *fait accompli* ('We are all involved in the Tao and it is idle to pretend otherwise') the Tao remains identifiable with Nature, but when he considers the Tao as something we *ought* to obey, something at once infinitely rich and horribly endangered, it is opposed to the 'merely natural'. When he writes that the Tao 'is Nature, it is the Way, the Road. It is the Way in which the universe goes on',[37] he comes very close, despite the august initial capitals, to a summary description of the world; the Tao is what happens. But a few pages later, provoked by the reductive naturalism of C. H. Waddington, his final gesture of contempt is to compare his adversary with the philosopher in *Rasselas*, who believed that the right way ('Way'?) in philosophy was to cooperate with the present system of things. Doubtless the word 'present' connotes an important difference, but there is no escaping the fact that Johnson's despised philosopher is a loyal disciple of the Tao. On page 44, when Lewis is thinking of the grotesque future product of psychological conditioning, he contrasts with it the pathetic surviving elements in the minds of the conditioners of 'the old *natural* Tao'. But on page 48 the elimination of the Tao is represented as a reduction 'to the level of mere nature'.

Lewis's own attempt[38] to map the possible opposites and hence the possible meaning of 'nature' does not resolve our difficulty, which concerns the question whether the Tao is or is not a given element in our constitution. Lewis is anxious to distinguish the rational obligation to preserve the species from the merely natural impulse to protect one's offspring. But when he comes in the course of his argument to the kind of scientific rationalism he dislikes, he is anxious that the sort of immediate repugnance we continue to feel towards vivisection – 'natural repugnance' seems an obvious way to express it – should be respected.

One suspects that in all this God or Supernature is a missing factor. Lewis's argument swings between ethical naturalism (either 'Do this because it is your nature to do it' or 'Do this because it is what people usually do') and non-naturalism ('This is what you ought to do, and no reason can ever be given'). As it is, it is a classic example of the subtle mutual interpenetration of descriptive and prescriptive argument which has always dogged ethical philosophy. Yet Christianity proclaims that *what ought to be* (seen from a human point of view) actually *is* (*sub specie aeternitatis*). Here, perhaps, is a non-subjective guarantor of another kind, more fitted to the task in hand. But Lewis was anxious to reach the Sceptic by natural reason alone, and therefore fought the fight with one hand tied behind his back.

Meanwhile, notice, the principal pillars of the building he raised remain. When we value things we refer outside ourselves. Even the claim that value is subjective involves a reference to that which is outside the subject. When every criticism has been heard, every needling qualification inserted, the sense of a great feat performed lingers. 'Done is a battel on the dragon blak.' Remember how in *The Pilgrim's Regress*, Reason did battle with the ogre, who was at once the Spirit of the Age and a heap of senseless rocks.[39] There the contest is seen, as it were, in profile. But in *The Abolition of Man* Lewis himself actually fought and, in the end, won. The intelligentisia does not yet know it, but subjectivism lies dead. Jack Lewis has killed the giant.

Notes

1. The point of greatest proximity to Barfield seems to be marked by a letter Lewis wrote to T. S. Eliot on 2 June 1931. In it he outlines a possible essay on metaphor and truth which would 're-affirm the romantic doctrine of imagination as a truth-bearing faculty'. Yet even here his mind twitched, and he added, 'though not quite as the romantics understood it'. See R. L. Green and W. Hooper, *C. S. Lewis? a Biography* (London: Collins, 1974), p. 126.
2. In his *Romanticism and Religion: the Tradition of Coleridge and Wordsworth in the Victorian Church* (Cambridge: Cambridge University Press, 1976).
3. *Parmenides*, 132, b–c.
4. See Stephen Medcalf, 'The coincidence of myth and fact', in *Ways of Reading the Bible*, ed. Michael Wadsworth (Hemel Hempstead: Harvester Wheatsheaf, 1981), pp. 55–78.
5. Op. cit., Oxford Paperbacks edn. (London: Oxford University Press, 1960), p. 1.
6. *Encounter*, XXVIII (Feb. 1962), pp. 97–102.
7. Alexander King and Martin Ketley, *The Control of Language* (London: Longmans, 1939), p. 19.
8. *The Abolition of Man, or, Reflections on education with special reference to the teaching of English in the upper forms of schools*, University of Durham, Riddell Memorial Lectures, Fifteenth Series, first published 1943. This quotation and all those which follow are taken from the 1962 reprint of the 'new edition' of 1946.
9. *Principia Ethica* (Cambridge: Cambridge University Press, 1903), ch. 1, section 13, p. 16.
10. Op. cit., first published 1912, the Oxford University Press paperback edn (1965), p. 67.
11. Op. cit., trans. J. H. Bernard, 2nd edn (revised) (London: Macmillan, 1914), p. 103.
12. Ibid., pp. 117–18.
13. *The Abolition of Man*, p. 7.
14. Henry Crabb Robinson recorded in 1810, 'Of Kant C[oleridge] spoke in terms of high admiration . . . and intimated that he should one day translate his work on the Sublime and Beautiful. His *Critik der Urtheilskraft* he considered as the most astonishing of his works.' See *Coleridge's Miscellaneous Crticism*, ed. T. M. Raysor (London: Constable, 1936), p. 386.
15. See his *Individuals: an Essay in Descriptive Metaphysics* (London: Methuen, 1959), pp. 9–11.
16. 'The poison of subjectivism', in *Christian Reflections*, ed. Walter Hooper (London Geoffrey Bles, 1967), p. 75.
17. Op. cit. (1908) p. 103.
18. See especially *The Abolition of Man*, p. 25.
19. *A Treatise of Human Nature*, III, i. 1, ed. L. A. Selby-Bigge (Oxford: Clarendon Press, 1888), pp. 469–70.
20. See 'Ethics' in *Christian Reflections*, p. 48.
21. *The Abolition of Man*, p. 33.
22. *Greek Studies* (1946), p. 67.
23. *Christian Reflections*, p. 77.

24. *The Abolition of Man* pp. 33–4.
25. Op. cit. (1954) (but delivered as lectures ten years before, i.e. close to the time of *The Abolition of Man*), p. 47.
26. *Christian Reflections*, p. 54.
27. In fact Pope's Indian receives similarly ambiguous treatment. See the *Essay on Man*, i. 99–112 and iv. 177–8.
28. Op. cit., p. 63.
29. *The Abolition of Man*, p. 23.
30. *A Preface to Paradise Lost*, p. 134.
31. See *English Literature in the Sixteenth Century, excluding Drama* (Oxford: Clarendon Press, 1954), p. 11.
32. *A Preface to Paradise Lost*, p. 10.
33. *The Abolition of Man*, p. 31.
34. E.g. *Principia Ethica*, ch. 1, section 7, p. 7.
35. 'Communitie'.
36. *The Abolition of Man*, p. 17.
37. Ibid., pp. 16–17.
38. Ibid., p. 48.
39. Op. cit. (London: Geoffrey Bles), the 1965 reprint of the seventh edition of 1950, p. 64.

PERSONALITY AND POETRY

The psyche

In Plato's *Phaedo*, Socrates, before taking the hemlock and dying, in obedience to the laws of Athens, draws his friends together and talks to them about immortality. He looks back on his life and remembers how in his youth he was tremendously attracted by physical explanations, and then how, as time went by, these became less and less satisfactory to him. It is as if, he says, in response to the question 'Why am I sitting here now' he were to be told, 'Ah, that's because your legs are flexibly constructed of bones and muscles so that they can be put in what is called a sitting position.' But, 'by the god of Egypt,' says Socrates, that's no use at all. I'm sitting here 'because the Athenians have condemned me and I think it right not to run away – *that's* why I am sitting here.'[1] Socrates thus steps from the material to the ethical, and suggests that the mere enumeration of physical conditions will never begin to explain any action of which the essence is ethical or moral. But actions of human personality are commonly thus. Much of the rest of the dialogue is taken up with discussion of the *psuchē* (psyche), often translated 'soul', but in some ways closer to 'personality'. *Psuchē* covers mind, intelligence, character, the subject-matter of psychology, which 'soul', with its increasingly restricted religious signification, tends not to do. So let us use the term 'psyche'.

The principal question asked in the dialogue is whether the psyche is mortal. Socrates offers a number of arguments for immortality, some of them very ingenious, and persuades almost no one. Among these arguments, which almost claim the status of proofs, is one which is nothing like a proof, looks hopelessly vague, but, to my mind, is the most persuasive of the lot. This is the one commonly known as the 'argument from affinity'.

Socrates says that visible things manifestly decay, but that anybody with any intelligence can see that the catalogue of visible things does not exhaust reality. Circularity (as distinct from 'that round wheel', say), justice (as distinct from so many bodies exchanging equal-sized objects), and so forth may be classed as illusions or culturally relative fictions by materialist philosophers with their backs to the wall, but they are never construed in this way by ordinary intelligent people in real life. It follows that the fabric of reality is in part physical, in part something else. Now if you look at the class of things which are not visible, these do not seem to be subject to decay in the same manner as visible things. The body of a particular judge may perish, but the justice of his one correct decision does not. Notice that the language here need not take on any sort of mystical resonance; there is no need for any special assertion of justice glowing through eternity or anything like that; all that is needed is an ordinary acknowledgement that certain sorts of universals operate achronically, without any involvement in the time sequence. Given this loose division into things that you can see and those that you can't see, says Socrates, which group does the psyche belong to? Socrates decides that it belongs with the invisibles, since you can see a person's body but never his psyche. I think Plato knows that there is a difficulty here, which arises from the fact that an individual's psyche is not a universal like circularity; on the other hand, the psyche of Michael Dummett is not as firmly removed from the universal Dummettishness as, say, that wooden wheel is removed from circularity. Plato implicitly grants, however, that there is some lack of fit. Otherwise he would have had another 'proof' of the form: invisible universals are timeless; the psyche is an invisible universal; therefore the psyche is timeless. But he does not presume to say that. Instead, more modestly, he suggests a certain, strange kinship between personality and timeless universals, a kinship in which the ever-decaying physical world cannot share.

Now I think I should say that I am not nearly as confident as Plato (who is himself less than certain) that the human psyche is immortal; I do feel, however, that the full idea of a person, or rather of any one person we know, is necessarily richer than almost any other idea in operation. If we fully attend to it, there seems to be more there than can be confidently assumed to fall under the ordinarily observable processes of death and decay. We feel this especially with people we love. After the death of his great friend Charles Williams, C. S. Lewis said that when the idea of Williams and the idea of death met in his mind, it was the idea of death that was changed. Mind you, when Lewis's wife died later on, it apparently didn't feel like that, because the sheer pain of loss was so great.[2] We late-born folk cannot but be aware of the various artillery brought to bear on the religious conception of immortality in the ages after Socrates. What does strike me, though, is that many of the seemingly 'hard-headed' rebuttals of the Platonic view could, in a matter of two or three decades, come to appear positively weak-minded.

The dissolution of the psyche

Consider, for example, Watsonian/Skinnerian behaviourism, in which the concept of the psyche is construed as a shorthand description of externally observable actions of bodies. The general idea was that if psychology was to be scientific, it should not concern itself with interior, 'introspectible' states of mind, but with external behaviour; most descriptions of individual human natures are based in practice on the things people visibly and audibly *do*, and not on their mental states. When we say that John is angry, we are not guessing at some inaccessible mental state; we are summing up the facts – for example, that he has just punched Fred on the nose and kicked his cat. At its most extreme, this form of behaviourism led to an actual denial of the very existence of thoughts and private mental states, leading some behaviourists to adopt an exaggeratedly nominalist view of universals. Skinner offered a violently reductive account of the universal 'probability', saying that those propositions (bits of verbal behaviour) were 'probable' which were uttered most loudly and most frequently by most people. Chomsky, in his famous review of *Verbal Behaviour*, mildly observed that perhaps Skinner could make his theories probable by training machine-guns on huge crowds of people in city squares and getting them to chant over and over again the basic principles of Skinnerian psychology.[3] Or, think of the old joke about the two behaviourists who make love, after which one says, 'That was marvellous for you; how was it for me?' What this brings out is the fact that inner experience is really quite different from experience of objects in the public world, not so much in Plato's sense as between the empirical and the non-empirical, as between different *modes* of the empirical (for if we divorce the psyche too firmly from experience, we shall end up with the mystified insulated conception *soul*, about which I was complaining earlier). My sense, nevertheless, is that Plato's argument continues to nag, to pluck at the sleeve of the mind, so to speak; for though it rapidly rises to an unmanageable vagueness and confusion, it has a surprisingly strong foundation.

In a word, I agree with Plato that if we confine ourselves rigorously to physical particulars, we cannot achieve anything like an adequate account of the real world. I would further agree that there is some sense, not yet adequately analysed by anyone, in which being human peculiarly and essentially involves a participation, as it were, in both the material and the non-material. Planets burn and then grow cold; but they never know that they do these things, never know what warmth is, what coldness. Clearly, a binary division into universals and physical particulars is far from adequate. There are too many intermediate entities. Compare a lump of coal with a clear view of a lump of coal; compare the view with a sensation (of being hit by the lump of the coal, say); compare that with a particular memory of a lump of coal, and that with the thought of coal, and that with the concept of coal, and that with intelligence or memory as such; or compare circularity with love, love with Beethoven's Eighth Symphony (Beethoven's Eighth Symphony exists all right; but where is it?). Now cross-compare; if you have been considering triangularity, say, the sensation of the lump of coal hitting you will seem physical; but if you have been comparing the sensation with the lump of coal itself, the sensation may appear to be a merely mental thing.

In all this the psyche is obstinately elusive, as ordinary universals are not. The relation between baldness, for example, and an actual bald head is perspicuous. Philosophers may argue about the ontological status of baldness, but there is a sense in which we understand the distinction between baldness and a particular bald head perfectly. But with the psyche, or personality, it is more difficult. I have already disparaged the attempts of early behaviourists to construe the psyche in terms of summary descriptions applied to complex behaviour, suggesting that they acknowledge a certain autonomy of inner experience. But then one thinks of Hume, who, with his usual candour, professed that he was very willing to look within for this thing called a 'self', or a 'soul'; but that when he did so, he never saw it.[4] Try as he might, all he got from introspection was bits and bobs, particular sensations, fragments of remembered conversation, appetites, resentments but never a unified 'self'. So here we have someone who was fully prepared to acknowledge and explore inner experience, but who, after a thoroughly honest endeavour, came up with precisely nothing. For Hume, the effect of introspection was not to discover the self, but to deconstruct it. We are left, it might be thought, in some disarray.

The dissolution of the poem

At this point, cued by the word 'disarray', I want to discuss the present state of English literary studies. At present a battle is being fought – a battle of Byzantine intricacy and Cimmerian obscurity. Every so often, journalists scent drama and conflict, and try to run articles explaining what is going on to the world at large. One is rung up by baffled, hard-pressed columnists, and the conversation usually ends with them saying, in a despairing way, 'You mean they are arguing about *that*?'

Roughly speaking, it is all about the replacement of New Criticism by a revived structuralism and the subsequent replacement of structuralism by deconstructionism. In the interest of brevity, I will use artificially simplified terms here; but in fact, it is characteristic of the debate that members of any party tend to see the opposition in precisely these simplified terms.

The New Critics believed by and large in a sort of autonomy of the poem. Study of the lives of poets, the history of ideas and the like were all, strictly speaking, forms of truancy from literary criticism, which, in its purest form, consisted of a close analytic reading of particular poems. They saw the authority of the poem as necessarily higher than that of the poet as a historical person. They delighted in test cases in which poets had said silly things about their poems, whereas the texts themselves demonstrably conveyed a richer, more coherent meaning. They liked to quote D. H. Lawrence's words, 'Trust the tale, not the teller.' Each poem was held to propose in effect the terms on which it should be read, as a separate work of art, unrelated to any other. It was this notion of separateness which was subverted by the new structuralism.

Structuralism initially grew out of Russian formalism, Lévi-Strauss's anthropology of differing cultural codes (usually binary systems), and Saussurian linguistics, with its stress on context as that which confers meaning (a mere noise usually means nothing; only as it forms part of a relational sequence does meaning begin to come through). The general thrust of this movement is to locate meaning in the relations rather than in the given chunks of a system. As we move up the hierarchy from linguistic to literary analysis, the effect of this relocation is to cast doubt on this very possibility of reading a poem as a thing-in-itself, an insulated thing. If the poem carries a meaning, it is by virtue of its relation, echoic or contrasting, to other poems, for literature is really a huge, ever-growing web; and what we call particular poems are merely points of intersection. So addressing the cultural context, far from being a form of truancy from literary criticism, is its primary task.

Of deconstructionism I will say very little. At one stage, structuralism had high, almost scientific, hopes. Just as in languages, according to some theorists, there are 'deep structures' which generate the variously differentiated systems of French, Italian, and so on, so in literature, it was thought, certain primary oppositions (of light and dark, say), or simple narrative sequences (injunction followed by transgression, for example) formed a matrix from which the richly differentiated structures of an actual literature might be derived. The idea was to analyse and set forth this generative grammar of literature, so that the phylogeny of art would be seen in its ultimate, necessary form; the codes of the great game in which individuals had participated for centuries without any general understanding would be identified and understood; and the deep structures permitting the formation of all the proliferating structures would be intelligible at last. What the deconstructionists did was to cast doubt on the dream of terminal understanding, often by showing that the very features which the structuralists supposed they were discovering were themselves merely the fluid product of yet another set of varying cultural codes. If meaning is located in context, it is endlessly deferred, because there is always a further context, and all definitions presuppose other definitions *ad infinitum*. In such an environment, one can no longer hope for certainty or truth but only throw oneself into the maelstrom with a sort of joyous despair. Deconstructive criticism (some of which is tremendously clever) is characterised by a most peculiar Nietzschean nihilist hilarity which I cannot hope to convey.

Real people and real poems

What is very noticeable in all this is a repeatedly applied process of dissolution. The New Critics set aside the living author as irrelevant: the poem was the thing. The structuralists actually 'dissolved the author outright and then merged the poem with its context: not the poem, but literature – which essentially propagates itself – is the thing. Deconstructionism dissolves the author, the reader, and the text, and also, in its metaphysically extreme moments, the very notions of meaning and truth. I should stress that it is only at these extreme moments that this fundamental dissolution occurs, for there is, so to speak, a house-trained deconstructive criticism which contents itself with emphasising detectable incoherence in literary works, rather than eliciting coherent patterns as previous criticism had done. This is all thoroughly cognitivist, in that it presupposes existence of a text about which certain true statements can be made. But the metaphysical extreme is my concern at present.

I will now try to pull the two bits of this paper together – the story of the philosophical investigation of the psyche, or soul, which seemed to end with losing the soul, and the story of the analysis of poetry, which seemed to end by losing the object of inquiry. It is as if the analytic intelligence, for considerable stretches of human history, operates as a sort of death-ray, withering all that lies in its path. Hume's method of highly focused introspection yielded no sort of 'self', but only a succession of bits. But the behaviourists' wild swing to the opposite extreme yields mere bloodless patterns of behaviour which no ordinary person finds adequate if an account of what it is to be human is being sought. In literary studies, the too highly focused work of certain New Critics presented isolated poems as intricate, yet somehow dessicated, things. The proper nourishment of cultural context was being denied. But the structuralist fled too abruptly to the opposite extreme, where there is in effect nothing but context. Something keeps going wrong, and it seems to be something to do with the artificial separation of different orders of being or discourse, and the subsequent wanton privileging of one order over all the rest. Certainly the basic philosophical challenges always seem to be readily reversible. 'Look,' says the structuralist, 'identity presupposes relation. You can't describe anything without describing its relation to other things; it's the relating that carries the meaning.' But, equally, relation presupposes thing, for a world in which nothing was related to any other thing would be a world without relations. The notion of relationship *in vacuo* is philosophically incoherent.

In ordinary life we operate not simply with primary atoms and their relations, or with ultimate particulars and pure universals, but with all kinds of intermediate wholes, two very important examples of which are persons and poems. These can be shown to be complex, involving different orders within them. But it does not follow from such analysis that they are, so to say, exploded. As we analyse, we must remember the necessity of integration, and here I am referring to an utterly fundamental necessity; indeed, the hardest analytic thinkers always use existing integrations at some point in their thinking, though not of course where the searchlight is shining most brightly. The intellectual purist may say that there is no method for weighing the importance of maintaining a cathedral, say, against a programme for improving council houses, because the arguments on each side are strictly incommensurable. They belong to different language games, to use Wittgenstein's term. But they occur, endlessly enmeshed, in one world. Outside the lecture room, we know that we must, can, and do weigh such considerations against each other within the complex whole called steward-ship.

It seems to me that in certain, quintessentially human fields the analytic intelligence becomes nothing more nor less than a technique for losing the goods – unless it is accompanied by a sense of the necessary integrations or wholes. This might sound like an attack on science which is not at all what I intend – not even an attack on scientific psychology. Occam's razor, controlled experiments, definition of the field of inquiry, specification of testable predictions, all these are of proven – indeed spectacular – intellectual utility. The danger is metaphysical: that when we hear the specified terms suddenly characterised as alone real, we acquiesce in the implication that all the rest is some sort of illusion. Good literature is not just an analogy, a secondary echo of the properly human, that retains both the complexity and the wholeness of personality; it also engages explicitly with meaning, and addresses the human in a manner quite different from that of analytic philosophical psychology.

Hume excluded from his picture the temporally diffuse awareness of continuous 'personal colour', duration, predisposition, and so on, which for most of us gradually grows into an awareness of selfhood. Or, at least, he does so in the famous passage in which he employs the fierce introspective searchlight. To be fair, there are signs in *The Treatise* that he recognised this, as when he says: 'In thinking of our past thoughts we not only delineate the objects of which we were thinking, but also conceive the action of the mind in meditation, that certain *je-ne-sais-quoi* of which 'tis impossible to give any definition or description, but which everyone sufficiently understands'.[5] And of course this more diffuse awareness is itself irremediably mixed up with our relationship to others – not with introspection, but with extrospection. But the self is not dissolved by this. Set against Hume (perhaps the greatest British philosopher) the greatest English poet. In *Hamlet* Shakespeare shows us a person who so thoroughly withdraws from ordinary relationships that his psyche, or soul, begins to decay. We see Hamlet engaging in introspection to the point of psychic self-destruction; whereas an actor can weep real tears for a fictitious Hecuba, Hamlet can feel nothing for a real dead father. It is a study in artificially intensified introspection. But because we are in the world of drama, in which, contrary to the principle of Occam's razor, entities are endlessly multiplied beyond a single immediate necessity, we can see what is surely a possibility, a person living as all persons must, among other human beings, but with an inner life that is going seriously wrong. Elsewhere, I have compared the plays of Shakespeare to Occam's beard.[6] Because of the context and an equally intense preoccupation with both a properly relative and an isolated inwardness, *Hamlet* the play (as opposed to Hamlet the person in the play) remains sane, so to speak. It corroborates and strengthens our sense of humanity. There is never any danger of that sense being lost. It takes – I won't say a scientist – a philosopher to do that.

Notes

1. Plato, *Phaedo*, 97E–99A.
2. C. S. Lewis, *A Grief Observed* (London: Faber and Faber 1961).
3. N. Chomsky, review of *Verbal Behaviour*, by B. F. Skinner, in *Language*, 35 (1959), pp. 26–58.
4. D. Hume, *A Treatise of Human Nature*, ed. L. A. Selby-Bigge, repr. of 11th edn. (Oxford: Clarendon Press, 1966), 1.iv. 6.
5. Ibid., 1. iii. 10.
6. A. D. Nuttall, *A New Mimesis* (London: Methuen, 1983), p. 181.

IS THERE A LEGITIMATE
REDUCTIONISM?

'Reductionism' has come to be used as a term of abuse, especially by non-scientists. Scientists, meanwhile, seem to be a little more reluctant to use the word in this way, perhaps because they cannot help being aware that, while bad or unsuccessful reduction certainly exists, there is also another kind of reduction to prior principles which can be conducted with a sort of tender vigilance, a profound respect for the phenomenon to be explained. Indeed, natural science itself is, to a considerable extent, a spectacular series of successful reductions, in which an immense variety of phenomena are explained in terms of relatively few conceptions or else in terms of 'lower-level' determinants. These acts of reduction are not achieved by suppressing data; rather they successfully incorporate and account for all relevant data. The technical language and conceptual intricacy of much science may often blind non-scientists to the fact that a reduction has occurred. Isaac Newton's *Principia* is a pretty stiff read. Nevertheless, in 1687 it appeared that he had accounted for an immense range of physical phenomena with a relatively small number of presumptions. Physical nature, it seemed, was not intractably random but exhibited certain principles and these principles could be contained within the covers of a single book.

The grand reduction of the *Principia*, however, is not in any clear way a reduction from one level to another which had previously been felt to be different *in kind*. Human language and thought has evolved different orders of discourse, implying different orders of reality. There is, so to speak, one language for physical objects, another for logical relations, another for number, another for living things, another for human beings, another for morality, another for religion, and so on. These patterns of discourse have their areas of overlap and intertexture but are nevertheless felt as logically separate and that separateness is further felt to imply a correlative division in the character of reality itself. At the same time, of course, this entire complex apparatus is applied in just one world, and can be operated by a single subject. Now, hackles rise when it is suggested that one of these orders of discourse can be 'collapsed' into one of the others (for example, when it is said that everything we say about thought can be re-expressed in chemical terms). As long as we put the difficulty in terms of discourse it may be thought that we are dealing only with what may be called 'formal reduction', that is the mere translation of one set of terms into another. But it is part of my point that such shifts are never felt as 'mere translations'; always, the formal reduction (in such cases) is felt to imply an ontological reduction, that is, it is felt to have an impact on the structure of the real world. Thus further examples of reduction from one fundamental order to another might be 'Conscience is really diverted *libido*', or 'Morality is disguised economics'. Newton's great enterprise was not, I think, seen as a reduction of this kind by most people. Rather he was seen as reducing the physically baffling to the physically intelligible: the physical was reduced to physics. I would guess that most of the readers and successors of Newton through the eighteenth and nineteenth centuries were unreflective Cartesian dualists, severely separating thought or mind from the physical, and therefore not vivdly aware of any great threat in Newton's science (I have said that hackles rise when one *order* is reduced to another; they rise highest of all, of course, when it is felt that human beings themselves have been reduced to a lower level).

Of course the picture I have just drawn can be qualified in various ways. Newton observed that a moving thing will naturally go on moving as long as nothing stops it (where Aristotle had thought that a moving object must either be propelled by some other object or else self-propelling and therefore alive). This insight of Newton must have helped to kill any lingering feelings that the heavenly bodies were either alive or else continually propelled by the living God. Here, if you like, as people looked up at the stars on clear frosty nights, a sort of reduction of the scope of theology or even biology might have been experienced as faintly desolating. And of course there were always some who were eager to infer, from the spectacular reduction so far achieved, that reductions greater still might follow: that everything would in the end be reduced to physics. This feeling survives today in our sense of a hierarchy in sciences according to which physics alone is fundamental; sociology is deemed to be implicitly reducible to socio-biology, socio-biology to biology, biology to chemistry and chemistry to physics. The presumed direction of reduction, through the sciences, seems tolerably clear (although it is sometimes disputed).

The general tendency of this kind of forcible reduction from one order to another is towards a physical materialism. The presumption is that a thing can be accounted for in terms of its component bits, so that if one knew everything about all the bits, considered *seriatim*, one could deduce everything about the complex wholes. The Roman atomist Lucretius provides a pleasingly primitive example of this way of thinking in his suggestion (taken of course from Epicurus) that some atoms must have hooks on them.[1] He does this precisely in order to account, at the lower level, for characteristics such as stability and coherence which might otherwise seem to belong only to large, visible objects. But for those hooks, it might have been thought that atoms alone could produce nothing but a sort of pea soup and that some Higher Agency was necessary to marshal them into stable objects like pebbles and iron bars.

Now let us look at the sorts of resistance which arise against forcible reduction.

First, even within the field of physics there is an immediate worry over laws of organisation. Even Newton had not confined himself to the description of corpuscles; he had gone further and had laid down the law of their behaviour, a law not deducible from a serial inspection of the primary constituents. The law of gravity is presented by Newton with a conscious, challenging blankness; 'Here it is; I've no idea why, but it happens; *Non fingo hypotheses*: I make no guesses'.[2] But of course subsequent physics may yet account for gravity in terms of the primary constituents themselves.

In biology there seems to be a recurrent worry, not about adapted-ness, which natural selection covers admirably, but about the extraordinary explosion in the living world of ever higher states of organisation. I note that Arthur Peacocke felt it necessary to fight a brisk little engagement on this point in his assumed defence of scientific reduction.[3] K. F. Schaffner, he explained, was forced to admit organisation itself as an extra, seemingly irreducible term, but then perhaps this was only a temporary stop-gap, covering a mass of environmental factors which are themselves in principle reducible. Watching from the sidelines, I am in no position to dispute the success of this rearguard action. All I do (a little helplessly) is remark the vigour with which it is fought (which seems to imply an opponent of some substance) and reflect on indistinct memories of arguments I have heard among biologists about whether, for example, the laws of form can or cannot be deduced from Darwinian first principles.

Thus, within the sciences themselves there seems to be a recurrent hiccup, so to speak, over the question whether laws of organisation can or cannot be deduced from the characters of the primary constituents. This intermittent difficulty (if it really exists at all) would be curiously parallel to the old dispute between the Realists and the Nominalists. Nominalists held that particulars alone exist and that universals or general ideas are mere fictions (*flatus vocis*); the Realists (conversely) held that universals are real. The grand seventeenth-century design of building a philosophy of 'things' (which seemed at first to imply a reduction of language not just to nouns but to proper names) ran into the fact that 'things' alone just would not build. It is as if they discovered the need for a logical equivalent to the hooks of Lucretian atoms, but this equivalent is, of course, the notion of relation itself, and that, *ex hypothesi*, cannot be attached exclusively to any one primary constituent. Thus one thinks also of certain twentieth-century philosophers who ruefully acknowledge that it is necessary to think of one's primary level as constituted not just by things, but by things-in-relation.[4] Again, one thinks of Bertrand Russell who believed at one time that he could dispense with all relations except – damn it – similarity.[5]

A difference between the scientific worry and the philosophic might seem to lie in the fact that the scientist can always postpone his difficulty and hope for some great advance in knowledge which may transform the entire field. Logical obstacles, on the other hand, are less easily dislodged. If the loose parallelism I have noted between the scientific problem and the philosophical springs from a fundamental identity, then it may be that no amount of additional knowledge will ever suffice to redistribute organisational factors among the primary elements, because organisation (on this hypothesis) simply is not that kind of thing. But (again I speak from the sidelines) it really does look much more like an empirical difficulty and not a logical one, in biology, say. It is not that one could not conceive any kind of higher level at all from a base of random molecular activity, but rather that this particular higher level which confronts us seems, in the very degree of its organisation, to present features which are empirically baffling to some (but not most?) biologists.

The principal logical obstacles to reductionism appear much more clearly when we move up the hierarchy. One such is G. E. Moore's celebrated Naturalistic Fallacy, according to which you cannot get an 'Ought' out of an 'Is'.[6] Ethical discourse is logically autonomous. An ethical conclusion can never be drawn from non-ethical premises. One might indeed conclude from the fact that smoking causes cancer that one ought not to pass cigarettes round at parties, but the conclusion follows only because of a tacit ethical premise (something like, 'It is wrong to cause pain'). The propositions of physical science are non-ethical. Therefore they can never provide an account of one's ethical obligation, e.g. to avoid gratuitous cruelty. In response to this argument a materialist might reply that Moore has only shown that a particular 'formal' reduction is impracticable. Formal reduction is the logical translation of a theory from the terms of a higher level into the terms of a lower level, the implication being that the same thing is successfully re-expressed in a different logical language. Ethical statements do not translate into non-ethical. But this need not mean that there is in fact an ontological area, a part of reality covered by ethical discourse which physics, somehow, cannot touch. Thus, if he were to argue in this way, the materialist might find himself urging that ethical talk is a sort of epiphenomenal game: there are physical people who say ethical things: a physical account can in principle be given of their behaviour but the content of their discourse is itself a mere web of illusions. If ethical contents are not translatable into physics, so much the worse for them. This position, naturally enough, is entirely consistent on its own terms, which is another way of saying that it is in fact a *petitio principii*; it begs the entire question. For, in truth, there is no such thing as a 'merely' formal reduction across a *logical* division. Our very attempt to speak of a logical language was itself a covert piece of forcible reductionism. Logical orders do not merely coexist, having a like relation to reality, as, say, French and Italian do. It becomes clear at once that the materialist has to rig the case ontologically. And indeed, if reality is by prior *fiat* restricted to material substance, it is scarcely surprising that ethics will turn out to be unreal. Remember the old rhyme,

> I am the Master of this College
> And what I don't know isn't knowledge.

The effect of Moore's Naturalistic Fallacy argument is to throw into prominence a necessary moment of forcible reductionism in absolute materialism. Newton's laws had seemed to take full and reverent account both of the sun rising and of the water as it swirled in the bucket; the sun *qua* sun and the water *qua* water were, so to speak, fully deferred to and acknowledged. The grand reduction at no point required that we relegate some of the data to the status of illusion. But a non-ethical account of ethical discourse does just that. To be told, for example, that one is a socialist only because one's parents were poor is to experience a painful cutting-down. Here the implicit theory is that beliefs we suppose to be founded on justice and charity are in fact a mere outgrowth, a sort of bubble or epiphenomenon, produced by non-ethical elements in our constitution. The very expression 'epiphenomenon' either concedes or betrays much (as, for example, in the observation, 'Our *consciousness* of obligation is a mere epiphenomenon upon certain chemical operations'). In decent physics, surely, there are only phenomena, no *epi*phenomena. The expression itself (etymologically 'on-top-of phenomenon' or 'extra-phenomenon') really concedes forthwith that the theory is incomplete, but the concession is often muffled by the polysyllabic obscurity of the term used (in particular it is possible to exploit an ancient ambiguity in the term 'phenomenon', which can mean semblance as well as datum, in order to insinuate that the matter in question is unreal). In fact different orders of discourse are normally felt to imply different ontological orders, that is to imply something about the real world, so that reduction of the ethical to the non-ethical has got to be either a piece of bad reductionism (the mere denial of a part of reality for the sake of simplification) or else a genuine demonstration that something we took to be real is not real at all.

Another sort of 'high level' resistance to absolute materialism was once expressed succinctly by, of all people, J. B. S. Haldane (though he later recanted (1954)):

> It seems to me immensely unlikely that mind is a mere by-product of matter. For if my mental processes are determined wholly by the motions of atoms in my brain I have no reason to suppose that my beliefs are true. They may be sound chemically, but that does not make them sound logically. And hence I have no reason for supposing my brain to be composed of atoms.[7]

There is, Haldane suggests, an unbridgeable gap between material motions and configurations on the one hand and truth on the other. Indeed this argument can be put in a sharper form. It is not so much that one cannot tell whether beliefs so constituted are true; one cannot see how one could meaningfully apply the word 'true' to such a state of affairs at all. No mere collection of bits, however complex, could ever be 'true'. Haldane was not the first person to present this view, of course. Ralph Cudworth said something very similar in the seventeenth century,[8] and Samuel Clarke in the eighteenth.[9] Many, likewise, have laboured to bridge the gap. Perhaps if one considers not just complex physical arrangements but complex-physical-arrangements-in-relation-to-other-complex-physical-arrangements, an operationalist version of truth as pragmatic success, say, might be achieved. But 'truth as pragmatic success' is itself a piece of forcible reductionism. In my view Haldane's argument is a real bone-crusher. Both Moore and Haldane, in fixing on logical discontinuity, have produced arguments which cannot be set aside with a mere gesture to the present, incomplete state of our knowledge. Both are saying, 'However much you learn, as long as your knowledge is of that kind, it will not serve.' But Haldane's argument is in one respect much more powerful than Moore's. The absolute materialist cannot give an account of ethical contents, but he can, if he is determined enough, set ethics on one side. Having consigned it to the darkness, he can proceed with the Work of Light. But the notion of truth cannot be set aside in this way. It is in fact an indispensable condition of materialism itself. I am careful to say 'of materialism' and not 'of matter'. Materialism, as long as it claims to be true, is itself irreducible to matter, since, as we have seen, mere matter can never be 'true'; it can only 'be'.

So far I have considered materialist reductionism and the ways in which we tend to resist it. Can forcible reductionism ever work in the opposite direction? Of course it can. For example, there is idealist reductionism. One of the great ironies of British Empiricism, the philosophy of experience, lies in the ease with which it can cross over from materialism to idealism. Earlier I pointed to an ambiguity in the word 'phenomenon'. There is a similar ambiguity in the word 'experience'. 'Experience' can connote either the thing experienced or the mental presentation. In the first book of Hume's *Treatise of Human Nature* the assimilation of all things to experience becomes an immense act of forcible reductionism, for in Hume 'experience' is only the stream of ideas in the mind. Some of these ideas are indeed classed as perceptions, others as mental images, but this distinction is not grounded on the fact that perceptions are of real existents. To look for an independent check on the veracity of experience is to step outside experience, and no self-respecting empiricist can ever do that. And so Hume is driven to say that perceptions differ from mental images only because they are more vivid, more forceful. The criterion of difference is itself purely ideational and as such can provide no basis for the normal distinction between the two, which rests on the fact that perception is of real existents, while mental images are fictions. Thus there is nothing in Hume's account to rule out the possibility that the isolated mind is confronted by two fictional displays, the one long-running, coherent and forcefully boring (like *Crossroads*), the other sporadic and unclear (like *Not the Nine O'Clock News*). The stable one is called the Perception Show, the unstable the Mental Image Show. Hume, before he gets to work with the so-called healing agents, feeling and imagination, in the latter part of the *Treatise*, is therefore a great forcible reductionist. His challenge consists in the running, implicit question, 'What else have you got?', which invites the answer given fifty years before by Locke in his *Essay concerning Human Understanding*:

> Since the mind, in all its thoughts and reasonings, hath no other immediate object but its own ideas, which it alone does or can contemplate, it is evident that our knowledge is only conversant about them.[10]

All our discourse, all our knowledge must consist of ideas, for we have nothing else. Thus Hume's sceptical philosophy dissolves, or 'reduces out' the three traditional substances, God, matter, mind. All three, even mind considered as a unitary substance, collapse into the flux, more or less vivid, of ideas. Hume is therefore the father of the phenomenologists. We may think also of Santayana's description of William James's philosophy: for James, he said, there is only one fact, 'the flying fact of our being'.[11] 'Being' here means subjective, not objective existence. Notice how violently reductive the process is, although the direction of the reduction runs counter to materialism. When I was considering materialism I drew attention to the way those who value consciousness can strike out against the reduction. With Hume, it is the lovers of matter who must fight back, for matter itself is reduced to its representative ideas (incidentally, Haldane's argument is fatal to radical idealism exactly as it is fatal to radical materialism). And all these things are done – initially at least – in the name of empiricism.

It may be said that Hume's idealism, in so far as it continues to smell of human psychology ('ideas'), is not the ultimate, most radical opposite to materialism. This (etymology suggests) will be not idealism but formalism. And indeed we can easily find, if we wish to, the philosophy in which the element of organisation (so awkward for the materialist) is so to speak given its head and allowed to eat up all the rest. This is structuralism, which teaches that the world consists not of bits but of various interwoven relations only. Sometimes, in structuralism and post-structuralism, language or writing is given privileged ontological status (think of Jacques Derrida's 'Il n'y pas de hors-texte').[12] But the purest of Structuralists was surely the ancient sceptic Pyrrho who held that 'nothing existed but convention, since nothing *in itself* was any more this than that'.[13]

Any discussion of materialist reductionism often leads people to conclude that theology must be the least reductive of all disciplines. As long as that sense rests only on the fact that theology deals with a more exalted (rather

than a more comprehensive) subject matter, it is vulnerable to attack. For, as
we have seen, reduction is a normative concept; we decide in which direction
the reduction shall run. In fact forcible reduction to the theological is possible.
I offer as an example Alexander Pope's notorious line,

> One truth is clear; 'Whatever is, is RIGHT'.[14]

It is curious how many of one's examples of radical reductionism come from
the eighteenth century, the century of clear thinking! Pope was striving to
reconcile the imperfection of the world with the fact that it was made and is
governed by an all-powerful, good God. He wrote at a time when Deist
criticism had rendered the myth of Adam's Fall virtually unusable in polite
society as an explanation. Pope's answer is, in effect, to 'reduce out' evil.
Since evil is incompatible with the universality of God's rule, evil cannot
really exist: what we take for evil is really good. Thus we have an attempt to
assimilate the character of the given to that of its underlying determinant.
The effect is an ethical reduction *upwards*, so to speak, to an undifferentiated
perfection.

In Calvin's theology, meanwhile, one finds a binary reduction. All good
belongs to God, but meanwhile there is evil and that belongs to man. The
effect of this on the available field of human concerns is powerfully reductive,
simplifying man to his bad impulses, for any good impulse, even the good
impulse of faith itself, is the work of grace; that is, it proceeds from God
working within us and is in no sense ours. The pious man who would love
God finds that he cannot do so. Only God can love himself, through the
corrupt vessel, man. Even Prayer, which one would suppose belongs by its
very essence to the human suppliant, belongs, in so far as it is virtuous, to
God. It is, as George Herbert put it, 'God's breath in man returning to his
birth'.[15] For Herbert, the Anglican, the believer in rich church furnishings
and saints' days, retains in his verse a radical Protestant sense of the total
depravity of man. The would-be lover of God finds himself harshly displaced
by this theology, much as the good socialist in my earlier example found the
moral impetus of his socialism displaced as that impetus was relegated to its
economic origin. In such moments of Calvinism, the moral agent finds
himself 'reduced out' by theology. Sometimes the effect is almost grotesque.
George Herbert proposes in the Dedication of *The Temple* to give his poems to
God, but then finds, in the course of the dedication, that he cannot give them
because they are God's already. He then produces the bizarre proposal that
he be allowed to compete with the poems in praising God. He is clamouring
for inclusion, for admission to the moral arena. But his proposal is
foredoomed by the pre-emptive theology, for if he were to produce any
worthy praise of God to set beside the poems, it would turn out that this too
had been wrought in him by God.

I have argued so far that reduction without suppression, without leaving an unassimilated remainder, which I take to be the essence of successful science, is a great good of the intellectual life. Such reduction normally occurs within a single major band of discourse. Of course these bands are themselves hierarchically structured or what takes place within them could not be described as a reduction. Reduction within a band will not encounter the kind of logical road-block put up by Moore and Haldane. Reduction, on the other hand, which involves the relegation to 'unreality' of relevant data in order to accomplish the desired transition to a more 'fundamental' level I regard as suspect. I cannot think of a reduction from one major band of discourse to another which does not employ these culpably Procrustean methods, unless it be Newton's demonstration of the inertial character of planetary motion.

We are, I have suggested, instinctively resentful of any reduction of the human (itself naturally a composite of all the bands of discourse) to a lower level. But instinct is not the opposite of reason. Some instincts are highly rational and this is one of them. Gilbert Ryle wrote with a fine sarcasm, referring to a period when Benthamite economic reductionism seemed strong,

> The brother, whom I ordinarily describe as hospitable, devoted to his branch of learning and unexcited about his bank-balance, must be a dummy-brother if I am to take science seriously. My real brother, my Economic Brother, is concerned only to maximise his gains and minimise his losses.[16]

This is forcible reduction to the economic. Contrast with it Christ's internal, non-forcible reduction of the labyrinthine moral law of the Jews to 'Love God and love thy neighbour'. As Newton reduced the (baffling) physical to (resplendently clarified) physics, so Christ reduces a proliferating system of moral laws to mere goodness. Like Newton's, this reduction is very nearly successful (there are elements of justice which, in my view, it fails to assimilate). The vicious kind of reductionism, on the other hand, fails to defer appropriately to the real richness of the available whole. Note that by 'available whole' I do not mean the field of consciousness. We have seen from the example of Hume how that concept can prove harshly exclusive and therefore the terminus of a peculiarly desolating reduction.

But the available whole, it would seem, is essentially intractable. We cannot operate intellectually, we cannot speak, without selecting certain features and omitting others. What Arthur Peacocke calls 'methodological reductionism'[17] is, in a manner, characteristic of all discourse.

But there are ways of selecting which do not imply suppression of the material which is left unspecified, ways which rather alert the mind to the presence of a possible, unuttered richness. Such, I would suggest, is the function of the great mimetic artist. Consider Shakespeare. The one thing that English literary criticism said about Shakespeare, when first it found its voice, was that he above all poets conveyed nature itself, the way things really are. The people who said this did not suppose that Shakespeare's plays were literally true, nor were they ignorant of the fact that the means employed in this feat of truth were conventional (the conventions of language rising to the more manipulable conventions of art). Yet, despite the evident presence of fiction and convention, Shakespeare produced in his auditors and readers a profound sense of the indefinite richness of reality. How he did this is a large and complex question. I will content myself, here and now, with pointing to two features. The first is his use of the device known as *variatio*, or variation. It is a curious experience to turn from Shakespeare's dramatic writing to a popular Renaissance handbook of style such as the *De Copia* of Erasmus. The *De Copia*, or to give it its full title, the *De Utraque Verborum ac Rerum Copia*, went through 180 editions, 150 of which were between 1512 and 1572.[18] One finds an immediate kinship with Shakespeare and, at the same time, an immense difference. Erasmus shows his reader how to say 'Your letter gave me great pleasure' in 148 different ways.[19] The general effect is of a frigid proliferation of mere forms. Yet it is similarly characteristic of Shakespeare (unlike, say, Racine, who is the master of the single, perfectly encapsulating, closed phrase) to offer a series of alternative phrases. In Erasmus the variations offered are so to speak variations only. There is no ontological implication. Their sole interest lies in the ingenious manner in which they differ from one another as forms. In Shakespeare we sense instead that these are alternative 'essays', shots at a target, nets cast out to catch some ulterior reality which is at once elusive and excitingly important. Thus at once, at the level of mere style, although we find convention and selection, the mode of that convention is one which *obtrudes its own incompleteness*, and so quickens our sense of transformal possibilities.

The second feature is Shakespeare's manner of presenting or implying motivation. His picture of human action is one of indefinite over-determination. Brutus in *Julius Caesar* is a Republican and his conscious Republican motives are fully respected by the poet. But he is also a sort of Stoic Narcissist. Further, there are recurrent hints of a queer excitability in connection with the shedding of blood. He is politically imperceptive and he is genuinely conscientious. Here we have a multiplication of levels and there is a kind of mind which, faced with such a multiplication, will instantly begin to hunt for some means of reduction, some way, say, of swallowing up the consciously ethical motives in the psychological. Shakespeare supplies all the data for the reductionist to work with, but he will not move a muscle to help with the reduction itself. Of course he selects and it follows that he has his own principle of economy. But this is not the economy of accounting for the greatest number of phenomena with the smallest number of explanatory principles. Rather it is an economy of suggestion, of implying the largest number of explanatory principles with the smallest number of phenomenal examples. Technically it is done by deliberate discontinuity (hopping continually from one order to another) and also by writing against the grain of earlier dramatic convention. The whole process is controlled by a sense of what is credible human motivation. This admits much, for the excellent reasons that human beings really are very complex.

All this is work of the intelligence, yet in another way it could be seen as labour to impede the intelligence, or at least to impede its more arrogant flights. It is as if Shakespeare's principle were the opposite of 'Occam's razor': 'Entities are not to be multiplied beyond necessity'. Here, if you like, is the fundamental methodological reductionism implicit in any act of positive explanation. If we want to know what, in any specific case, is causing a given effect, we always – rightly – try to exclude variables. Bacon's hostility to controlled experiment, his wish to let the wind blow through and the rain rain in on the laboratory, was really ill conceived. But we need to retain, in all our specific efforts at explanation, some sense of the hypothetical possibilities. Shakespeare multiplies entities with a will and reminds us of this range of possibles. His works may thus be likened to Occam's beard, golden, luxuriant, happily unsubdued by the famous razor. Indeed, Shakespeare explains nothing. Bentham was a hard-headed realist, who believed in getting down to brass tacks. Shakespeare was 'of imagination all compact'. But none of us has ever met Bentham's man. Indeed, if we did so, I fancy we should decide in a very short time that he was not in fact a member of the human species at all, but a disguised visitor from another planet. But Falstaff we would recognise at once.

Is there a legitimate reductionism? Of course there is. Not just science but ordinary practical life could not proceed without it. Nor is it always merely methodological. I believe myself that much religious language really can be 'reduced out' and therefore assent to a large part of the naturalising movement of the last three centuries. But we must never, in our hunger for unity and 'usable' explanations, relax our awareness of the real richness of the universe. It is a rather boring way to end, but I really feel that we need both kinds of mind, the reverently reductive and the other (I will not call it 'inflationary') which is always here, ready to catch at one's sleeve and ask, 'But have you noticed this?' *Amicus Newton, sed magis amicus Shakespeare.*

There is I think an educational moral in what I have been saying. There is a sense in which the available field, the phenomenal *qua* phenomenal, is irreducible[20] and it can be the function of great mimetic art to remind us of this. Great mimetic art sometimes looks intellectually weak, because it never tells us anything we did not already know. I want to suggest that indeed it tells us what we know, but telling us what we know can be, given the danger of illicit or forcible reductionism, an urgent, even a practical intellectual operation. If our education became closed within a reductive conception of 'the useful' there is a sense in which it would die. Our children and young people should learn to conduct experiments, to make machines that work, but they should also look at the paintings of Vermeer, at the plays of Shakespeare and at the faces of their friends.

Notes

1. *De Rerum Natura*, ii. 444f.
2. Newton, The General Scholium to Book iii of the *Principia* in Florian Cajor's revision of Motte's translation (Berkeley: University of California Press, 1962) vol. II, p. 547.
3. A Peacocke (ed.), 'The case for reductionism in the sciences', in *Reductionism in Academic Disciplines* (Guildford: Society for Research into Higher Education and NFER-NELSON, 1985), pp. 7–16.
4. See e.g. W. T. Stace, *The Theory of Knowledge and Existence* (Oxford: Clarendon Press, 1932), pp. 38–9.
5. B. Russell, 'On the relations of universals and particulars', *Proceedings of the Aristotelian Society* (New Series), vol. XII (1911–12), p. 9.
6. G. E. Moore, *Principia Ethica* (London: Cambridge University Press, 1959), pp. 10, 13–14, 18–20, 38–9, 66–7, 72–3.
7. J. B. S. Haldane, 'When I am dead', in *Possible Worlds* (London: Chatto and Windus, 1930), p. 209.
8. R. Cudworth, *The True Intellectual System of this Universe*, ed. Thomas Birch (London: Richard Priestley, 1820), vol. III, pp. 274, 398; vol. IV, pp. 94, 118.
9. L. Stephen, *History of English Thought in the Eighteenth Century* (London: Rupert Hart Davis, 1962), vol. I, p. 240.
10. J. Locke, *An Essay Concerning Human Understanding*, ed. A. C. Fraser (Oxford: Oxford University Press, 1894), vol. II, p. 167.
11. G. Santayana, *A Brief History of my Opinions*, in *The Philosophy of Santayana*, enlarged edition by Irwin Edmar (New York: Scribners, 1953), p. 121.
12. J. Derrida, *De la Grammatologie* (Paris: Les Éditions de Minuit, 1967), p. 227.
13. Diogenes Laertius, *Lives of the Eminent Philosophers*, Loeb edition, with a translation by R. D. Hicks (London: William Heinemann, 1925), vol. II, p. 474.
14. *Essay on Man*, I. 294.
15. 'Prayer I'.
16. G. Ryle, 'The world of science and the everyday world', in his *Dilemmas* (Cambridge: Cambridge University Press, 1960), p. 69.
17. A. Peacocke, *Higher Education Newsletter*, 4. Dec., 1982, pp. 21–4.
18. Cf. H. D. Rix, 'The editions of Erasmus's *De Copia*', *Studies in Philology*, vol. XLIII (1946), pp. 595–618.
19. Cf. Erasmus, *De Copia*, translated by D. B. King and H. D. Rix as *On Copia of Words and Ideas* (Milwaukee: Marquette University Press, 1963), pp. 39–42.
20. Cf. Thomas Nagel's observation concerning experience as it is lived: 'It is not captured by any of the familiar, recently devised reductive analyses of the mental, for all of them are logically compatible with its absence,' 'What is it like to be a bat?' in *The Mind's Eye*, composed and arranged by D. R. Hofstadter and D. C. Dennett (Harmondsworth: Penguin Books, 1982), p. 392.

DID MEURSAULT MEAN
TO KILL THE ARAB?

The intentional fallacy fallacy

I

This essay is an attempt to resolve a complex and sophisticated question – is the artist's intention relevant to a critical appraisal of his work? – by answering what is, at first sight at least, a much simpler question: did Meursault, in Camus's *L'Etranger*, mean to kill the Arab? W. K. Wimsatt Jun. and Monroe C. Beardsley published in 1946[1] a singularly difficult and tortuous essay on the first of these questions. It is called 'The Intentional Fallacy' and has become famous; indeed the phrase 'intentional fallacy' has passed into the language and found a warm welcome even before its meaning has become clear, and one could hardly ask for greater fame than *that*. In the same year the first English translation of Camus's *L'Etranger* appeared. Perhaps more than one university lecturer, wearied by the theoretic involutions of Wimsatt and Beardsley, turned for solace to the latest novel and found instead of solace the red sand and pitiless sun, the stark mortality of Meursault's world. Such a reader would have the experience of passing from evident complexity to enigmatic simplicity; of moving from an abstract disquisition on the relation between intention and public performance to a scrupulously observed concrete instance; instead of the intricate cogitations of Wimsatt and Beardsley, an implied question, itself more radical than any they had thought to ask: what is an 'intentional' action?

II

A great part of the difficulty of the essay 'The Intentional Fallacy' springs naturally from the intrinsic complexity of the subject. It is, however, consistent with this view to suspect that a certain amount of our difficulty may be traced to a less respectable source, that is to confusions in the thought of the essay itself. Many of these have already been publicly discussed, perhaps most effectively in Mr Frank Cioffi's admirable article.[2] I wish here to isolate just one of them.

Wimsatt and Beardsley seem to oscillate between two essentially opposed views. The first is relatively straightforward and, in my opinion, erroneous. It is this: the critical reading of a poem and the acquisition of 'background information' have nothing to do with each other; judgements formed in criticism are, in principle, not modifiable by arguments drawn from 'background information'. Thus the authors cite with approval Matthiessen's contention that T. S. Eliot's contrasting of the modern Thames with the Elizabethan river requires no reading of Spenser for its proper appreciation, although (as a matter of merely historical interest) Spenser's line, 'Sweet Thames, run softly till I end my song' is actually quoted in Eliot's poem. The notion here seems to be that although poems may be constructed, like mosaics, from fragments of other authors, to point out this fact is to say something about the psychological genesis of the poem, certainly, but nothing material to a critical reading. If an objector were to say 'Do you hold to this view even if it could be shown that Eliot was writing with a clear awareness of the context, in the original author, of his quotation?' Wimsatt and Beardsley might well reply, 'When you say Eliot has this awareness, are you merely describing Eliot's state of mind at the time of writing? If so, our answer must be that this is of purely psychological interest. If, on the other hand, you mean that Eliot's awareness shows in his writing, then of course it is of interest to us as critics; but then, if it shows, it shows; there is no need for Dryasdust to point it out.' It is not hard to expose the sophistry of this possible reply: it is often impossible to tell whether an awareness of context is shown or not without first obtaining information about the original passage. There need, of course, be no question here of investigating Eliot's state of mind at the time of writing. All that is necessary is that certain turns of phrase, certain echoes will click into place with a coherency which suggests a complex relationship between archetype and ectype. Such echoes and correspondences could not have been perceived at all by a reader entirely ignorant of the original. Moreover, to cite a single instance in which (to grant for the moment Matthiessen's contention) the background information is of no critical value is scarcely the most effective way to convince a sceptic. Wimsatt and Beardsley have, in effect, put the following case: 'Background information cannot, in principle, have any effect on our critical judgements, and to show that this is so we offer a line where it has none.' Plainly, an ordinary confirming instance carries no cogency in such a situation; what is rather needed is an *invidious* instance, which can yet be made to yield the required lesson. Wimsatt and Beardsley ought to be saying '. . . to show that this is so we offer a line where everyone has always assumed that the background information is critically relevant but where we can demonstrate that, essentially, it is not'.

But this Wimsatt and Beardsley cannot do; not because of the insufficient reading or weak memory, but because no one can; because it is impossible.

III

Certainly there is a difference for most people between reading *The Waste Land* before and after reading a commentary (I have in mind here not Eliot's notes but the sort of commentary provided in the Norton Anthology of English Literature). Now if we hold that the first reading, *sans* commentary, is the right one, what are we to say to a man who, by some strange chance, happens to have read the Sanskrit *Upanishads, From Ritual to Romance*, and *The Golden Bough?* Does his knowledge *unfit* him for reading the poem?

Perhaps we should limit ourselves for the moment to speaking, not of the right and the wrong reading, but of better and worse readings.

But Wimsatt and Beardsley do not commit themselves to the view I have just attacked. Instead, as I have said, they oscillate. After commending Matthiessen, they note: 'Eliot's allusions work when we know them – and to a great extent even when we do not know them, through their suggestive power.' The phrasing of this suggests scholarly caution, but what is really happening here? That qualifying 'to a great extent' in fact gives away the whole principle. If it is only in the majority of cases that background information has no critical relevance, there must remain a minority of cases when it *has*. Obviously no conscientious critic could afford to neglect the commentaries and background information as long as that were true. An apparently radical – even revolutionary – thesis has shrunk to a platitude: that historical information is often dry and unexciting, but occasionally it can illuminate a line of verse.

Our authors seek to remedy this unhappy situation by means of an epigrammatic distinction. We must separate, they say,[3] evidence relating to the meaning of words (ironically enough called internal evidence) from evidence concerning the biography of the poet, the circumstances of composition, etc. (ironically enough – for it all derives from private or idiosyncratic sources – called external evidence). They also admit the possibility of a third kind, to which I shall turn in a moment. Of the two kinds so far described the first is critically useful while the second is not. This is a neat distinction, but very vulnerable. The authors have achieved their paradox only by blurring the normal distinction between internal and external evidence. 'Internal evidence' means simply 'evidence provided in the work'. The solemn-secretive tone of Donne's 'A Valediction: forbidding Mourning' is internal evidence for the dating of that poem; Walton's *Life* is external.[4] The reference in Act Four of *Macbeth* to the union of the Kingdoms is internal evidence for the date of that play; Dr Simon Forman's description of the performance he saw is external. Glossarial information about the meaning of words in a poem normally utilises external evidence – that is, it collates other uses of the same word from other writers. The evidence used in determining the meaning of words in our older literature is usually external.

Secondly, it looks as if this distinction will not in any case do the work for which it was designed. Even the biographer cannot safely be ignored by the critic. Certainly I am willing to grant at once that biographical work done on, say, Shakespeare has contributed very little to our critical understanding of that poet. The contribution to criticism made by the immense work of E. K. Chambers is grotesquely small; grotesque, that is, in comparison with the richness of the scholarship employed. Theories about the Dark Lady of the Sonnets have been critically barren. But (and this is the point) we cannot be confident that they will always be barren. Oscar Wilde's theory[5] that Mr W.H. was an actor called Willie Hughes who played the part of Rosalind in *As You Like It* would certainly, if it were established, modify our reading of the Sonnets. The imagery of shadows and glasses, in particular, would be enriched by the presence of an unsuspected theme – the relation between the creator and the interpreter of a drama, the maker and the mask, the magician and his creature, poet and player. The sonnet beginning 'What is your substance whereof you are made' *feels* different to a man who has just read Wilde's essay. Similarly, Leslie Hotson's conjecture about the identity and history of Shakespeare's 'Mr. W.H.' could, if true, alter the whole character of Sonnet 125 – alter, and in this case diminish. But these are weak examples, partly because their historical support is weak. Let us take one which is strong and clear. Can any reader doubt that Milton's line 'O dark, dark, dark, amid the blaze of noon'[6] carries a special power because it is the utterance either of a blind poet or of one shortly to become so? The fact that this is a commonplace piece of information is beside the point. It is largely because of the work of historians that it is commonplace. What, in these circumstances, is the conscientious anti-intentionalist to do? Repress his human reaction to the poet he knows? Endeavour to forget Milton's blindness? Restrict himself to the pure reading? But why should we, any more, believe in the pure reading? Such literary asceticism has nothing to commend it. Indeed, it can lead, I am sure, to mortification of the sensibility.

IV

But perhaps I have been too hasty. It could be argued that all my objections were anticipated by Wimsatt and Beardsley when they provided that third category of evidence, the category I omitted to describe. Under this heading falls all evidence of a private or semi-private nature which can clarify special meanings given to a word, either by an individual author, or by a coterie of which he is a member. The critical relevance of this sort of evidence is readily admitted by Wimsatt and Beardsley on the ground that it teaches us not just the intention of the author (which *is* irrelevant) but also the meaning of the words. The crucial criterion here, however, seems at first sight to be semantic: that biographical information which makes no contribution to philology, to our knowledge of word-meanings, is without critical relevance. But in none of the cases I cited is our knowledge of the *meaning* of the words modified, in the ordinary dictionary sense of that term. Milton did not use the word 'dark' in a special, private *sense* because of his blindness. Thus, if the criterion is interpreted strictly, the theories of Wilde and Hotson and the biographical information about Milton do not satisfy it. The evident fact that these several considerations do effect our critical interpretation then becomes an embarrassment to Wimsatt and Beardsley, which their provision of a third category has failed to scotch. If on the other hand we relax our terminology and allow 'meaning' to cover impact, resonance, effect and the like, then all my examples might well be admitted to the status of critical relevance. But at what cost? It seems that we have been diverted once again with the now familiar party-trick of the disappearing thesis. We are left with the proposition that biographical information is not critically relevant unless it affects our critical judgement – a disguised tautology from which few will trouble to withhold their assent.

Of course biography and literary criticism are two different things. The biographer wants to know who (in fact) was X, where (in fact) did he do what he did. The critic usually wants to know: what is the precise tenor of this passage, how does it achieve its effect, how good is it? As long as we confine ourselves to the distinction of aims and processes, the distinction between the two disciplines will be perfectly clear. Confusion enters when we try to extend our distinction to the material handled, and argue that the stuff dredged up by the biographer cannot be relevant to the critics' enquiry. The fact that a biographer is actuated by biographical motives does not mean that he can never turn up a new fact of more than biographical interest. Facts (in this world) tend to be three-dimensional. They can be looked at from different angles. The historian, the scholar, the philologist, all throw up, once in a while, three-dimensional facts which, if they engage our interest, can modify our reading of a work of literature.

V

In arguing for the possible importance of biographical material, I have tried to follow my own advice to choose the invidious example. If such limited investigations can yield critically relevant information, then *a fortiori* how much more may not the history of ideas yield? Here the simple question 'Do you want to know what the words mean?' (the status of which is disguised in Wimsatt's and Beardsley's essay) should make my point sufficiently clear. The meaning of the word ἀγαθός in Sophocles is supplied by a chapter from the history of ideas. The given meanings of the word 'wit' in the poetry of Pope come to us from the same source. The fact that the critic who has completed his homework on 'background' still has before him the task of following out what Pope does with those meanings does not destroy the relevance of background information as a prerequisite. But, to be sure, Wimsatt and Beardsley have already virtually granted this.

Which makes their analysis of Coffin on Donne all the more puzzling. The lines in question are from the 'Valediction: forbidding Mourning':

> Moving of th' earth brings harmes and feares,
>   Men reckon what it did and meant,
> But trepidation of the spheares,
>   Though greater farre, is innocent.

Coffin interpreted this as a reference to the Copernican hypothesis that the earth goes round the sun, which people found disturbing. Wimsatt and Beardsley, quite rightly dissenting from this view, tell us that Coffin's reading has been perverted by astronomical knowledge, and that the lines go much better if taken, in a commonsense fashion, as Ptolemaic throughout. The irony should be already evident. Wimsatt's and Beardsley's rebuttal of Coffin's use of the history of ideas itself involves the use of the history of ideas. Coffin's misinterpretation is not the fault of historicism, it is the fault of Coffin. It is not just bad criticism, it is bad history of ideas. Conversely, the interpretation of Wimsatt and Beardsley, so far from refuting the claims to critical relevance of the history of ideas, is a reasonably good specimen of it. Wimsatt and Beardsley clearly avail themselves of the information that trepidation of the spheres is, as a translunar phenomenon, in ethical and spiritual contrast with the sublunary character of earthquakes and the like. Moreover I would guess that the very phrase 'trepidation of the spheares' would be virtually meaningless to the average, intelligent man, unlearned in the history of literature and ideas. Ask your bank manager what it means when next you see him.

VI

I am, however, very close to agreement with Wimsatt and Beardsley on one particular, that is, the general critical irrelevance of the author's state of mind at the time of writing. I am not sure, however, that I would erect even this into a principle. I can conceive of a situation in which information about a poet's state of mind (presumably supplied by the poet himself) could supply a richer reading. But to reflect on this point is to realise that the word 'intention' can be understood in two distinct ways. Here in fact lies the crux of the whole question. I will call these the dualist way and the quasi-behaviourist way. I suspect that there is a confusion of these two ways latent in the following sentence (which occurs near the beginning of Wimsatt's and Beardsley's article):

> How is [the critic] to find out what the poet tried to do? If the poet succeeded in doing it, then the poem itself shows what the poet was trying to do.

Now if the authors hold a dualist view of the nature of intention – if, that is, they think that in every intentional performance there is, first, a pre-existent, identifiably relevant state of mind and, second, an overt action having some appropriate relation to the state of mind – then it seems that the above sentence contains an illegitimate inference. According to the dualist view, success in fulfilling an intention can be measured only by the degree of correspondence between the state of mind and the public action. No one who was ignorant of the prior state of mind could measure this correspondence.

According to the quasi-behaviourist view, however, we do not need to be admitted to the introspective field of the agent before we decide whether his action is intentional or not; one always has and always will decide such questions by referring to public criteria. Let us suppose that a man is watching, from a window, an armed terrorist advancing up his garden path; he crosses the room, takes down a gun, stations himself where he can see both his sleeping wife and the stranger, waits until the stranger enters the room and draws close to the wife, and at that point shoots him. Should we not say that the husband shot the terrorist intentionally? Yet in reaching this conclusion we have made no reference whatever to what was going on in his head. But now let us suppose that we can, *per impossible*, see what is happening in the husband's mind. And suppose we discover that what is introspectively available to him is not, e.g., the repeated proposition 'If he gets close I'll shoot him' but simply a series of disconnected images and reflections: 'The light's bad; will dawn come soon? That clock ticks loudly; I may hear the dog bark in a moment.' If we discovered this, would we decide that the husband's action was not intentional after all? I very much doubt it. Indeed, I suspect that in most of the actions quite properly called intentional there need be no corresponding scheme in the mind at all. The man who answers a telephone may have any of a hundred things in his mind as he does so; yet he answers intentionally; certainly not by accident.

VII

I have already asked, in effect, the question which forms the title of this essay. Camus, in *L'Etranger*, showed us how a philosophical novel ought to be written. Instead of the spongy theorising of *La Nausée*, with its ceaseless metaphysical directives to the reader, we are given a *specimen*, a concrete instance minutely and scrupulously observed, for each philosophical reader to construe as he thinks fit. My own question about *L'Etranger* is not the only philosophical question raised by that book. It is not even the most important. It is enough, however, to extricate us from our Wimsattian difficulties.

For Camus has provided precisely the data we require: both the public story and the private one; the steady thread of public action, paid out in the full blaze of the Algerian sun, and the strange, discontinuous lucidity of

Meursault's private thoughts. He has even added an actual trial in which we readers can, armed with our special interior knowledge of Meursault, sit beside the jurors of the novel and despise – or not despise – their judgements, reached by such crude external paths. At the trial Meursault says that he had no intention of killing the Arab and the president receives his observation as 'an affirmation'. This may be thought to settle the question forthwith, but as we shall see, there are reasons (in which Meursault's own brand of simplified introspectionism will figure) for suspending judgement. The external story of the killing is pretty simple. Meursault attends the funeral of his mother. His behaviour at the ceremony suggests to those who watch that he feels no particular grief at her death. Shortly afterwards he becomes acquainted with a shady character named Raymond Sintès, who asks him to help with a plan. Raymond's scheme is to humiliate his mistress in a peculiarly disgusting manner, by way of revenging her infidelity. It is an essential part of his plan that the mistress be first tricked into a loving repentance, but this can only be brought about by means of a specially eloquent letter 'avec des coups de pied et en même temps des choses pour la faire regretter'.[7] Meursault readily agrees to write this letter for the unliterary Raymond. Raymond's plan is a partial success, although it ends in his beating up the mistress and undergoing an embarrassing interview with the police. A more frightening consequence, however, is that certain Arabs, one of whom is the brother of the girl humiliated by Raymond, begin to make threatening appearances. Meursault learns about this and implicitly ranges himself beside Raymond by promising to warn him if necessary.[8] Later in the story, when the Arabs reappear, Meursault agrees[9] to help his friend if a fight breeaks out. A fight follows but proves inconclusive. Meursault is not drawn into it. Some hours after, however, Raymond and Meursault meet the Arabs once more. Meursault, anxious to prevent bloodshed, says '. . . Mais s'il ne sort pas son couteau, tu ne peux pas tirer.'[10] – that is, 'You can't shoot unless he draws his knife.' The implication, clearly, is that if the Arab does draw, you can shoot. A few seconds later, Meursault makes the point clear by adding: 'Prends-le d'homme à homme et donne-moi ton revolver. Si l'autre intervient, ou s'il tire son couteau, je le descendrai.' However, Raymond and Meursault get back safely to the bungalow they are using. Raymond goes inside but Meursault chooses to prowl about outside for a while. It is at this point that he encounters the Arab. Meursault sees the Arab draw his knife and shoots him. After the Arab falls, Meursault fires four more shots into the inert body. The whole incident is played out in intense heat, under a glaring sun. So much for the external story.

Now for the internal: we can pass over Meursault's private feelings at his mother's funeral with the single observation that they do not markedly contradict the conclusions drawn by outside observers. The evidence of the interior story as it relates to Raymond's scheme is again, in a manner, negative. Meursault experiences no repulsion from the idea, entertains no exonerating counter-plot. When we come to the skirmish and the killing, his mind is chiefly filled with a suffocating awareness of heat and light. At one moment only is this distinctly qualified. That is the point at which Meursault tries to restrain Raymond; here, we are told, he feels a real anxiety. The standard English translation by Stuart Gilbert gives another moment – this time a mood of definite, implacable defiance, as Meursault refuses to re-enter the bungalow with Raymond and continues his walk. This, however, rests on an inference from the French 'mes mâchoires se crispaient' and as such could be contested. To this should be added the negative information that Meursault's state of mind is such that he can perceive no moral distinction between staying or going away, between shooting or not shooting. At the moment of the killing itself, the interior story erupts from its dry, Hemingway style in an explosion of imagery.[11] Meursault, surprised to see the Arab again, grips the gun in his pocket and halts under the fierce sun. The tension rises, and the heat grows more oppressive, reminding Meursault of the heat at his mother's funeral, until at last he irrationally takes a step forward. The Arab at once draws his knife. The light of the sun rebounds from the glittering blade, 'transfixing' Meursault's forehead. Blinded by the glare and deafened by the 'cymbals of the sun', Meursault's grip tightens on the gun. The five shots follow.

These stories, the public and the private, can be reduced to two simple sentences. First, Meursault had armed himself in case something went wrong, and when something did go wrong he fired five times. Second, during the incident his head was full of the light and heat of the sun, of feelings of oppression, flickering anxiety and memory, awareness of a knife drawn before him, desperation. It seems that if we had only the first story to go on we should entertain no doubts about the answer to our title-question. The problem which now arises is this: does the second story exonerate Meursault? Let us take a moment to imagine what *any* close account of the introspective accompaniment of a murder – not an accidental killing – would be like. To my mind, the answer after we have scrutinised the interior account remains unchanged. Although there is room for argument about the degree of responsibility involved, Meursault's action was, in the ordinary sense of the word, an intentional performance. I thus opt for the 'quasi-behaviourist' view (which obviously owes more than a little to Professor Gilbert Ryle).

VIII

To take once again the invidious instance: even when I am trying to decide whether an action *of my own* was intentional or not, I do not necessarily proceed by looking for a particular state of mind. If I ask myself, 'Did I intend to contradict that man so bluntly?' I find myself searching, not for a memory of an inwardly framed project, 'Now contradict him', but rather for memories of the precise tenor of our conversation: was I pressed for time, had *he* just contradicted me? There is, I suppose, a sense in which this *is* scrutinising my own state of mind, but, if so, it is a surprisingly Rylean sense.

But perhaps I should fight one more round before I leave the point. Often an attempt to remember whether an action was intentional or not will take the form not of a search for an appropriate previous mental state but simply of an effort to remember whether or not one was surprised by what happened. Here it might be objected that the word 'surprise' betrays my case. 'Surprise', it will be said, 'occurs when the event contradicts the expectation, that is, what you think will happen – in fact, the previous mental state. Your antithesis between the search for a previous mental state on the one hand and the attempt to discover whether or not one was surprised on the other accordingly collapses, since the very word "surprise" presupposes a reference to a previous mental state.' My reply is as follows: it is doubtful whether an 'expectation' is necessarily, or even usually, the sort of introspectible phenomenon which your argument requires. Often enough we become conscious of an expectation only when it disappointed. Thus I should be surprised if I saw a dog on the roof of the National Gallery. This would, in a perfectly normal sense, be contrary to my expectation. But this does not mean that all the way from Victoria to Trafalgar Square I was saying to myself, 'There will be no dog on the roof of the National Gallery.' The fact that the National Gallery never entered my head would not mean that the surprise was not a surprise, nor would it mean that I lied if I said 'That's unexpected!' 'Expectation' is not typically the name of a conscious mental state; it is a word which is useful in situations where a course of rational action has been interrupted, or in some way intruded upon. It follows that my antithesis between looking for a mental state and looking for a surprise should be allowed to stand.

IX

Let us now look again at Wimsatt's and Beardsley's observation that if a poet succeeds in fulfilling his intention the poem itself will show it. Clearly, the quasi-behaviourist can make sense of this: an action is intentional when it makes sense, when one part rationally precedes another; that is what 'intentional' *means*. A poetic effect is intentional when it hangs together, when it *goes*; that is what 'intentional' *means*. But if Wimsatt and Beardsley avail themselves of this saving interpretation, it can only be at the cost of sacrificing their main contention. The Intentional Fallacy would cease, forthwith, to be fallacious. On this hypothesis it makes perfectly good sense to ask 'What did Shakespeare intend here?' where 'intend' will be explained in terms of the coherence, the movement and order of the images and ideas *as expressed*, and will have nothing to do with the question 'What was streaming through Shakespeare's consciousness at 6 p.m. on the 14th of November 1604?' To say 'Keats clearly intended *x*' is as simple as to say 'The train-robbers clearly intended *y*'.

The same analysis could, naturally, be applied to *The Personal Heresy* (1939) by C. S. Lewis and E. M. W. Tillyard, an earlier version of the same controversy. Tillyard maintained that the proper object of the critic's attention in reading *Paradise Lost* is the mind of the poet. Lewis replied that he cared little for Milton's *mind*, being more interested in angels, devils and the movement of the poem. 'Mind' is here ambiguous in exactly the same way as 'intention'. If 'mind' means 'Milton's stream of consciousness from second to second', Lewis is right. If it means all the marvellous things that Milton said and wrote, or might say or write, then Tillyard's right; but only tautologously right in that his position could now be expressed in the following form: 'We read Milton in order to read Milton – all the ideas and images of his poetry.'

What about consulting the poet himself? My position on this follows from my position on ordinary intention. There are some hyper-Ryleans who hold that a man is no better judge of what he intends than an outsider is; that the knowledge is identical in kind in either case. There are others who hold that a man's statement that he intended a thing is in principle not corrigible since *ex hypothesi* the agent is the unique authority. I reject both these extremes and suggest that the agent has a special but not indisputable access to his own actions. Similarly, the poet is in an especially good position for watching the movement of a poem, but his judgements on it are not infallible. So, if in doubt, why *not* ask the poet? He could help.

Postscript. I have at no point in this article referred to M. C. Beardsley's more recent treatment of the problem of literary intention in his *Aesthetics: Problems in the Philosophy of Criticism*, New York, 1958. Beardsley in this work makes it perfectly clear that his view of intention is dualist; on p. 19 he criticises Edmund Wilson for oscillating between the discussion of the author's mind and his performance, having laid down in advance (p. 17) that 'the artist's intention is a series of events or psychological states in his mind'. My own plea for a quasi-behaviourist view of intention is therefore equally relevant to the early and to the later work.

Notes

1. *Sewanee Review*, LIV (Summer, 1946); the essay is also printed in W. K. Wimsatt's *The Verbal Icon* (1954), pp. 3–18. All references in this article are to *The Verbal Icon*.
2. 'Intention and interpretation in criticism', *Proceedings of the Aristotelian Society*, New Series, LXIV (1963), pp. 85–106.
3. p. 10.
4. See Helen Gardner's edition (1965) of *The Elegies and the Songs and Sonnets* of John Donne, p. xxix.

5. Wilde's scholarly fantasy, 'The portrait of Mr. W.H.' is in *The Complete Works of Oscar Wilde* (1966), pp. 1150–1201.

6. *Samson Agonistes*, 80. The early date ascribed to this poem by such scholars as Allan H. Gilbert, William R. Parker and John T. Shawcross, even if correct, would not really affect what I have to say about it here. Even if the line I quote *could* have been written as early as 1646, and was not added in the postulated revision of 1653, it would still be the work either of a blind poet or of a poet living in fear of total blindness. We know that Milton's sight began noticeably to fail in the autumn of 1644.

7. *L'Etranger* (Paris: Gallimard, 1942), p. 50.

8. Ibid., p. 63.

9. Ibid., p. 80.

10. Ibid., p. 83.

11. This point is well made by John Cruickshank, following W. M. Frohock, in his *Albert Camus and the Literature of Revolt* (1959).

PUBLICATIONS

This list, with a few exceptions, excludes reviews.

Books

A Common Sky: Philosophy and the Literary Imagination (London: Chatto and Windus for Sussex University Press, 1974).

A New Mimesis: Shakespeare and the Representation of Reality (London: Methuen, 1983).

Dostoevsky's Crime and Punishment: Murder as Philosophic Experiment (Edinburgh: Scottish Academic Press for Sussex University Press, 1978).

Milton: The Minor Poems in English, Introduction, pp. 17–60 (London: Macmillan, 1972).

Overheard by God: Fiction and Prayer in Herbert, Milton and St John (London: Methuen, 1980).

Pope's Essay on Man (London: George Allen & Unwin, 1984).

Shakespeare: The Winter's Tale (London: Edward Arnold, 1966).

Timon of Athens, Harvester New Critical Introductions to Shakespeare (Hemel Hempstead: Harvester Wheatsheaf, 1989).

Two Concepts of Allegory: A Study of Shakespeare's The Tempest and the Logic of Allegorical Expression (London: Routledge & Kegan Paul, 1967).

Articles

'Adam's dream and Madeline's', in *The Religious Imagination*, ed. James P. Mackey (Edinburgh: Edinburgh University Press, 1986), pp. 125–41.

'An answer to Mr Magarey', *Southern Review*, 4 (1971), pp. 255–64.

'Did Meursault mean to kill the Arab?' – The intentional fallacy fallacy', *Critical Quarterly*, 10 (1968), pp. 95–107.

'Fishes in the trees', *Essays in Criticism*, 24 (1974), pp. 20–38.

'Gospel truth', in *Ways of Reading the Bible*, ed. Michael Wadsworth (Hemel Hempstead: Harvester Wheatsheaf, 1981), pp. 41–54.

'Gulliver among the horses', *Yearbook of English Studies: Pope, Swift and their Circle: Special Number*, 18 (1988), pp. 51–67.

'Is there a legitimate reductionism?', *Reductionism in Academic Disciplines*, ed. A. Peacocke (Guildford: The Society for Research into Higher Education and NFER-NELSON, 1985), pp. 113–24.

'Jack the giant-killer', *Seven*, 5 (1984), pp. 84–100.

'Loam-footed English Empiricism', *Renaissance* 37 (1985), pp. 193–7.

'*Measure for Measure*: Quid pro quo?', *Shakespeare Studies*, 4 (1968), pp. 231–51. Reprinted in *Shakespeare Criticism*, ed. L. L. Harris and M. W. Scott (Detroit, 1986).

'*Measure for Measure*: The bed-trick', *Shakespeare Survey*, 28 (1975), pp. 51–6.

'Moving cities: Pope as translator and transposer', in *The Enduring Legacy: Alexander Pope's tercentenary essays*, ed. G. S. Rousseau and Pat Rogers (Cambridge: Cambridge University Press, 1988), pp. 151–70.

'Neo-Darwinism', *Theoria to Theory*, 13 (1979), pp. 197–202.

'Ovid Immoralised: The method of wit in Marvell's "The Garden"', in *Essays in Honour of Kristian Smidt*, ed. Peter Bilton *et al.* (Oslo: University Oslo Institute of English Studies, 1986), pp. 79–89.

'Personality and poetry' in *Persons and Personality*, ed. A. Peacocke and Grant Gillett (Oxford: Basil Blackwell, 1987), pp. 164–71.

'Philosopher as hero' (Review of 2nd volume of Bertrand Russell's *Autobiography*), *New Christian*, 13 June 1968, pp. 18–19.

Realistic Convention and Conventional Realism in Shakespeare, *Shakespearean Survey*, 34 (1981), pp. 33–8.

Review of Jackson Cope's *The Theatre and the Dream*, *Shakespeare Studies*, 1975, pp. 292–6.

'Shakespeare's Richard II and Ovid's Narcissus', in *Ovid Renewed: Ovidian Influences on Literature and Art from the Middle Ages to the Twentieth Century*, ed. Charles Martindale (Cambridge: Cambridge University Press, 1988).

'Solvents and fixatives', *Modern Language Review*, 82 (1987), pp. 273–85.

'The argument about Shakespeare's characters', *Critical Quarterly*, 7 (1965), pp. 107–20; reprinted in C. B. Cox and D. J. Palmer (eds), *Shakespeare's Wide and Universal Stage* (Manchester: Manchester University Press, 1984), pp. 18–32.

'Two unassimilable men', *Shakespearian Comedy, Stratford-Upon-Avon Studies* 14, ed. Malcolm Bradbury and David Palmer (London: Edward Arnold, 1972), pp. 210–40.

'Virgil and Shakespeare', in *Virgil and his Influence: Bimillenial Studies*, ed. Charles Martindale (Bristol: Bristol Classical Press, 1984).

INDEX